FOUR WITNESSES

ROD BENNETT

FOUR WITNESSES

The Early Church in Her Own Words

IGNATIUS PRESS SAN FRANCISCO

Unless otherwise noted, all Scripture quotations (except those included within the patristic texts themselves) have been taken from the Revised Standard Version of the Holy Bible, the Old Testament © 1952, and the New Testament © 1946, by the Division of Christian Education of the National Council of the Churches of Christ in the United States of America.

Excerpts from the English translation of the *Catechism of the Catholic Church* for use in the United States of America copyright © 1994, United States Catholic Conference, Inc.—Libreria Editrice Vaticana. English translation of the *Catechism of the Catholic Church: Modifications from the Editio Typica* copyright © 1997, United States Catholic conference, Inc.—Libreria Editrice Vaticana. Used with permission.

Cover art by Christopher J. Pelicano
Cover design by Roxanne Mei Lum

ISBN 0-89870-847-8
Library of Congress Control Number 2001088858
Printed in the United States of America ∞

This book is gratefully dedicated to the memory of

John Henry Newman

The Fathers are primarily to be considered as *witnesses*, not as *authorities*. They are witnesses of an existing state of things, and their treatises are, as it were, *histories*—teaching us, in the first instance, matters of fact, not of opinion. Whatever they themselves might be, whether deeply or poorly taught in Christian faith and love, they speak, not their own thoughts, but the received views of their respective ages.

Primitive Christianity: Essays and Sketches, 1833–1836

Contents

Introduction

The early Church is no mystery. As a matter of fact, most believers would be astonished to learn just how much we do know about the first three hundred years of Christian history. We have, for example, much inspiring history about the founding of her many congregations throughout the ancient world. We actually know the names of some of her earliest pastors, and in a few cases we have their writings to read. We still have harrowing accounts of her persecution by the Pharisees and by the pagan Romans. We know what sorts of heresies attacked the early Church and, once again, the very names of the heretics who stood against her. We have hymns and prayers and poetry preserved from this period. We have epitaphs from Christian tombs. We have doctrinal statements, Bible commentary, and sermons dating from these days. We have responsive readings used in church; in fact, we have a good deal of information about how the Sunday services were conducted. To put it briefly, we have (contrary to popular belief) a very vivid picture of primitive Christianity—and a picture that is open for investigation by anyone. Some Christians speculate that when Constantine legalized the faith in A.D. 313 many half-converted pagans corrupted the Church by introducing elements retained from their old beliefs. If you are anything like me, you will be amazed to discover that we have literally thousands of pages of documentation dating from long, long before this legalization—much of which is, to the emperor

Constantine, as distant backward in time as the Declaration of Independence is to President George W. Bush. And this information is reliable. Most of us have heard, I suppose, of "apocryphal" Christian writings from the first and second centuries; spurious books like *The Gospel of Thomas* and *The Acts of Paul*. These were pseudo-scriptures manufactured by early cults like the Gnostics and Manichees to shore up their false teachings; they were condemned by the Church as soon as they appeared. But this same Church produced post-New Testament writings; works that, while not to be classed with the inerrant Word of God, do accurately represent the character, teachings, and practices of the very earliest Christians. Priceless artifacts such as *The Martyrdom of Polycarp*, *The Epistle of Barnabas*, and *The Shepherd of Hermas*—all of these come down to us with as much trustworthiness as any ancient document, as reliable as the *Jewish Antiquities* of Josephus or Plutarch's *Lives of the Noble Romans*. All of today's Christian scholars agree that these invaluable records really are authentic productions of the early Church. There is nothing "apocryphal" about them. They have all the authority—not, indeed, of Scripture—but of history.

And yet, like most modern believers, I have lived practically all of my Christian life knowing next to nothing about any of this. Until I discovered these writings a few years ago any vague ideas I might have had about the early Church came straight out of old C. B. DeMille movies. I honestly did not think it was possible to know much more—or I believe I would have tried harder. Looking back, I can see that I had a very sincere (but completely ungrounded) conviction that the period from Revelation to Constantine was *Terra*

Incognita—a gaping "Dark Continent" on the map of history. After all, I had spent quite a lot of time in denominations, para-church movements, and "home-cell" groups whose publicly announced intention was "to restore the pure Christianity of the early Church". Not one of them had ever sent me back to any first- or second-century documentation for evidence. So who knew? Who could have imagined—with so many competing versions of "pure New Testament Christianity" on the market out there—that finding out what the early Church was like might be as simple as opening up the records and having a look?

Like many of you readers, I suspect, I have been familiar with the Scriptures since childhood—to my eternal benefit. Raised in a strong, Bible-believing branch of Protestant Evangelicalism, I was taught to glory in the famous Reformation rallying cry of "*Sola Scriptura*"—the fiery conviction that the Bible and the Bible alone constitutes the basis for Christian belief. We saw this as the only way to prevent mere "traditions of men" from creeping into our religion. But was it perhaps this honorable passion to defend the uniqueness of Scripture that eventually led us to neglect such a huge treasure chest of testimony about the early Church? In our sincere eagerness to be "Bible Christians", had we perhaps come to undervalue the witness of God's hand in Church history? I really had to start taking this possibility seriously when I learned that even my Reformation heroes had not hesitated to reference these ancient writings. Even Luther and Calvin—the very men who taught us *Sola Scriptura* in the first place—knew and respected these venerable saints whom ancient custom has given the title *Fathers of the Church*. They quite often used the writings of early giants like

Ambrose and Augustine to bolster their various arguments. In fact, I eventually discovered that John Calvin had not only affirmed the testimony of these Church Fathers but unequivocally declared that for the first six hundred years of her existence on earth the Church had remained "pure and undefiled".

This was good enough for me—good enough, in fact, to start at least one old-fashioned Baptist from the Bible Belt looking into the lives and teachings of exotic sounding characters like "Cyprian of Carthage", "Gregory Nazianzen", "Epiphanius of Salamis", and "Didymus the Blind". Poking around in a local Christian bookshop one rainy afternoon, I stumbled upon a set of books entitled *The Ante-Nicene Fathers* ("ante-Nicene" refers to the period prior to the Council of Nicaea, held in A.D. 325). They were squirreled away on a back shelf—at least ten volumes, reprinted from an old nineteenth-century edition issued in England by an Anglican publisher. I gingerly cracked the covers, apparently the first customer to do so. Within five minutes I knew that I had just dropped down the rabbit hole into Wonderland. Two whole volumes in this set—big, fat, hard-bound library books stuffed with tiny print—did not have a word in them written later than A.D. 200. I do not mind saying that I leapt in with both feet.

The first thing to go was my "gap theory"—that is, my nebulous notion that a tactful three-hundred-year silence keeps "pure, early Christianity" locked safely away in the Platonic world of ideals. Right off the bat I encountered four eloquent witnesses squarely straddling this alleged gap between apostolic and postapostolic Christianity. To begin with there was **Clement of Rome** and his *Epistle to* *the Corinthians*—a book written, by conservative estimates, about the same time as the Gospel of John. I also discovered **Ignatius**, an early pastor of the church at Antioch and a man described by several ancient writers as "a hearer of the apostles". We have at least five certified epistles of Ignatius; all of them composed in or about A.D. 107 . . . which dates them to within a decade of the close of the apostolic age. **Justin Martyr** reports that the Church had spread across the known world by his time—the year 150. And **Irenaeus of Lyons**, in his massive, five-volume work *Against Heresies*, wistfully recalls studying his theology at the feet of Polycarp. Polycarp was personally taught by John the Beloved, who was personally taught by Jesus Christ, who was personally taught by God the Father Almighty, Maker of heaven and earth. Which, obviously, kicked my convenient "gap" beliefs right in the pants. There is no gap. My four witnesses had eliminated this option forever. And I suddenly realized, with a little trepidation, that I was actually going to have to start dealing with the early Church from now on . . . rather than just identifying myself with her.

Pushing ahead, I moved beyond my initial encounter into a period of intense study. In fact, for nearly a year I read little else but the Bible and these four Apostolic Fathers. Clement of Rome, Ignatius of Antioch, Irenaeus of Lyons, and Justin Martyr became my constant daily companions, and I let the spirit of their "pure and undefiled" Christianity wash over me like a bath. I actually seemed to live for a while in this, the Church's holiest and most Spirit-filled age; the age of secret baptisms in the catacombs, of the figure of a fish knowingly etched in the dust between friends, of Christians thrown to the lions and Peter crucified upside-down.

But as I did—as I immersed myself in this faith nineteen centuries younger than my own—I slowly began to notice that I was doing a great deal more than just investigating an interesting subject; I was undergoing a profound spiritual transformation.

I had expected, I think, to hear and be moved by the well-known stories of heroes and martyrs. What I had not expected to hear was clear, unambiguous teaching from these heroes and martyrs—the actual doctrine of primitive Christianity set down in black and white. Yet here it was, nevertheless: plain, substantive instruction about what the early Church actually believed—and much of it on "hot-button" topics that have become hopelessly controversial in our own time. I found that these four witnesses were not a bit shy about interpreting the holy Scriptures written so recently by the Apostles in whose steps they followed. They interpreted them vigorously, boldly, and with authority . . . leaving me, I'm afraid, in something of a pickle when I noticed that their interpretations often differed considerably from my own. Don't get me wrong. I still held firmly to *Sola Scriptura*. But honestly, what's a young fellow to do when he finds himself in a theological disagreement with four men who got their Bible training more or less directly from the Apostles? Looking back, I can see that when I first opened these books I was thinking of myself as an archeologist, perhaps breaking the ancient seal of King Solomon's Mines to plunder his dusty relics. But before long I felt as if my flashlight beam had fallen upon King Solomon himself sitting among his treasures—alive, energetic, and still ready to impart his royal wisdom to anyone with ears to hear.

How I dealt with this remarkable encounter—how it

changed me forever and how it renewed the youth of my spirit—I really won't be able to explain until you have experienced something of these four witnesses for yourselves. Which, of course, is my excuse for writing the book you now hold in your hands.

It occurred to me that if this information were just a bit more accessible—if there were not quite so much of it buried under purple Victorian translations or petrified by lifeless, clinging academic critique—then ordinary believers like me would not have to work quite so hard to get at it. In fact, I thought I could see a compelling human *drama* entangled in all this dusty fine print; a drama that might go on to work its rejuvenating magic in many more lives if only someone could write it up in a more approachable style. This is where I began to feel that I might be of help. The Lord knows that I am no scholar. In fact, I am not much more than a Christian bookworm, with an amateur's interest in history. But I will own up to a certain knack for storytelling—along with an intense persuasion that this particular story needs telling right now. This, I suppose, is what finally gave me the courage foolishly to rush in; an impatient conviction that this material is simply too amazing to remain a "best-kept secret" any longer, even if it has to be presented by an author whose only real qualification is *enthusiasm*.

Way back in the early 1960s, writer Margaret T. Monro penned a few short but prophetic words that seem to me very appropriate for quoting here. In the introduction to her excellent little book *Enjoying the New Testament* she wrote:

> The progressive paganization of society is now putting twentieth-century Christians in close rapport with their first-century brethren. The world has not quite relapsed

> into its pagan state, but it has gone far enough to give us a new sense of kinship with these spiritual ancestors of ours. Dark as our sky is, theirs was darker, for they lacked all the encouragement of Christian history, to us such a precious support.[1]

Has the dark sky done anything but darken since then? And as Monro's twentieth-century now becomes our twenty-first, do we not need the encouragement of Christian history more than ever?

My fervent hope is to spread this precious support just a bit farther abroad. May the Holy Spirit use this new book to kindle in your hearts—as He has in mine—a bit of the fire and passion of your spiritual ancestors as they write to us from across the centuries *in their own words*.

The early Church is no mystery . . . thanks be to God!

> Can any who spend several years in the seats of learning, be excused if they do not add to that of the languages and sciences, a knowledge of the Fathers?—the most authentic commentators on Scripture, as being both nearest the fountain, and eminently with that Spirit by whom all Scripture was given.
>
> John Wesley—*An Address to the Clergy*

[1] Margaret T. Monro, *Enjoying the New Testament* (Garden City, N.Y.: Image Books, 1962), p. 15.

A Note about Historical Accuracy

In these pages I have proposed to tell the authentic story of early Christianity by presenting large verbatim excerpts from the four earliest non-canonical Christian writers whose works have survived down to our own time—the "four witnesses" of my title. In doing this my goal has been (as far as possible) to let the early Church speak for herself. But I have also felt the need to set each excerpt in its historical context as well. Who were these books written to, and under what circumstances? What emergencies were being dealt with? What hopes and dreams and fears were being addressed? I felt that it was only by portraying these things—sketching out the landscape, so to speak, behind each excerpt—that I could hope to make the ancient writings truly understandable. I have based these reconstructions solidly upon the very best scholarship available to me. Naturally however, any additions to or explanations of the naked text itself would necessarily admit a certain amount of subjectivity into the work. Choices had to be made between competing scholarly opinions and judgments had to be drawn up when clear documentary evidence was lacking. I frankly own up to this subjectivity—and also to using certain novelistic devices imported from the storyteller's art that would be inappropriate in a more scholarly work. All this should be understood in the context of my previously stated goal; to tell *a true tale*, certainly—but also to tell a tale that engages the heart as well as the mind.

Acknowledgments

I had the opportunity to submit this text to several genuine experts on the early Church, most notably to Mr. Mike Aquilina, whose wonderful book *The Fathers of the Church* (Basilica Press) I heartily recommend to anyone who might wish to delve deeper into the subject at hand. Many other kind, intelligent people offered their thoughts, prayers, and encouragement as well; chief among these were Mark Shea, Jim Henry III, Geoff Horton, Mike Hertenstein, Fr. Tim Hepburn, Gary and Kathie Lundquist, Jim Peavy, and Erick Soto.

Several members of the Church Triumphant need mentioning also, writers whose profound effect on *Four Witnesses* will be obvious to anyone familiar with their works: Msgr. Robert Hugh Benson, G. K. Chesterton, St. Francis de Sales, and, particularly, Hilaire Belloc.

Finally, I wish to extol the patient virtue of my devoted wife, Dorothy, who brought a timely word from the Lord at a crucial moment, keeping *Four Witnesses* alive. May God bless and keep her.

Therefore, since we are surrounded by so great a cloud of witnesses, let us also lay aside every weight, and sin which clings so closely, and let us run with perseverance the race that is set before us.

Hebrews 12:1

Abbreviations

ACW — Ancient Christian Writers series. Mahwah, N.J., Paulist Press.

ANF — *Ante-Nicene Fathers.* 10 vols. Edited by Alexander Roberts and James Donaldson, revised by A. Cleveland Coxe. Peabody, Mass.: Hendrickson Publishers, 1995.

CCC — *Catechism of the Catholic Church*, 2d ed. Rome: Libreria Editrice Vaticana, 1997.

CEC — Chadwick, Henry. *The Early Church.* London: Penguin Books, 1973.

EHC — Eusebius Pamphilus. *History of the Church.* Translated by G. A. Williamson. London: Penguin Books, 1989.

FEF — *The Faith of the Early Fathers.* 3 vols. Translated and edited by W. A. Jurgens. Collegeville, Minn.: Liturgical Press, 1970–1979.

NPNF1 — *Nicene and Post-Nicene Fathers.* 1st series. 10 vols. Edited by Philip Schaff. Peabody, Mass.: Hendrickson Publishers, 1995.

NPNF2 — *Nicene and Post-Nicene Fathers.* 2d series. 14 vols. Edited by Philip Schaff and Henry Wace. Peabody, Mass.: Hendrickson Publishers, 1995.

Clement of Rome

Let us fix our gaze upon the Blood of Christ and understand how precious it is to the Father, because, poured out for our salvation, it brought to the whole world the grace of conversion. Let us pass in review all the generations and learn the lesson, that from generation to generation the Master has given an opportunity for conversion to those who were willing to turn to Him.[1]

A man named Clement, pastor of the church at Rome during the decade of the 90s A.D., wrote these tender words to his fellow Christians living in the Greek city of Corinth—the very same Corinthians to whom the Apostle Paul had addressed two New Testament epistles about thirty years earlier. Both Origen, the third-century scholar, and Eusebius, author of the world's oldest book of Church history (written in A.D. 325), knew this letter of Clement well. They tell us that its author is the same Clement mentioned by name in the Bible as the fellow worker of Paul, who **"labored side by side . . . in the gospel"** with the great Apostle and **"whose names are in the book of life"** (Phil 4:3).[2] But notice how

[1] Clement of Rome, *First Epistle of Clement to the Corinthians*, chap. 7, nos. 4–5, in *The Epistles of St. Clement of Rome and St. Ignatius of Antioch*, trans. James A. Kleist, ACW, vol. 1 (Mahwah, N.J.: Paulist Press, 1948), p. 13. [Please be aware that the notes and corresponding italics added to the text by Dr. Kleist have not been used in this present book.—Ed.]

[2] Though no fewer than seven of the earliest Church Fathers make this same identification without hesitation, many modern scholars are inclined to doubt, citing various chronological difficulties. Nevertheless, the Protes-

even at this early date the Church feels the need to turn the eyes of her people backward in time to marvel at the saving works of God in history. It seems fitting, then, as the Church enters her third millennium, to take these ancient words to heart again for ourselves. Let us begin this exploration of the testimony about the early Church by "passing in review all the generations" back to Clement's own time, where his *Epistle to the Corinthians* preserves a fascinating snapshot of the gospel of Christ being lived out by believers who received it from the lips of Christ's own disciples.

Feed My Sheep

To understand Clement's role in God's plan for the early Church we really need to begin even farther back—by reliving some of the "childhood" of the congregation he eventually came to shepherd. Sadly, the actual details of our subject's life have been lost to history; all that survives with certainty is the *Epistle* itself. Yet if we look very carefully at the pages of Scripture and at the history of those amazing times, we do begin to see an *outline*—the life and times, not of Clement himself perhaps, but of his family in Christ. It is true that without an actual biography of Clement much of the backdrop of his priceless letter has to be sketched in with hypothesis and speculation. The story of Clement's *home church*, however, is known with quite a bit of accuracy, and with this story guiding the way we can at least learn

---

tant scholars Roberts and Donaldson, in their introduction to Clement's letter in the *Ante-Nicene Fathers*, summarize the still valid traditional view: The Epistle "is to be regarded as an authentic production of the friend and fellow-worker of St. Paul" (ANF 1:2).

about the events that would have shaped the course of his Christian adventure here on earth.

In fact, it may be that the best place to begin Clement's story is found within the pages of the New Testament itself. There, in the final chapter of the Gospel of John, we find recorded the single event that seems chiefly to have forged the pattern of his destiny. Significantly, it is an event, not from the life of Clement himself, but from the life of the Apostle whom Tertullian (writing about A.D. 200) tells us ordained him for ministry by the laying on of his own hands.

> **Jesus said to Simon Peter, "Simon, son of John, do you love me more than these?" He said to him, "Yes, Lord; you know that I love you." He said to him, "Feed my lambs." A second time he said to him, "Simon, son of John, do you love me?" He said to him, "Yes, Lord; you know that I love you." He said to him, "Tend my sheep." He said to him the third time, "Simon, son of John, do you love me?" Peter was grieved because he said to him the third time, "Do you love me?" And he said to him, "Lord, you know everything; you know that I love you." Jesus said to him, "Feed my sheep."** (Jn 21:15–17)

The scene is a private breakfast along the shore of Tiberias. The Bible tells us that a "charcoal fire" burns on the beach: on the menu—some simple bread and one or two of 153 miraculous fishes just pulled out of the lake at the word of Christ. Present at this apostolic meal are Simon Peter, Thomas, Nathanael of Cana, and two other unnamed disciples; also James the son of Zebedee and his younger brother John—the eyewitness who will later record the episode in the Gospel that bears his name. John pauses here to tell us

"This was now the third time that Jesus was revealed to the disciples after he was raised from the dead" (21:14).

It is sobering to notice that the Lord asks His heart-rending question three times—once for each of Peter's three denials on the night before the crucifixion. Surely the phrase "Peter was grieved" must be putting the matter mildly. But notice also that even in his grief the Apostle shows his great faith. "Look within me", he seems to cry out. "Look with all your omniscience, Son of the living God. Though I am a sinful man, though I betrayed you as badly as Judas, whatever else may be true, you *know* that I love you." And Jesus does know it. Ultimately, this scene is not about the past but about the *future*.

"Feed my sheep." These words are full of profound meaning. All through His Passion and right up to His Ascension, Jesus seems to be acutely concerned—even beset—over the future of His fragile little flock. Recall that earlier, on the night in which He was betrayed, Jesus, "deeply troubled", had lifted His eyes to heaven and called out a great high-priestly prayer for this ragged band of working men and ne'er-do-wells:

> **"Father, the hour has come; glorify thy Son that the Son may glorify thee. . . . I have manifested thy name to the men whom thou gavest me out of the world; thine they were, and thou gavest them to me. . . . I have given them the words which thou gavest me, and they have received them and know in truth that I came from thee; and they have believed that thou didst send me. I am praying for them; I am not praying for the world but for those whom thou hast given me, for they are thine. . . .**

And now I am no more in the world, but they are in the world, and I am coming to thee. Holy Father, keep them in thy name which thou hast given me, that they may be one, even as we are one. While I was with them, I kept them in thy name. . . . But now I am coming to thee. . . . Sanctify them in the truth." (Jn 17:1b, 6a, 8–9, 11–12a, 13a, 17)

Sanctify them in the truth. Jesus has come to give humanity the words of truth given to Him by His Father. But now that the Son is going back to the Father, how will the world know that He was ever here? And that He really was sent by God? How will His work be preserved and continued? How will future generations learn "the words of eternal life" that belong to Jesus alone, and, just as importantly, how can they know that they have learned them correctly? And understood them correctly?

It has been too little commented upon, but when Jesus made the simple statement, **"I am the good shepherd"** (Jn 10:11), He made one of His most startling claims to divinity. Every Jew in Palestine would have been familiar with this ancient prophetic title—a prophecy that when the Messiah did finally come, He would come as *God in the flesh*.

"The word of the LORD came to me: 'Son of man, prophesy against the shepherds of Israel, prophesy, and say to them, even to the shepherds, Thus says the Lord GOD: Ho, shepherds of Israel who have been feeding yourselves! Should not shepherds feed the sheep? You eat the fat, you clothe yourselves with the wool, you slaughter the fatlings; but you do not feed the sheep'" (Ezek 34:1–3). So begins one of God's greatest pledges to His wayward people, given late in Israel's history through the prophet Ezekiel. Over long ages of time He has sent them prophet after prophet in hopes of turning their hearts toward home. But the warnings of these true shepherds have been continually undercut by false shepherds—false prophets who **"prophesy out of their own minds"** (Ezek 13:2), who **"follow their own spirit, and have seen nothing"** (13:3), who say, **" 'Says the LORD,' when the LORD has not sent them"** (13:6), who prophesy **" 'Peace,' when there is no peace"** (13:10). Against these evil shepherds the Lord rises to continue:

> **"As I live, says the Lord GOD, because my sheep have become a prey, and my sheep have become food for all the wild beasts, since there was no shepherd; and because my shepherds have not searched for my sheep, but the shepherds have fed themselves, and have not fed my sheep. . . . Behold, I, I myself will search for my sheep, and will seek them out. As a shepherd seeks out his flock when some of his sheep have been scattered abroad, so will I seek out my sheep; and I will rescue them. . . . I myself will be the shepherd of my sheep, and I will make them lie down, says the Lord GOD. I will seek the lost, and I will bring back the strayed, and I will bind up the crippled, and I will strengthen the weak, and the fat and the strong I will watch over; I will feed them in justice. . . . I will save my flock, they shall no longer be a prey. . . . And I will set up over them one shepherd, my servant David, and he shall feed them: he shall feed them and be their shepherd. . . . And they shall know that I, the LORD their God, am with them."** (Ezek 34:8, 11–12a, 15–16, 22–24b, 30)

It was into this context—a culture steeped in Old Testament literacy—that Jesus, the humble carpenter out of Nazareth, dropped the words that must have resounded like thunderclaps:

> **"I am the good shepherd. The good shepherd lays down his life for the sheep. He who is a hireling and not a shepherd, whose own the sheep are not, sees the wolf coming and leaves the sheep and flees; and the wolf snatches them and scatters them. He flees because he is a hireling and cares nothing for the sheep. I am the good shepherd; I know my own and my own know me, as the Father knows me and I know the Father; and I lay down my life for the sheep. And I have other sheep, that are not of this fold; I must bring them also, and they will heed my voice. So there shall be one flock, one shepherd."** (Jn 10:11–16)

That Christ's hearers knew full well what was implied by His claim to Ezekiel's famous epithet is obvious from their response: **"Many of them said, 'He has a demon, and he is mad; why listen to him'"** (Jn 10:20). Their shock is perhaps understandable in the face of such an astounding assertion: Emmanuel—the "God with us" who was to come—claims to have arrived at last. As Jesus had said to them a short time earlier, **"Do not murmur among yourselves. . . . It is written in the prophets, 'And they shall all be taught by God'"** (Jn 6:43, 45).

But what then becomes of the sheep when the Good Shepherd returns to heaven? **"I came from the Father and have come into the world; again, I am leaving the world and going to the Father"** (Jn 16:28). As we wondered before, how will Christ's work be continued? If God's sheep starved for truth at the hands of false religious teachers under the Old Covenant, will not His New Testament flock again be defenseless after the Shepherd ascends back **"to my Father and your Father, to my God and your God"** (Jn 20:17)?

The answer, according to the testimony of the early Church, lies in these words, spoken by the Good Shepherd to Simon Peter, representative of a simple band of Galilean fishermen:

"Feed my sheep."

Little Lost Sheep

Clement of Rome, in all likelihood, was born and raised a heathen idol worshipper—born, by the best estimates, about A.D. 30; possibly the very year that the risen Lord gave His solemn charge to Peter. And though (as we mentioned before) reliable details about his early life are hard to come by, there do seem to be at least a few authentic traditions preserved in an ancient book called *The Itinerarium of St. Clement.*[3]

---

[3] The *Itinerarium of St. Clement* (often referred to as *The Book of Recognitions*) is one of three major second-century works about the life of Clement; two of them are more or less orthodox, the third is a heretical work created by a Judaizing sect called the Ebionites. These books are certainly not, as they purport to be, autobiographies written by Clement himself—but this falsification may have been simply a literary device rather than a deliberate deception. Still, most modern scholars hold these documents suspect, and I frankly admit that this material is much less dependable than the other sources I will be quoting in this chapter. The fact that all three works agree in basic outline, however, strongly suggests that they were shaped by recollections of genuine events in the life of the real Clement.

This book tells us that Clement was born at the very center of the greatest cosmopolitan empire the world has ever known, at the city of Rome itself. If this is true, our subject would have reached manhood at a point in history that echoes with strong parallels to our own troubled times.

In A.D. 50 Imperial Rome was perhaps at the peak of its political, economic, and military might—sole surviving "superpower" in a world of once-formidable but now forgotten enemies. The famous *Pax Romana* had been established; a "new world order" of peace and prosperity sprawling from the crashing shores of the Atlantic in the west to the barbaric steppes of Scythia in the east, from foggy Londinium in Britannia to the sun-parched Sahara in the south. But this vast transcontinental civilization had been forged by a hardier crop of Romans; by soldiers and frontiersmen from a healthier, happier era. Clement's own sickly generation, fatally addicted to luxury and excess, inherited an empire without external enemies, but was destined to watch helplessly as this legacy began to rot like so much overripe fruit under the influence of new adversaries springing up from within.

Romans of the first century were surprisingly modern in many respects. They had running water and flushing toilets in their homes, they had a tabloid "press" dishing up the latest dirt on celebrity divorces, and so on. They had billboards, traffic jams, and (if their ruins are any indication) a serious problem with graffiti. Stunning recent discoveries seem to prove that they even had elaborate mechanical calculating devices that can only be called *computers*. Perhaps it should not be too surprising, then, to learn that they also faced an all too familiar tangle of intractable social ills:

crime, unemployment, slums, high taxes, political corruption, class and race divisions, pornography, and prostitution.

Religion for the Romans, which had at one time been a homey, agrarian affair of friendly household gods, took one of two recognized courses during Clement's youth—both of them ugly. Under the influence of Lucretius and his school (who taught the Romans a strikingly complete theory of evolution) many citizens of the Empire became sophisticated, world-weary skeptics who abandoned religion altogether—except of course for the obligatory pinch of incense offered to the approved civic pantheon once a year. Contrariwise, the other prevalent trend in Roman spirituality was to *embrace the chaos*. A new synthesis of all cults began to emerge—a first-century New Age movement, so to speak. In this stream the old-fashioned harvest gods once worshipped with sheaves of wheat and jugs of wine degenerated steadily into fashionable sex gods to be worshipped with acts of perversion and infant sacrifice. Late Roman paganism became a sad, sordid blend of riotous demonism, on the one hand, and cold, cynical sophistry, on the other.

It was within this hopeless religious climate, then, that Clement of Rome came of age—Clement who (the *Itinerarium* tells us) was a seeker after truth from his childhood. As a matter of fact, this particular account of Clement's youth reads a little like a tale out of our own turbulent 1960s. By A.D. 50 Clement would have reached about what we call "college age". He is depicted here as a young man from an upper-class background, with important family connections in government and business. His surviving writings strongly suggest that someone provided him with a quality classical education once upon a time, and there would have been, no doubt, some expectations incumbent upon such a bright, promising lad. Yet Clement seems suddenly to have abandoned it all in an idealistic search for "answers". Like Christian in the opening chapter of Bunyan's *Pilgrim's Progress*, we soon find young Clement "dropping out", as it were, from his dying culture—compelled to "flee from the wrath to come" onto the arduous road that leads to the Celestial City.

Sadly, answers were hard to come by in first-century Rome. Quite beyond the aforementioned religious chaos, even the most sincere seeker of truth would have found himself swamped by a hundred mutually exclusive philosophical systems clamoring for attention. The *Itinerarium* vividly describes the anguish and perplexity that grew in Clement's heart as he tried one current school of thought after another and found "nothing but disputings, contradiction, and uncertainty". Specifically, we are told that he was tortured by the puzzle of how the world came to be, by what its ultimate destiny might hold, and by whether he himself might reasonably expect to encounter anything at death beyond a cold, dark hole in the ground.

In other words, Clement of Rome, a desperate pagan living in a desperate city, was obviously one of those "little lost sheep" the Good Shepherd came to save—one from that "other fold" to whom He also promised to send His Apostles.

The Kingdom of Heaven at Hand

The Apostles came. Sometime between A.D. 50 and 60, Clement heard a rumor spreading among the local street-corner philosophers that there had arisen in distant Judea a group of Jewish wise men preaching in the name of a mysterious new deity called *Christus*. In fact, these Apostles and their followers were already said to be busily importing this new faith into Rome itself. And though Clement had undoubtedly heard many preachers by this time (representing every exotic "mystery religion" of the day, from Zoroastrianism to the cult of Mithras) these new sages from the East reportedly came confirming their teaching with *miraculous signs*. To someone floundering, as Clement seems to have been, in a sea of empty words, the mere rumor of a doctrine preached with heaven's own authority must have been enough to send a man on a mission from God.

Where might these "Apostles" be found? Their new movement was, after all, still secretive. The hatred of the Pharisees had driven Christianity underground by ensuring that its name would always be associated (at least in the minds of Roman officials) with tumult and civil unrest. Nevertheless, a bit of scratching around among Clement's metaphysical cronies would probably have turned up a lead or two; these Roman sophists were, after all, the kindred spirits of the Athenians Paul met on Mars Hill, who **"spent their time in nothing except telling or hearing something new"** (Acts 17:21). Did one of these leads send Clement to some half-ruined barn out along the Appian Way? Or did "the friend of a friend" direct him to some hushed, firelit encampment under a rural aqueduct? We will probably never know the actual details this side of heaven. But this much we *do* know: Clement of Rome did eventually take his tormenting questions to the Church of Rome—that local body of first-century believers whom Paul had so recently praised for great faith, a faith **"proclaimed in all the world"** (Rom 1:8).

In *Quo Vadis?*, his famous novel of the early Church, author Henryk Sienkiewicz sends his protagonist, the headstrong pagan soldier Marcus Vinitius, to this very same Church of Rome at about the same period we have been discussing. Basing his re-creation of such a scene on meticulous research, Sienkiewicz admirably succeeds in painting a vivid picture of just the sort of experience someone like Clement might have had at *his* first church service.

> They walked by way of Vicus Patricius along the Viminal near the plain on which Diocletian later built his famous baths. . . . Then turning to the left towards the Via Salaria, they found themselves among the sandpits and graveyards. . . . At the gate two men accepted the password and they entered within. . . . The crowd was huge, so they all had to gather outside of the crypt itself. . . . Someone lighted some torches made of pitch around the crypt and suddenly it became much lighter and warmer. Songs were sung now at different locations. Vinitius had never heard such songs before. . . . [The music] soon filled the whole cemetery, penetrating and immense, as if together with the people, the pits, the hills around and the whole region itself was filled with yearning. . . .
>
> Vinitius had seen many different temples, in Asia Minor, Egypt as well as in Rome. . . . but here for the first time he heard people, not fulfilling some kind of ritual, but calling from the heart with sincere yearning as children seek their father or mother. One had to be blind not to see that these people not only honored their God but also loved Him with their hearts and souls. Vinitius had never seen anything like it. . . . Meanwhile, more torches were lit and it became lighter still. At the same time an old man who wore

a hooded mantle with bared head came from the crypt. He mounted a stone in order to be seen by all. The crowd swayed before him.

Voices near Vinitius whispered, "Peter . . . Peter." Some knelt, others extended their arms toward him. There followed a silence so deep that one heard every charred particle that dropped from the torches, the distant rattle of wheels on the Via Nomentana and the sound of the wind through the pines which grew close to the cemetery.

[One of his companions] bent toward Vinitius and whispered, "This is he . . . the foremost disciple of Christ . . . a fisherman."[4]

How much had Clement heard about this *Simon Cephas*—handpicked representative of the shadowy Christus of Judea? Had he heard him called a miracle man? That he had walked on water? Made the blind to see? Raised the dead? We do not know. Perhaps it was Peter's simplicity that shone strongest. In the fondly remembered 1951 film version of *Quo Vadis?*, Scottish actor Finlay Currie portrays the Big Fisherman in this scene. As he begins to preach, Currie's strong highland flavor beautifully suggests the weathered dignity with which an old seaman like Peter might have impressed a city-slicker like Clement.

Jesus has guided my feet to Rome so that together we can begin to build his Church here. I give thanks for the faith you have in Him whom you have never seen but whose voice you have heard and answered in your hearts.

I heard His voice by the Sea of Galilee. My brothers and I were fishermen. All the night through we had been fish-

[4] Henryk Sienkiewicz, *Quo Vadis?*, trans. Stanley F. Conrad (San Francisco: Ignatius Press, 1993), pp. 153, 155–56.

ing and had caught nothing. We were cold and very tired. As our boat was coming into the shore I heard someone call my name. I looked up and a man stood there. At the sight of Him the cold and weariness left me and my heart grew light. I answered "Yes, friend?" and He called and asked that He might come into our boat so that He could speak better to the people who were pressing round Him on shore. We bade Him enter. He spoke to the people about the kingdom of heaven at hand. And suddenly my heart leapt in my breast and I knew that He was the Christ to come. When He had finished He said to me, "Go out into deep waters and let down your nets." In a moment the nets were full, as if by a miracle. He looked at my wonderment and said, "Do not be afraid. From henceforth you shall be a fisher of men." He told me to follow Him and I did, I and my brethren James and John. Throughout the length and the breadth of the land we followed Him. Others joined us until, besides Himself, we were twelve. To the hungry and thirsty He gave food and drink. To those who were sick and worn and weary He gave peace.

Who but the Son of God could have brought such gifts to man? Who but the Son of God could have commanded the storm to be calm? Who but He could have raised Lazarus from the dead and given peace to the heart of Mary Magdalene? And yet . . . I lived to deny this man. He Himself foretold that I would on the night of our last supper. "Lord," I had said, "I am willing to follow you both to prison and to death." But He answered, "Peter, this night, before the cock crows, you will deny me thrice." And I did—three times outside the house of His judges. When they accused me of being with Him I said, "I know not the man"—with a curse for the weakness of my body in the face of death. Then, they weighed Him down with a cross and scourged Him.

As Peter begins to speak of the sufferings of Christ, Sienkiewicz sends a holy fear upon his hero; though still skeptical, Vinitius finds in Peter's face "a convincing power as pure as truth itself". Clement, too, must have listened in awe as the broad-shouldered old Galilean began to share—not esoteric speculations on the nature of the divine—but his own *memories*.

> At a place called Calvary they crucified Him with a crown of thorns upon His head. But even in the midst of His suffering Jesus said, "Father, forgive them for they know not what they do." Only the Son of God could have forgiven them, as He forgave me for my denial of Him. But He who raised the dead could not be conquered by death. The room in which we later sat in silence and in sorrow was filled suddenly with a great light, and the risen Lord stood before us. We saw His hands that the nails had pierced and His wounded side and we knew indeed that it was the Lord.

Gradually, Marcus Vinitius feels "something strange happening within his soul". "When Peter spoke to the people about the Resurrection, some uttered cries of joy and raised their arms to the heavens. . . . Christ lived and lives now! Christ to them was everything. . . . Only Christ mattered, and He it is Who fills them with complete happiness." But as Peter's sermon nears its climax, the aged Apostle goes on to do far more than simply evoke the past. He begins to exhort Christ's present-day flock to imitate His example in the here-and-now:

> Obey those who govern you and the laws by which they govern, even though under them you suffer cruelties and witness maliciousness beyond your mind's dimensions. Make no threat of violence in return. And in the words of Jesus

> I further say to you, "Whosoever shall smite thee on thy right cheek, turn to him the other also." "Love thy neighbor as thyself." "Whatsoever you would that men should do unto you, do ye also unto them." "Love your enemies." "Bless them that curse you. Do good to them that hate you and pray for them that despitefully use you and persecute you."
>
> Oh, believe in Him! Endure all things in His name so that you may dwell in blessedness even from everlasting to everlasting![5]

Did Clement of Rome first respond to the call of Christ under circumstances like these? Once again, we can only speculate. But the ancient books that tell us of his conversion all agree in at least one particular: *Clemens Romanus*, citizen of the Empire, was baptized into the "one flock" by Peter himself and then personally instructed by the Apostle in the pure doctrine of Jesus Christ, God's "True Prophet".

Sojourning in Babylon

Some of us may have been a bit surprised to find Peter pastoring the Church of Rome. The Bible says little, if anything, about such a state of affairs, and the subject has been at the center of much controversy. Obviously, today's Protestants still have a big problem with the Catholic belief that Peter was the first pope. In their zeal, however, many preachers have gone beyond this to deny that Peter was ever in Rome at all. This is unfortunate; serious scholars—Catholic, Protes-

---

[5] Peter's sermon here has been transcribed from the MGM film, screenplay by S. N. Behrman, Sonya Levien, and John Lee Mahin.

tant, or entirely secular—have long agreed that the historical evidence for Peter's Roman ministry is unimpeachable.[6]

It is true that our only *infallible* book of Church history is the New Testament book of Acts, written as it was by the evangelist Luke under the inspiration of the Holy Spirit. But Acts leaves more than half of Peter's apostolic career undocumented, turning away at chapter 13 to focus the spotlight almost entirely on Paul and his great missionary journeys. For any further details about the life of the Big Fisherman, we are forced to rely upon merely human sources. Nevertheless, a good deal of very trustworthy material remains, preserved by the ordinary methods of history. Eusebius sums up these early traditions in his venerable *History of the Church*: **"In the . . . reign of Claudius** [emperor from A.D. 41 to 54] **the all-good and gracious providence which watches over all things guided Peter, the great and mighty one among the Apostles, who, because of his virtue, was the spokesman for all the others, to Rome."**[7] In another place, the same historian records that in the **"second year of the two hundred and fifth olympiad: the Apostle Peter, after he has established the Church in Antioch, is sent to Rome, where he remains as bishop of that city, preaching the gospel for twenty-five years."**[8] The scholar Jerome, who

---

[6] The distinguished antiquarian Lanciani wrote this: "For the archaeologist the presence and execution of SS. Peter and Paul in Rome are facts established beyond a shadow of doubt by purely monumental evidence" (Rodolfo Lanciani, *Pagan and Christian Rome* [Boston: Houghton, Mifflin, 1893], p. 123.

[7] Eusebius Pamphilus, *History of the Church*, bk. 2, chap. 14, no. 6, in FEF 1:292, no. 651dd.

[8] Eusebius Pamphilus, *The Chronicle, Ad An. Dom.* 42, in FEF 1:291, no. 651aa.

died in 419, also preserves interesting details. He writes that **"Peter, the Prince of the Apostles, after his episcopate in the church of Antioch, went to Rome in the second year of Claudius, and continued there for 25 years up to the end of his life in the fourteenth year of Nero."**[9] This would put the Apostle's arrival in Rome about A.D. 42 and his death in 67. Even earlier is the testimony of Irenaeus of Lyons (of whom much more will be said later). Irenaeus wrote his five-volume work *Against Heresies* as early as A.D. 180, and in it he plainly states that **"the greatest and most ancient Church known to all, [was] founded and organized at Rome by the two most glorious Apostles, Peter and Paul."**[10] Tertullian, too, weighs in on this subject of Peter at Rome: **"How happy is that Church, on which Apostles poured out their whole doctrine along with their blood, where Peter endured a passion like that of the Lord, where Paul was crowned with a death like John's [the Baptist]."**[11] Epiphanius, Origen, Cyprian, and many more of the earliest Church Fathers treat this information as if it were common knowledge, and by the third century the tombs of Peter and Paul were already being visited at Rome by pilgrims from across the world. In all honesty (and putting partisan quarrels aside), there really does not seem to be any good reason why Peter should not have been shepherding Christ's flock

---

[9] Quoted by D. I. Landslots, *The Primitive Church* (Rockford, Ill.: TAN Books, 1980), p. 118.

[10] Irenaeus of Lyons, *Against Heresies*, bk. 3, chap. 3, no. 2, in FEF 1:90, no. 210.

[11] Tertullian, *Demurrer against the Heretics*, chap. 36, no. 1, in FEF 1:122, no. 297.

at Rome when Clement's hour of need arrived—as all the ancient literature insists.

The very first Christians in Rome were probably Jewish expatriates returning to their adopted city after being converted by Peter's Spirit-filled preaching at Jerusalem on the Day of Pentecost. The Bible explicitly mentions that present in the crowd that day were **"visitors from Rome"** (Acts 2:10). But such early Roman converts would truly have been sheep without a shepherd, returning to face the prospect of life as the only believers in a pagan metropolis of half a million souls. They probably met together in their homes for prayer—two or three gathered in Christ's name—but entirely without instructed leadership. Twenty-five years later, however, when Paul addressed his most profound epistle to **"all God's beloved in Rome, who are called to be saints"** we find a much different situation. Written about A.D. 57, the Epistle to the Romans speaks to a church large and well organized, consisting of several house-congregations knit together in complete unity under the oversight of seasoned elders, or *presbyters*. Who accomplished this work of organization? Who discipled these presbyters and trained them in the correct doctrine? As we have seen, history answers that it was Peter. After his miraculous release from Herod's prison in Acts 12, we are told that Peter **"departed and went to another place"** (12:17), and this verse is pretty much his "swan song", scripturally speaking.[12] Was this "other place" Rome? If so, then "the Prince of the Apostles" launched his

[12] Peter does make a brief reappearance a few years later, returning to Jerusalem with the other Apostles to take part in the great Church council recorded in Acts 15. This council was held not later than A.D. 50.

crusade to conquer the Imperial City for Christ sometime between A.D. 42 and 45—just the moment pinpointed by our extrabiblical witnesses.

With these witnesses leading the way, it *is* possible to deduce from the pages of the New Testament at least a few additional facts about Peter's Roman mission. We know, for example, that he was *not* present in Rome when Paul sent the Epistle to the Romans from Corinth. How to account for this absence? Probably he continued, like Paul, to make extended missionary tours occasionally, leaving the care of his home church in the hands of other approved men. Another theory is that his fiery preaching, not sparing the delicate feelings of either Jew or pagan, made Peter a marked and hunted man. Like the celebrated leaders of the French Resistance during World War II, a man like Peter would have been forced to "disappear" from time to time to save his life. We know, for example, that while Paul was in Corinth writing the book of Romans he met Priscilla and Aquila, refugees **"lately come from Italy . . . because Claudius had commanded all the Jews to leave Rome"** (Acts 18:2).[13] Peter himself was quite possibly displaced in this same purge.

Yet notice that, wherever he may have been, the true shepherd cannot be kept away from his flock for long. Shortly after this, we find Peter sending his first general epistle to

[13] Suetonius, pagan author of the *Life of Claudius*, may possibly provide a secular confirmation of this event. He writes: **"Since the Jews continually made disturbances at the instigation of Chrestus** [the Latin for Christ is *Christus*], **Claudius expelled them from Rome"** (*Life of Claudius*, quoted in CEC 41). The pagans continued for many years to regard Christianity as just another Jewish sect, and thus they were inclined to see persecutions of the early Church by the Pharisees as religious infighting among rival factions.

the churches of the world, known familiarly to us as First Peter. In signing off at the end of this letter, the Apostle provides cryptic but compelling evidence (and our strongest bit of canonical evidence) that he is now back with his people in the "City of the Seven Hills": **"She who is at Babylon . . . sends you greetings"** (1 Pet 5:13).

As can be observed in the pages of the book of Revelation, the early Church had a mystical "code name" for the debauched city that was pagan Rome. Chapter 17 speaks of **"a woman sitting on a scarlet beast"**, a beast with seven heads (17:3). It goes on to reveal that **"the seven heads are seven hills"** (17:9) and that the woman herself is **"the great city which has dominion over the kings of the earth"** (17:18). The name of this great city? **"Babylon the great, mother of harlots and of earth's abominations"** (17:5). Peter's "Babylon", then, was his own chosen mission field of Rome. This was the unanimous opinion of all the ancient commentators concerning this passage, and, in more recent times, even such a disinterested witness as John Calvin reaffirmed this interpretation.

Turning to the rest of the Apostle's New Testament writings, one sees right away that this was indeed Peter's vision of the Christian life: believers are strangers and pilgrims sojourning in Babylon. First Peter itself is addressed (borrowing a Jewish metaphor) **"To the exiles of the Dispersion in Pontus, Galatia, Cappadocia, Asia, and Bithynia"** (1 Pet 1:1), and in it Peter beseeches his readers **"as aliens and exiles"** (2:11) to abstain from the worldly allurements of their surrounding culture. Peter's colleagues in the apostolic ministry also emphasized the wayfaring nature of Christ's Church on earth. The Apostle John, for instance, wrote:

"Do not love the world or the things in the world. . . . The world passes away, and the lust of it; but he who does the will of God abides for ever" (1 Jn 2:15, 17).

Looking ahead in time, we can see Peter's teaching about this "Babylonian Captivity" taking permanent root in the church he founded; the literature associated with Latin Christianity will ring with this theme for hundreds of years to come. One particularly striking example is an ancient document known as *The Epistle to Diognetus.* This anonymous letter was an appeal on behalf of persecuted believers addressed to a high Roman official by someone who describes himself as **"a disciple of the Apostles"**.

Interestingly enough, several scholars have held that this beautiful epistle was composed by Clement himself. Be that as it may, it does certainly express this pilgrim religion we believe Clement would have learned from his newfound family in Christ:

> **Christians . . . reside in their respective countries, but only as aliens. They take part in everything as citizens and put up with everything as foreigners. Every foreign land is their home, and every home a foreign land. . . . Their board they spread for all, but not their bed. They find themselves in the flesh, but do not live according to the flesh. They spend their days on earth, but hold citizenship in heaven. They obey the established laws, but in their private lives they rise above the laws. They love all men, but are persecuted by all. They are unknown, yet are condemned; they are put to death, but it is life that they receive. They are poor, and enrich many; destitute of everything, they abound in everything. They are**

> **dishonored, and in their dishonor find their glory. They are calumniated, and are vindicated. They are reviled and they bless; they are insulted and render honor. Doing good, they are penalized as evildoers; when penalized, they rejoice because they are quickened into life. The Jews make war on them as foreigners; the Greeks persecute them; and those who hate them are at a loss to explain their hatred.**[14]

Unhappily, this mad inexplicable hatred is a passionate living thing among those who prefer darkness to light—and *The Epistle to Diognetus* failed in its object. The persecution of the church at Rome was destined, in God's gracious providence, to continue for over 250 years, ending only with Galerius' Edict of Toleration in 311.

But here at the turn of the sixth decade of the first century A.D., the great Apostle Peter and Clement of Rome, his newborn son in Christ, still have a church to build at this lost city called "Babylon"—come what may. And with a little imagination it is not difficult to picture the Apostle strengthening his new friend for the journey with these gentle words included in his first epistle:

> **Beloved, do not be surprised at the fiery ordeal which comes upon you to prove you, as though something strange were happening to you. But rejoice in so far as you share Christ's sufferings, that you may also rejoice and be glad when his glory is revealed. If you are**

---

[14] *The Epistle to Diognetus*, chap. 5, nos. 1, 5–17, in *The Didache, The Epistle of Barnabas, The Epistles and The Martyrdom of St. Polycarp, The Fragments of Papias, The Epistle to Diognetus*, trans. James A. Kleist, ACW, vol. 6 (Mahwah, N.J.: Paulist Press, 1948), p. 139.

reproached for the name of Christ, you are blessed, because the spirit of glory and of God rests upon you. (1 Pet 4:12–14)

A Wolf in the Fold

Elsewhere in Rome, another shepherd has also been working tirelessly among God's lost sheep. Like Peter, his given name is Simon. As a matter of fact, to most Roman minds he will seem cut from precisely the same cloth as our Big Fisherman. Both men, after all, refer to themselves as "apostles". Both have been associated with reports of miracles and other unexplained happenings. And both have come to Rome preaching in the name of Jesus the Nazarene, crucified God of the Christians. Though Simon of Gitto is technically a Samaritan rather than a Jew, the majority of the pagans will regard him as simply another Semitic prophet out of the same hot, distant backwater.

Yet in the memory of the Church herself Simon of Gitto is *Simon Magus*—Simon the Magician—founder (according to the Fathers) of the ancient heresy called *Gnosticism*, Christianity's oldest and most obstinate rival.[15] Former disciple of Philip the evangelist, Simon apostatized to become the first

[15] While it is true that the actual term "Gnosticism" does not come into use until after Simon's day, nearly all first- and second-century heresies shared the central Gnostic tenet that matter itself is inherently evil and incapable of redemption. This fact alone would seem to favor the idea that they all sprang from a common origin. But note that Irenaeus of Lyons, the Church's first expert on Gnosticism, is himself quite explicit: **"[The spiritual man] shall also judge the vain speeches of the perverse Gnostics, by showing that they are the disciples of Simon Magus"** (*Against Heresies*, bk. 4, chap. 33, no. 3, trans. Alexander Roberts and James Donaldson, in ANF 1:507). **"Although [some] do not confess the name of their master,**

person in recorded history to teach falsehood in the holy name of Jesus. He was, in fact, the original fulfillment of one of Christ's darkest warnings: **"Beware of false prophets, who come to you in sheep's clothing but inwardly are ravenous wolves. You will know them by their fruits"** (Mt 7:15).

> **Simon the Samaritan** [writes Irenaeus about A.D. 180] **was that magician of whom Luke, the disciple and follower of the apostles, says, "But there was a certain man, Simon by name, who beforetime used magical arts in that city, and led astray the people of Samaria, declaring that he himself was some great one, to whom they all gave heed, from the least to the greatest, saying, This is the power of God, which is called great. And to him they had regard, because that of long time he had driven them mad by his sorceries"** [Acts 8:9–11]. **This Simon, then —who feigned faith, supposing that the apostles themselves performed their cures by the art of magic, and not by the power of God . . . offering money to the apostles, thought he, too, might receive this power of bestowing the Holy Ghost on whomsoever he would. . . . [He] was addressed in these words by Peter: "Thy money perish with thee, because thou hast thought that the gift of God can be purchased with money: thou hast neither**

---

in order all the more to seduce others, yet they do teach his doctrines" (ibid., bk. 1, chap. 27, no. 4, ANF 1:353). **"All these heretics, taking their rise from Simon, have introduced impious and irreligious doctrines into this life"** (ibid., prologue to bk. 2, ANF 1:359). Eusebius has this to add: **"Of such vices was Simon the father and contriver, raised up at that time by the evil power which hates all that is good and plots against the salvation of mankind, to be a great opponent of great men, our Saviour's inspired apostles"** (*History of the Church*, bk. 2, chap. 14, EHC 48).

part nor lot in this matter, for thy heart is not right in the sight of God; for I perceive that thou art in the gall of bitterness, and in the bond of iniquity" [Acts 8:20, 21, 23]. **He, then, not putting faith in God a whit the more, set himself eagerly to contend against the apostles, in order that he himself might seem to be a wonderful being, and applied himself with still greater zeal to the study of the whole magic art, that he might the better bewilder and overpower multitudes of men.**[16]

Justin Martyr, writing about A.D. 153, addressed an impassioned defense of Christianity to the emperor himself; we call this book Justin's *First Apology*. In it he preserves some further details, this time about the Magician's baleful advent at Rome:

After Christ's ascension into heaven the devils put forward certain men who said that they themselves were gods. . . . There was a Samaritan, Simon, a native of the village called Gitto, who in the reign of Claudius Caesar, and in your royal city of Rome, did mighty acts of magic, by virtue of the art of devils operating in him. He was considered a god, and as a god was honored by you with a statue, which statue was erected on the river Tiber, between the two bridges, and bore this inscription, in the language of Rome: "Simoni Deo Sancto— To Simon the holy God." And almost all the Samaritans, and a few even of other nations, worship him, and acknowledge him as the first god.

Justin goes on to provide the actual names of some of Simon's co-conspirators; the pillars, so to speak, of an insid-

[16] Irenaeus, *Against Heresies*, bk. 1, chap. 23, no. 1, in ANF 1:347.

ious "anti-church" in actual competition with Peter's work at Rome:

> **A woman, Helena, who went about with him at that time, and had formerly been a prostitute, they say is the first idea generated by him. And a man, Menander, also a Samaritan, of the town of Capparetaea, a disciple of Simon, and inspired by devils, we know to have deceived many while he was in Antioch by his magical art. He persuaded those who adhered to him that they should never die, and even now there are some living who hold this opinion of his. And there is Marcion, a man of Pontus, who is even at this day alive, and teaching his disciples to believe in some other god greater than the Creator. And he, by the aid of the devils, has caused many of every nation to speak blasphemies, and to deny that God is the maker of this universe, and to assert that some other being, greater than He, has done greater works. All who take their opinions from these men, are, as we before said, called [by the pagans] "Christians"; just as also those who do not agree with the philosophers in their doctrines, have yet in common with them the name of philosophers given to them.**[17]

In this last comment, we can appreciate the real tragedy of Simon's "ministry"; the Gnostics pass themselves off as Christians, and Justin is forced to report that the average Roman cannot tell the difference. Here, right at the very

---

[17] Justin Martyr, *First Apology*, chap. 26, trans. Alexander Roberts and James Donaldson, in ANF 1:171–72.

source of Jesus' river of life, Satan is already back at his old business of *muddying the waters*.

How did the early Church respond to this new generation of false shepherds? Interestingly, several of the ancient histories relate that it was Simon's evil work at the Imperial City that first drew Peter himself to Rome. Leaving his original ministry at Antioch in the hands of other approved men, the Fisherman followed Simon Magus to the capitol in order to combat his malignant influence there among the gentiles. But what about ordinary believers—recent converts like our own Clement? How would they have reacted to the bewildering presence of a second set of "Christian" apostles preaching on their streets? Simon did not come, after all, in a black cloak, twiddling a stage villain's mustache. He was a charming figure by all accounts; an eloquent orator preaching a sophisticated message. Would it have been so very obvious that there was a wolf under the sheepskin? Yes, Jesus had said that we would know them by their fruits —but what if the fruits themselves can be counterfeited? Recall that Simon had many "miracles" to his credit and a large number of converts as well. Clement's future mentor, the Apostle Paul, seems to have been addressing this very dilemma in his second letter to the church at Corinth. There he warns about men **"who would like to claim that in their boasted mission they work on the same terms as we do."** He calls them **"false apostles, deceitful workmen, disguising themselves as apostles of Christ. And no wonder, for even Satan disguises himself as an angel of light"** (2 Cor 11:12, 15).

The predicament, then, was very real; if all the prospective shepherds look like angels, just how exactly are the sheep supposed to choose between them? How on earth are common Roman laymen in A.D. 50—only just hearing of Jesus Himself for the first time—supposed to know which are His true disciples and which the false? Once again, we who live two thousand years downstream must be careful not to let our hindsight cause us to underestimate this problem. From a distance of centuries, for example, we might casually imagine that these early believers had only to pull out their pocket New Testaments to send these dangerous pretenders packing, tails between their legs. In reality, this was completely impossible—simply because the New Testament did not exist in Clement's day. It is a neglected fact, perhaps, but the Church had been preaching the gospel, saving souls, and founding congregations all over the Near East for at least ten years before a single line of the New Testament was written. She had been doing these things for over *fifty* years before the final line was completed. At the time of Clement's conversion a new believer might possibly have been introduced to Matthew's Gospel and perhaps one or two letters from Paul—but even these would have been circulating loose as individual works; over three hundred years would have to pass before they ever came to be bound together in one authoritative canon.[18] So clearly, the traditional appeal to the Christian Bible as we know it today just was not an option. True, the Hebrew Old Testament (in the

[18] Various New Testament canons were proposed and gained widespread usage in the early Church before the final list of inspired books was formally recognized at the Third Council of Carthage, A.D. 397.

Greek translation known as the *Septuagint*) *was* available to first-century believers; Clement's surviving epistle gives us ample proof that he came to know it very well indeed. But unfortunately the puzzle just gets more tangled at this point: most of the Gnostics never openly contradicted the Scriptures. In fact, like today's Jehovah's Witnesses, they invoked them constantly and ingeniously twisted every text to suit their own purposes. They, of course, would have insisted that it was Peter and his Galileans doing the twisting; according to Gnostic exegesis the Old Testament was an excellent source for strong, conclusive proofs . . . of Gnosticism. It was all simply (in a phrase fated to become tragically familiar in the centuries ahead) *a matter of interpretation.*

But surely the Holy Spirit was present in the early Church —would not He have been there to guide genuine believers into all truth? Indeed He was, in a fullness unequaled before or since. Yet no orthodox Christian today believes that the Spirit does this guiding independently of the Bible; we rightly insist that individuals must test their private spiritual insights against the written Word of God. So what filled this crucial role in the first-century Church—a Church where the Word of God for Christians would not be fully known for literally *centuries?* What kept the Body of Christ from collapsing into doctrinal chaos in a world where most (if not all) believers lived their entire lives without even knowing what the New Testament was?

Are we back to *prophet vs. prophet*, your word against ours, "peace, peace, when there is no peace"? Does the wolf now go back on the prowl just as before—eating the fat, clothing himself with the wool, slaughtering the fatlings?

Somehow, Clement of Rome did not think so. His surviving writings show no sign of a man still tortured by "disputings, contradiction, and uncertainty".

What was *his* answer?

How did he personally—and the thousands like him—make the all-important choice *between the two Simons?*

The Household of God

The solution to this seemingly insoluble conundrum turns out to be deceptively simple—indeed, to Clement's generation it would have been the plainest fact about the whole matter:

"This man was with Jesus of Nazareth." (Mt 26:71b)

In the beautiful irony of God, the words that once drove Peter to deny his Lord before men were now the very words that would bind the two of them together in the eyes of humanity for all time: **"And a maid came up to him, and said, 'You also were with Jesus the Galilean'"** (Mt 26:69b). Not a theological theory. Not a story out of a book. When even the milling crowds in Caiaphas' courtyard could recognize one of Christ's chosen men—well, then, perhaps the problem of who could and could not legitimately claim to come in His name was not so very perplexing after all.

In short, Jesus' public ministry had been just that—*public*. And though He was much more than a mere rabbi, the Rabbi Jesus did follow the established rabbinical practice of the day by publicly committing His teaching to *disciples*. Just as Paul of Tarsus had been personally discipled by the great Pharisee Gamaliel (Acts 22:3), so Peter of Galilee, along with the rest of the Twelve, had been personally discipled by Christ. Unfortunately, this word *discipleship* carries an almost exclusively religious meaning today; but not so in the ancient world. This was the great age of Master and Apprentice, of Scholar and Novice; where everything, from furniture to philosophy, was *handcrafted* and the time-honored tricks of every trade were painstakingly handed down to the next generation, person to person. This had two practical results. The first was that each disciple in any field carried the name of his master with him like a "maker's mark", like a Stradivarius violin or a Brumby rocking chair. The second is even more to the point: this institution of discipleship produced a whole society of canny, "educated consumers". The first question the public asked about any workman—butcher, baker, or Hebrew theologian—was always the same: Who had been his master? Which guild had accepted him as member? If the founder of a particular school was still living, people wanted to know whom he recommended. If the founder had gone on, people wanted to know which men were carrying on his traditions. Clement's task, then, as a pagan but sensible Roman citizen, had not really required deep insight or special revelation. He had simply to pose the traditional query: Which men had been with Jesus? That fact alone, once truly established, banished all doubt. Summarizing this understanding in the early Church, Tertullian wrote the following simple but penetrating words: **"If the Lord Jesus Christ sent the Apostles to preach, no others ought to be received except those appointed by Christ: For no one knows the Father except the Son, and him to whom the Son gives a revelation** [Mt 11:27]. **Nor does it seem that the Son has given revelation to any others than the**

Apostles, whom He sent forth to preach what He had revealed to them."[19]

Obviously, Simon and his Gnostics could not even credibly claim to have been authorized in this way—and, in point of fact, they never did: such a claim would have been immediately contradicted in Clement's day by the many living witnesses to Jesus' life and ministry. What then did the Gnostics have to offer when confronted by their lack of credentials? What did they have to say for themselves? Invariably, they fell back on an appeal to human pride. The very name itself reveals this tactic: *gnosis* is the Greek for *knowledge*. Rather than contradicting them outright, Irenaeus tells us that Simon and company preferred to represent themselves as **"improvers of the apostles"**.[20] After all, were these simple fishermen not plain, unlettered peasants? Would it be so surprising if such men had been unable to grasp fully the subtleties of their Teacher's message? Accordingly, the Gnostics maintained that the Galileans had **"preached before they possessed 'perfect knowledge'"**[21] and **"intermingled the things of the law with the words of the Saviour"**.[22] They themselves, on the other hand, were **"purer and more intelligent"**[23] and had **"discovered more than the apostles"**,[24] rescuing **"the unadulterated truth"**[25] that had eluded these ignorant and carnal Jews. **"Inflated with the false name**

[19] Tertullian, *Demurrer*, chap. 21, nos. 1–2, in FEF 1:120–21, no. 293.
[20] Irenaeus, *Against Heresies*, bk. 3, chap. 1, no. 1, in ANF 1:414.
[21] Ibid.
[22] Ibid., chap. 2, no. 2, in ANF 1:415.
[23] Ibid., chap. 12, no. 12, in ANF 1:434.
[24] Ibid.
[25] Ibid., chap. 2, no. 2, in ANF 1:415.

of 'knowledge'", continues Irenaeus, they **"do certainly recognise the Scriptures; but they pervert the interpretations."**[26] **"By transferring passages, and dressing them up anew, and making one thing out of another, they succeed in deluding many through their wicked art in adapting the oracles of the Lord to their [own] opinions."**[27] And when challenged in this? **"They proclaim themselves as being 'perfect,' so that no one can be compared to them with respect to the immensity of their knowledge, nor even were you to mention Paul or Peter, or any other of the apostles. They assert that they themselves know more than all others, and that they alone have imbibed the greatness of that knowledge of that power which is unspeakable."**[28]

In dramatic contrast to this kind of windy flimflam was the sound Clement heard among Jesus' true Apostles; voices less interested in their own "unspeakable greatness" than in simply testifying to the life-changing miracle they had experienced together. **"We are witnesses to all that he did"**, Peter once told another Roman convert, Cornelius the Centurion. **"They put him to death by hanging him on a tree; but God raised him on the third day and made him manifest; not to all the people but to us who were chosen by God as witnesses, who ate and drank with him after he rose from the dead"** (Acts 10:39–41). Likewise the Apostle John, who once clung to the Messiah's breast like a child at their last supper, based his right to a hearing squarely on his status as an eyewitness to the Incarnation: **"That which was from the beginning, which we have heard, which we**

[26] Ibid., chap. 12, no. 12, in ANF 1:435.
[27] Ibid., bk. 1, chap. 8, no. 1, in ANF 1:326.
[28] Ibid., chap. 13, no. 6, in ANF 1:335.

have seen with our eyes, which we have looked upon and touched with our hands, concerning the word of life—that life was made manifest, and we saw it, and testify to it, . . . so that you may have fellowship with us; and our fellowship is with the Father and with his Son Jesus Christ" (1 Jn 1:1–2, 4). Even Paul, who truly *was* enlightened with a special revelation direct from heaven, nevertheless carefully grounded his ministry on the verifiable, public *fact* of his companionship with Christ's chosen spokesmen: **"I delivered to you as of first importance what I also received, that Christ died for our sins in accordance with the scriptures . . . and that he appeared to Cephas, and then to the twelve. Then he appeared to more than five hundred brethren at one time, most of whom are still alive, though some have fallen asleep. Then he appeared to James, and then to all the apostles. Last of all, as to one untimely born, he appeared also to me"** (1 Cor 15:3–8). Elsewhere, the same Paul directly contrasts the authority of the genuine apostolic band with the crafty trickery of their shabby competitors: **"Our appeal does not spring from error or uncleanness, nor is it made with guile; but just as we have been approved by God to be entrusted with the gospel, so we speak, not to please men, but to please God who tests our hearts"** (1 Thess 2:3–4).

Yes, these were the men who had been with Jesus . . . and that fact makes all the difference in the world. Listen, for example, as Peter responds to the charge that he and the other Galileans had "misunderstood" the Scriptures: **"We did not follow cleverly devised myths when we made known to you the power and coming of our Lord Jesus Christ, but we were *eyewitnesses* of his majesty"** (2 Pet

1:16, emphasis added). Speaking of the miracle known as the Transfiguration (Mt 17:1–8), Peter continues: **"When he received honor and glory from God the Father and the voice was borne to him by the Majestic Glory, 'This is my beloved Son, with whom I am well pleased,' we *heard* this voice borne from heaven, for we were with him on the holy mountain. And we have the prophetic word made more sure. You will do well to pay attention to this as to a lamp shining in a dark place, until the day dawns and the morning star rises in your hearts"** (2 Pet 1:17–19, emphasis added). Going on, the Apostle delivers his *coup de grace*, so to speak, against any self-appointed "improvers" who might seek (as they had with Christ Himself) to turn God's Old Testament message against His New Testament messengers: **"First of all you must understand this, that no prophecy of scripture is a matter of one's own interpretation, because no prophecy ever came by the impulse of man, but men moved by the Holy Spirit spoke from God. But false prophets also arose among the people, just as there will be false teachers among you, who will secretly bring in destructive heresies, even denying the Master who bought them, bringing upon themselves swift destruction"** (2 Pet 1:20—2:1). And what is to be the Christian's safe bulwark against such deadly error? Peter speaks it clearly a few paragraphs later: **"Remember the predictions of the holy prophets and the commandments of the Lord and Savior through your apostles"** (2 Pet 3:2).

Eventually, these Apostles will commit the commandments of the Lord and Savior to writing, in their letters, in books, and in strange accounts of their prophetic dreams and revelations. And eventually, through the inspiration of the Holy Spirit, these writings will be gathered together and will come to constitute for later generations a sacred and inerrant link to that apostolic age. Yet even now, with the Bible still an unfinished symphony for years to come, the holy gospel of Jesus abides safely just where Jesus Himself deposited it—in the hearts of the men He called *friends*.

The fact is that what Christ left behind when He went to sit at His Father's right hand was a *thing*, not a theory . . . something more like a *family* than a philosophy. The Scriptures refer to this family as **"the household of God, built upon the foundation of the apostles and prophets, Christ Jesus himself being the cornerstone"** (Eph 2:19–20). And it was to this household—and none other—that Jesus delivered His precious gifts; gifts to be enjoyed, of course, but also to be cherished for the future like priceless family heirlooms. In his pride, Simon Magus will despise this family, drawing disciples away to himself even as he ignores the disciples Jesus made. And sadly, this spirit will live on into today's world. Anywhere that modernists and higher critics propose their "historical Jesus" whose "original message" (strangely similar to their own) was gradually "corrupted" by misguided followers into organized Christianity—there you find the spirit of the Gnostics alive and well. But Clement of Rome learned better. Yes, the Magician can still come with biblical expertise, with powerful preaching, with "signs and wonders" and an impressive degree from the school of Athens. But the one thing he cannot claim to come with is *Jesus' own stamp of approval*. For that astonishing distinction, the proud city of Rome must learn to look where Clement looked—to the simple man to whom the Good Shepherd said, **"Feed my sheep."** Personally discipled by God-in-the-flesh; set apart for truth by His fervent prayers; empowered at Pentecost by the Comforter He promised—it was Peter and his apostolic companions to whom the Savior said, **"All authority in heaven and on earth has been given to me. Go therefore . . ."** (Mt 28:18–19).

These twelve were with Jesus.

And for at least one of Rome's hopeless religious orphans that simple reality put an end to a lifetime of confusion. Doubts and fears, of course, would come again, as they must to all disciples, as they did to Jesus Himself in Gethsemane. But the haunting question that had been driving Clement slowly mad; the taunting query that is, even today, license to the wicked and torment to the seeker; the question, specifically, of: "Who's to say?"

That mocking riddle has now been banished forever, for the first century and beyond, like the bad dream that it is.

A Teacher of the Gentiles

After becoming a disciple of [the] Apostles, I am now becoming a teacher of the Gentiles. What has been handed down I deliver exactly to such as become disciples of the Truth. Really, can anyone who has been correctly taught and has fallen in love with the Logos, fail to strive to learn exactly what has been plainly shown by the Logos to disciples to whom the Logos appeared in person and made revelations in plain language? He was not understood by unbelievers, but gave a detailed explanation to disciples, and these, reckoned by Him as trustworthy, came to know the mysteries of the Father.[29]

[29] *The Epistle to Diognetus*, chap. 11, nos. 1–2, ACW 6:145.

Jurgens, 248

This fascinating passage is from, once again, the *Epistle to Diognetus*—and if Clement really is the author of that letter then we have here our subject's own "personal testimony" preserved. But whoever the writer may have been (and the epistle is undoubtedly very ancient, dating from not later than A.D. 150), he does clearly spell out the vital importance of discipleship in this pre-New Testament Church. Notice also how the author, writing to pagans rather than to Jews, speaks of Jesus and His mission in terms that would be meaningful to pagans. Ezekiel's Good Shepherd—who comes to teach and to establish trustworthy teachers—is now spoken of as the *Logos*, a term familiar from Greek philosophy, a title that might be loosely translated as *Wisdom Personified*.[30] The astounding good news, then, is one and the same for both Jew and Gentile: hope against hope, the Eternal Mind has cracked open the heavens and "appeared in person". He walked among us for a season, uncovering mysteries in "plain language", silencing the babble of human religious speculation. And most importantly of all—while He was here He made *apprentices*. This being the case, all those who "have fallen in love with the Logos" (all true seekers after wisdom, that is) will surely not hesitate when Wisdom's own disciples come calling at last.

It seems natural, of course, that someone with Clement's background and abilities might soon have been steered into the role of a teacher. After all, somebody was needed to train the steady stream of converts flowing into the Church at Rome, and who better than a man so intimately familiar

---

[30] The first and most famous use of this term, *Logos*, as a name for the Eternal Christ is, of course, John 1:1: **"In the beginning was the Word [Logos], and the Word was with God, and the Word was God."**

with their thought forms and ideas? Perhaps they would not have called him a "Sunday School" teacher back then; but something of the sort must always have been necessary in the Church, and it is a pleasing thought to imagine our earnest young philosopher, up early on a bright Italian Lord's Day, faithfully discharging his first job in "full-time ministry" by teaching a little circle of his countrymen all about Noah's Ark and Joseph's Coat of Many Colors. This is actually more than just a pleasant scene, however. Though Clement's exact role will perhaps always be guesswork, we do know for a fact that the early Church did conduct "catechism classes" of this kind—for the very good reason that she has left us the actual textbook from one of them!

As it happens, the book that is thought to be the single earliest Christian document to survive outside the pages of the New Testament really is a *catechism*; that is, a brief synopsis of Christian faith and morals designed for use by new believers. It is called *The Teaching of the Lord to the Gentiles through the Twelve Apostles*, or, more commonly, the *Didache* (pronounced *DIH-duh-kay*, from the first word of the title in Greek). Composed, as most experts believe, not later than A.D. 90 and possibly as early as 60, the *Didache* comes therefore directly out of the period during which Clement himself would have been teaching Christianity.[31] That makes this little book our best and earliest window into what our

[31] The *Didache* has an exceptionally interesting history. A lost work for centuries, it was nevertheless well known from numerous lengthy quotations appearing in such established early works as *The Epistle of Barnabas* and the *Apostolic Constitutions*. The complete text, however, was rediscovered only in the late nineteenth century, hidden away in a neglected medieval library in Constantinople. As to its antiquity, the translator, Dr. James A. Kleist, has this to say: "It is impossible to disprove the statement of some scholars that the *Didache* was written, if not in whole, at least in

"teacher of the Gentiles" might actually have taught his students—and also a priceless peek at actual Christian practice sometime in the mid to late first century.

"Two Ways there are," the ancient text begins, **"one of Life and one of Death, and there is a great difference between the Two Ways.**

"Now, the Way of Life is this: first, love the God who made you; secondly, your neighbor as yourself: do not do to another what you do not wish to be done to yourself."[32]

From here, the *Didache* launches into a remarkable digest of all the precious and familiar precepts of the Sermon on the Mount: love thy neighbor, turn the other cheek, go the extra mile; indeed, everything that we imagined Peter himself preaching at Clement's conversion. But soon the document turns to very clear specifics, tailoring its message directly to former pagans still struggling to disentangle themselves fully from a culture of death Clement knew only too well:

> **Do not murder; do not commit adultery; do not practice pederasty; do not fornicate; do not steal; do not deal in magic; do not practice sorcery; do not kill a fetus by abortion, or commit infanticide. Do not covet your neighbor's goods. Do not perjure yourself; do not bear false witness; do not calumniate; do not bear malice. Do not be double-minded or double-tongued, for a double tongue is a deadly snare. Your speech must not**

part, between 60 and 70. . . . It should, therefore, be admitted that we have a thoroughly conservative, and altogether reliable, estimate in the statement of many leading scholars that the *Didache* was written 'before the end of the first century'" (Introduction, *The Didache*, ACW 6:5–6).

[32] Ibid., chap. 1, nos. 1–2, ACW 6:15.

be false or meaningless, but made good by action. Do not be covetous, or rapacious, or hypocritical, or malicious, or arrogant. . . . Hate no man; but correct some, pray for others, for still others sacrifice your life as a proof of your love.

My child, shun evil of any kind and everything resembling it. . . . Be gentle, for the gentle will inherit the land. Be long-suffering, and merciful, and guileless, and quiet, and good, and with trembling treasure forever the instructions you have received. Do not carry your head high, or open your heart to presumption. Do not be on intimate terms with the mighty, but associate with holy and lowly folk. Accept as blessings the casualties that befall you, assured that nothing happens without God.[33]

The danger of Simon Magus and his ilk is addressed in these pages as well, albeit obliquely:

My child, day and night remember him who preaches God's word to you, and honor him as [you would] the Lord, for where His lordship is spoken of, there is the Lord. Seek daily contact with the saints to be refreshed by their discourses. Do not start a schism, but pacify contending parties. . . . Do not by any means neglect the commandments of the Lord, but hold fast to the traditions, neither adding nor subtracting anything.[34]

---

[33] Ibid., chap. 2, no. 2—chap. 3, no. 1; chap. 3, nos. 7–10, ACW 6:16–17.

[34] Compare this statement to these important verses: **"I commend you because you remember me in everything and maintain the traditions even as I have delivered them to you"** (1 Cor 11:2). **"So then, brethren, stand firm and hold to the traditions which you were taught by us, either by word of mouth or by letter"** (2 Thess 2:15).

In church, confess your sins, and do not come to your prayer with a guilty conscience. Such is the Way of Life.[35]

Now the tone darkens; the sober warnings begin:

The Way of Death is this. First of all, it is wicked and altogether accursed: murders, adulteries, lustful desires, fornications, thefts, idolatries, magical arts, sorceries, robberies, false testimonies, hypocrisy, duplicity, fraud, pride, malice, surliness, covetousness, foul talk, jealousy, rashness, haughtiness, false pretensions, [lack of the fear of God]. It is the way of persecutors of the good, haters of the truth, lovers of falsehood; of men ignorant of the reward for right living, not devoted to what is good, or to just judgment, intent upon not what is good but what is evil; of strangers to gentleness and patient endurance; of men who love vanities, and fee hunters; of men that have no heart for the poor, are not concerned about the oppressed, do not know their Maker; of murderers of children, destroyers of God's image,[36] **of men that turn away from the needy, oppress the afflicted, act as counsels for the rich, are unjust judges of the poor— in a word, of men steeped in sin. Children, may you be preserved from all this!**

See that no man leads you astray from this Way of

[35] *Didache*, chap. 4, nos. 1–2, 13–14, ACW 6:17–18.

[36] Another reference to abortion. An old Latin translation actually uses the word *abortuantes* (abortionists). The testimony of the early Church is quite clear on this subject; Tertullian, about A.D. 200, wrote: "We acknowledge . . . that life begins with conception, because we contend that the soul begins at conception. Life begins when the soul begins" (*The Soul*, chap. 27, no. 1, in FEF 1:144).

the Teaching, since any other teaching takes you away from God.[37]

Do not pray as the hypocrites do, but pray as the Lord has commanded in the Gospel: *Our Father, who art in heaven; hallowed be Thy name; Thy kingdom come; Thy will be done on earth as it is in heaven; give us this day our daily bread, and forgive us our debts as we also forgive our debtors; and lead us not into temptation, but deliver us from evil;* for Thine is the power and the glory for evermore.

Say this prayer three times a day.[38]

The *Didache* seems to come out of a relatively tranquil period for early Christianity; and we do know that, with two important exceptions, the first century itself was not one of continuous, active persecution. Nevertheless, as the author brings his lesson to a close he strikes this unmistakable note of *warning*:

Watch over your life; your lamps must not go out, nor your loins be ungirded; on the contrary, be ready. You do not know the hour in which Our Lord is coming. Assemble in great numbers, intent upon what concerns your souls. Surely, of no use will your lifelong faith be to you if you are not perfected at the end of time. For in the last days the false prophets and corrupters will come in swarms; the sheep will turn into wolves, and love will turn into hate. When lawlessness is on the increase, men will hate and persecute and betray one another; and then the Deceiver of this world will appear.[39]

---

[37] *Didache*, chap. 5, no. 1— chap. 6, no. 1, ACW 6:18–19.

[38] Ibid., chap. 8, nos. 2–3, ACW 6:19.

[39] Ibid., chap. 16, nos. 1–4, ACW 6:24.

Undoubtedly, these words have reference to the actual end of the world, far in the future from Clement's day. But like most such end-times prophecies there is also a more immediate application; just as Matthew 24 prophesies both the final apocalypse and also the fall of Jerusalem in A.D. 70, so the Didachist's warnings have both a contemporary and an eschatological dimension. Yes, a great antichrist will appear to tempt the nations at the end of time. But history shows us that the spirit of antichrist has been active from the beginning and was, even for Clement's generation, preparing a great and imminent trial. This being the case, the gentle Sunday School teacher of the *Didache* (whoever he may have been) would not have his children ignorant: **"Then humankind will undergo the fiery test, and many will lose their faith and perish; but those who stand firm in their faith will be saved by none other than the Accursed.[40] And then the proofs of the truth will appear."[41]**

Partakers of the Glory

Even as her pilgrim son Clement was finding new life and sanity among the Christians, the once-vital nation of the Romans was slipping farther and farther down the slopes of madness. Material prosperity and external peace were not enough; then, as now, they made poor substitutes for hope and idealism. Ever more fragmented, daily more frightened, helplessly angry and pathologically skeptical—the Roman people soon began to retreat into morbid

[40] By Jesus, who became accursed for our sake. *Didache*, chap. 16, no. 5, ACW 6:24–25. Cf. Deut 21:23, Is 53, and 2 Cor 5:21.

[41] *Didache*, chap. 16, no. 6, ACW 6:25.

individualism. Every man did what was right in his own eyes. The government, presented with an exploding population of ungovernable libertines and hopelessly hamstrung by political gridlock, did what governments always do under such circumstances: incapable of believing in a Shepherd, they started looking for a Strongman.

The process had begun under Caesar Augustus, emperor at the time of the Savior's birth. After his signal defeat of Antony and Cleopatra at Actium, Augustus was emboldened to declare himself "master of all things" and took steps that would eventually transform the democratic Roman Senate into a mere "rubber stamp" committee. His successor, Tiberias (under whose reign Christ was crucified), furthered this concentration of power. But the successors of Tiberias —these men constituted nothing less than a judgment upon the entire civilization. Tiberias was followed in rapid succession by Gaius Caligula, a psychotic pervert; Claudius, a mentally retarded simpleton who became the puppet of his scheming wife, Agrippina; and finally, by Agrippina's monstrous son Nero.

> **Many writers have recorded the facts about him in minute detail,** [writes Eusebius of this legendary tyrant] **enabling anyone who wishes to get a complete picture of his perverse and extraordinary madness, which led him to the senseless destruction of innumerable lives, and drove him in the end to such a lust for blood that he did not spare even his nearest and dearest but employed a variety of methods to do away with mother, brother, and wife alike, to say nothing of countless other members of his family, as if they were personal and public enemies.**

All this left one crime still to be added to his account—he was the first of the emperors to be the declared enemy of the worship of Almighty God.[42]

It started on the evening of July 18, A.D. 64, when Clement had been a Christian perhaps ten to fifteen years. Some old buildings caught fire in Rome, in the warehouse district behind the Circus Maximus. Aided by windy weather conditions, the blaze spread quickly and all through the night. Before it finally burned itself out ten days later, this fire had utterly consumed ten of the city's fourteen districts and had established itself as one of the most catastrophic events in human history. Thousands upon thousands were killed; asphyxiated by the smoke, trampled in the panic, or burned alive by the flames themselves. The survivors emerged from the ashes looking for someone to blame.

Certain rumors began to be heard. Nero had been away from the city when the fire broke out, in his holiday villa at his hometown of Antium. And several eyewitnesses turned up claiming to have glimpsed sinister agents moving among the billowing black clouds—agents carrying torches, threatening with the sword anyone who attempted to extinguish the blaze. Could it be possible that the fire had been deliberately set by the emperor himself? It was well known that Nero fancied himself an artist and an architect and that he often rhapsodized to his advisors about building a new and more glorious Rome and calling it Neronia. Worst of all for Nero were the persistent reports, preserved for us by a contemporary historian, that **"at the very time when the city was in flames, the emperor appeared on a private stage**

---

[42] Eusebius, *History of the Church*, bk. 2, chap. 25, in EHC 62.

and sang of the destruction of Troy, comparing present misfortunes with the calamities of antiquity."[43]

This historian was the grim and fatalistic Tacitus, who had been a boy of ten years at the time of the disaster. And ironically, it is to this pagan scribe that we owe most of our knowledge, not only of the fire, but also of its cataclysmic sequel:

> **All human efforts, all the lavish gifts of the emperor, and the propitiations of the gods, could not banish the sinister belief that the conflagration was the result of an order. Consequently, to get rid of the report, Nero fastened the guilt and inflicted the most exquisite tortures on a class hated for their abominations, called *Christians* by the populace. Christus, from whom the name had its origin, suffered the extreme penalty during the reign of Tiberias at the hands of one of our procurators, Pontius Pilatus, and a most mischievous superstition, thus checked for the moment, again broke out not only in Judea, the first source of the evil, but even in Rome, where all things hideous and shameful from every part of the world find their centre and become popular.[44]**

The "abominations" Tacitus speaks of were imaginary, created in the minds of the pagans out of the secrecy practiced by early Christians and their reputation for being "unpatriotic". But the hatred stewing in Roman hearts, so skillfully exploited by the shrewd dictator, was very real indeed.

---

[43] Tacitus, *The Annals*, bk. 15, trans. Alfred John Church and William Jackson Brodribb (New York: Random House Modern Library, 1942), pp. 242–43.

[44] Ibid., p. 243.

Accordingly, an arrest was first made of all who pleaded guilty; then, upon their information, an immense multitude was convicted, not so much of the crime of firing the city, as of hatred against mankind. Mockery of every sort was added to their deaths. Covered with the skins of beasts, they were torn by dogs and perished, or were nailed to crosses, or were doomed to the flames and burnt, to serve as nightly illumination, when daylight had expired. Nero offered his gardens for the spectacle, and was exhibiting a show in the circus, while he mingled with the people in the dress of a charioteer or stood aloft on a car. Hence, even for criminals who deserved extreme and exemplary punishment, there arose a feeling of compassion; for it was not, as it seemed, for the public good, but to glut one man's cruelty, that they were being destroyed.[45]

This supposed compassion, however, seems to have done little to abate the fury of the violence; most scholars believe that it lasted in full force until Nero's own death four years later. The result was a period of persecution unequaled in the young Church's history up to that time. In fact, this was the Church's original "Great Tribulation", and Nero her first antichrist. His persecution here in the first century became the model she would always return to in the centuries to come when picturing the Body of Christ glorious under suffering.

It seems probable that Clement of Rome was absent from his home city at the time of this outbreak. Paul's epistle to the church at Philippi was written just a year or two earlier

[45] Ibid.

—and if the Fathers are correct in identifying his "fellow worker" there with our own Clement, then it would appear that our subject had been sent abroad from his home church as a foreign missionary. In fact, Clement may actually have become by this time one of the pastors at Philippi; though still a youngish man, his status as one of Peter's own personal disciples would likely have given him prominence. Did he lead the congregation there in a great outpouring of intercessory prayer when the news from Rome arrived? Or did he hastily return to his home church in order to be with his friends and pupils in their time of testing? Once again, we do not know. There is, however, an ancient tradition that Simon Peter did just that—going back to the great metropolitan congregation he had founded and thereby setting the stage for the fulfillment of the last prophecy he had received from his Divine Master.

Several second-century works record that "the two most glorious apostles" Peter and Paul were on mission in the East when word reached them of the events at Rome. By these accounts, Paul survived his first imprisonment there —that confinement to which he is headed when the book of Acts closes so abruptly—and lived on to make at least one more of his epic missionary journeys. But when the Apostle learned of the fiery trial at the Imperial City, he traveled to Corinth to meet with Peter. The two agreed to leave for Rome immediately, intent on lending their combined strength to the suffering flock there and of dying with them at Nero's hand, if that be the will of God.

Peter's second New Testament epistle was written from Rome during this period, and Paul's second to Timothy was actually sent at this time from a Roman prison. In fact, it seems that both of them were in jails and awaiting martyrdom not long after their arrival. This may have been deliberate on their part; jail, after all, was where most of the Christians were by then. And both of these inspired letters contain *farewells*, as it were: powerful last words to the churches from Jesus' two favorite champions. Two great pastors, two men full of burning love for their lambs in the Lord, send heart-rending good-byes from Rome, preserved forever in the imperishable pages of Scripture.

"I am already on the point of being sacrificed", Paul writes, from his final foul dungeon. **"The time of my departure has come. I have fought the good fight, I have finished the race, I have kept the faith. Henceforth there is laid up for me the crown of righteousness, which the Lord, the righteous judge, will award to me on that Day, and not only to me but also to all who have loved his appearing"** (2 Tim 4:6–8). The globe-trotting missionary, the man thrice shipwrecked, the wanted fugitive who eluded every snare, has finally had his last adventure. Yet like his Lord before him, the Apostle also takes care to ensure that his work will be continued after he is gone. **"Rekindle the gift of God that is within you through the laying on of my hands"**, Paul urges his disciple Timothy; **"for God did not give us a spirit of timidity but a spirit of power and love and self-control. . . . Be strong in the grace that is in Christ Jesus, and what you have heard from me before many witnesses entrust to faithful men who will be able to teach others also. . . . Continue in what you have learned and have firmly believed, knowing from whom you learned it"** (2 Tim 1:6–7, 2:1–2, 3:14).

Peter, too, sees death approaching. **"I know that the**

putting off of my body will be soon, as our Lord Jesus Christ showed me" (2 Pet 1:14). The long sunlit path of his life—that glorious miracle-spangled life that began so long ago by the Sea of Galilee—will now end here at "Babylon" as well. But Peter also has taken steps to see that his life's work will not be for nothing. Surely he must have reiterated here at the end, to Clement and to all the younger men who will be forced to try and fill his shoes, the solemn charges made in his earlier letter: **"I exhort the elders among you, as a fellow elder and a witness of the sufferings of Christ as well as a partaker in the glory that is to be revealed. Tend the flock of God that is your charge, not by constraint but willingly, not for shameful gain but eagerly, not as domineering over those in your charge but being examples to the flock. And when the chief Shepherd is manifested you will obtain the unfading crown of glory"** (1 Pet 5:1–4). How poignant to realize that our Big Fisherman, shortly before being reunited at last with the Good Shepherd, got his own opportunity to tell his disciples, "Feed my sheep."

Exactly how long the two Apostles languished in prison is not known. But most writers believe that it was sometime during the summer of A.D. 67 when Paul of Tarsus was finally roused from his coal-black cell and taken, blinking in the sun, to a lonely spot along the Ostian Way for execution. Being a Roman citizen, he was allowed a dignified Roman death, kneeling over a block or a stump for the headsman's sword. A remarkably consistent Christian tradition identifies the exact spot of his burial; just over a mile outside the old city gates, where a magnificent church has stood in his honor since early in the fourth century.

Peter, on the other hand, was not a citizen. He was simply a troublesome barbarian, preaching treasonous nonsense during a time of unrest. Eusebius tells us that he was taken and **"crucified, head downwards at his own request"**.[46] Apparently, the Apostle felt unworthy to die in exactly the same manner as his Lord and thus asked for the strange variation. Even so, we cannot help but notice that his symbolic identification with Christ is startlingly complete; if it is true that believers are called to take up their crosses and follow Jesus, then Simon Peter answered the call in the most astonishingly literal way. The traditional account of his martyrdom says that he preached from the cross to whoever would listen, and that he lived for nearly two days before giving up the ghost. After he was gone, his friend John recalled a cryptic exchange overheard between Peter and the Lord thirty years before: **"Jesus said to him, '. . . Truly, truly, I say to you, when you were young, you girded yourself and walked where you would; but when you are old, you will stretch out your hands, and another will gird you and carry you where you do not wish to go.' (This he said to show by what death [Peter] was to glorify God)"** (Jn 21:17–19). And glorify Him he did. The site of his crucifixion is marked today by a pagan obelisk from Nero's garden, an obelisk that an old tradition says was the very last thing on earth that Peter saw with his own eyes. When the Prince of the Apostles opened them again, it was on the Celestial City—that City which shames "the glory that was Rome" as the face of the sun shames a smoky candle.

One by one and all across the known world, the rest of the Master's chosen Twelve met similar fates—or so Christians

---

[46] Eusebius, *History of the Church*, bk. 3, chap. 1, in EHC 65.

have always believed. James, brother of John, had been the first to go; beheaded by Herod in about the year 42 in the only such account actually included in Scripture (Acts 12:2). Less certain, but still creditable in the main, are the traditional accounts of the deaths of the less prominent names on the list. Thomas is said to have taken the gospel to India, arousing the jealousy of the Brahmin priests there, who rose as a mob and pierced him with spears. Nathanael went to cruel, half-civilized Armenia, where—singing hymns all the while—he was tortured to death with flaying knives. According to Eusebius, the Apostle Andrew chose what is today Russia as his mission field and died there, like his older brother, on a wooden cross. Matthew and the lesser James, by various reckonings, are said to have been stoned to death by the Jews or burned at the stake, and Simon Zealotes, like the prophet Isaiah, to have been sawed in half. Probably all of them were gone by A.D. 70, all save John Bar Zebedee, the Gospel writer, who had been the youngest. And to the churches of the world even John might just as well have been dead—indeed, he may have wished, in moments of temptation, that he were dead. Banished by an imperial edict to Patmos, the dreaded "Devil's Island" of the ancient world, John underwent a living martyrdom in slow motion. And the churches went without their founders.

Clearly this was a crucial moment in Church history. Her living links with Jesus were passing away, and she was still without a complete, authoritative Bible. Within the Empire, pressure mounted to compromise with the government; after all, Christians had only to offer a little symbolic sacrifice, perhaps allow Jesus' name to be added decorously to the list with Jupiter and Mercury, and all would be forgiven. And the Judaizers, whom Paul had battled so vigorously, were still there, too; now that their old nemesis was gone they looked for more flexible leadership to emerge. New Church officers might be more reasonable, might agree to have everyone circumcised, satisfying the law of Moses and thus allowing Christians to be received safely back into the synagogue as one more Jewish denomination. Simon's Gnostics were waiting in the wings as well, standing by patiently for the chance to make their own mark on Christ's fragile legacy. . .

Though speaking in a different context, Paul's old schoolmaster Gamaliel put the situation aptly. His advice to his fellow Pharisees some years earlier really applies equally well to all enemies of the Christians everywhere: **"If this plan or this undertaking is of men, it will fail; but if it is of God, you will not be able to overthrow them"** (Acts 5:38–39). The next few years would tell the tale.

A Very Strong Letter

"After the martyrdom of Paul and Peter," records Eusebius, **"the first man to be appointed Bishop of Rome was Linus. He is mentioned by Paul when writing to Timothy from Rome, in the salutation at the end of the epistle"** [2 Tim 4:21].[47] Then, **in the second year of Titus's reign Linus, Bishop of Rome, after holding his office for twelve years yielded it to Anencletus."**[48] Practically nothing is known about either of these two men; probably they

---

[47] Ibid., chap. 2, in EHC 65.

[48] Ibid., chap. 13, in EHC 80.

were ordained early by the Apostles, perhaps as deacons, and had matured through persecution and faithful service into strong, steadfast leaders. Finally, **"in the twelfth year of the same principate Anencletus, after twelve years as Bishop of Rome, was succeeded by Clement."**[49]

At last, our subject himself steps clearly upon the stage. Our callow pagan idealist of the sixties (A.D.) finds himself called upon to take up responsibility for Peter's own flock; he was roughly sixty years of age, about the year 92, if Eusebius' numbers are accurate. And much like the sad, haunted Abraham Lincoln, who assumed the American presidency on the eve of great calamity, Clement is handed the shepherd's crook at a dire and desperate hour.

After twenty-five years of relative peace (since the suicide of the now disgraced and hated Nero) persecution broke out again in the mid-90s under another tyrannical Roman emperor, Domitian. Domitian was the first of the Caesars to proclaim himself officially *Dominus et Deus*, "Lord and God", and he moved with swift severity against all objectors, or "atheists" as he called them. Sweeping through the churches of Asia Minor with particular fury, he beheaded large numbers of believers in a general round-up, but no part of the Empire seems to have been truly spared. Yet significantly, the Church's greatest threat at the start of Clement's bishopric came from elsewhere. No amount of anger from the pagans could shake her; as a matter of fact, external per-

[49] Ibid., chap. 15, in EHC 80. Several Fathers record this succession in a slightly different way, placing Clement *before* Anencletus (who is sometimes called just "Cletus") and immediately after Linus. The reported lengths of their respective pastorates vary as well. Eusebius' account, however, is the most widely accepted.

secution has always strengthened the Church. But schism and factions, pride and partisanship—these are poison to the Body of Christ. And the celebrated letter of Clement that has brought him to our attention in these pages was occasioned by the struggle against these dark forces.

Across the Adriatic Sea, at the church of Corinth, an event that Irenaeus of Lyons describes as **"no small dissension"**[50] took place—the start of a budding "church split", to use the modern parlance. The venerable Corinth, a congregation founded by Paul himself, was in turmoil. Such events are traumatic enough in the best of times, but here, at such a critical juncture in the Church's life, this kind of strife was a luxury she could ill afford. We have no details at all except what we can gather from the epistle itself. It seems however, that a party with "new ideas" had arisen within the congregation there.[51] Corinth, alas, had something of a history of this kind of thing. Recall that even in the days of the

---

[50] Irenaeus, *Against Heresies*, bk. 3, chap. 3, no. 3, in ANF 1:416.

[51] Just what these new ideas may have been is not known. There is, however, one ancient account of the trouble during Domitian's reign that places the blame squarely with—you guessed it—the Gnostics. It is taken, according to Eusebius, from the lost memoir of Hegesippus, written about A.D. 170: **"In describing the situation at that time Hegesippus goes on to say that until then the Church had remained a virgin, pure and uncorrupted, since those who were trying to corrupt the wholesome standard of the saving message, if such there were, lurked somewhere under cover of darkness. But when the sacred band of the apostles had in various ways reached the end of their life, and [most of] the generation of those privileged to listen with their own ears to the divine wisdom had passed on, then godless error began to take shape, through the deceit of false teachers, who now that none of the apostles was left threw off the mask and attempted to counter the preaching of the truth by preaching the knowledge [*gnosis*] falsely so-called"** (Eusebius, *History of the Church*, bk. 3, chap. 32, in EHC 96).

Apostles her members were already dividing up into theological cliques ("'I belong to Paul,' or 'I belong to Apollos,' or 'I belong to Cephas'", and so on [1 Cor 1:12]). But this new affair was something else again; Domitian's persecution was hardly over, and the leaders of the uprising had already gained enough support to overthrow the church's original pastors and replace them with men of their own choosing. The other churches looking on could see that a turning point was being reached at Corinth, a door was opening to something entirely new. What Paul or Peter would have done in these circumstances was clear to everyone . . . but Paul and Peter were gone. What would happen now?

Looking back on the crisis in retrospect, from the distance of one long lifetime later, Irenaeus tells it this way: **"[Clement of Rome] had seen the blessed Apostles and was acquainted with them. It might be said that he still heard the echoes of the preaching of the Apostles, and had their traditions before his eyes."** Taking up pen and parchment then, **"he sent a very strong letter to the Corinthians, exhorting them to peace and renewing their faith."**[52] That epistle, preserved to this very day, illumines, like a flash of lightning, the precise moment in time at which the mighty Church of God successfully survived into postapostolic history.

Here now are some excerpts: Clement's own words from the *Epistle to the Corinthians*, circa A.D. 96:

> **The Church of God which resides as a stranger at Rome to the Church of God which is a stranger at Corinth; to those who are called and sanctified by the will of God through our Lord Jesus Christ. May grace and**

[52] Irenaeus, *Against Heresies*, bk. 3, chap. 3, no. 3, in FEF 1:90, no. 211.

peace from Almighty God flow to you in rich profusion through Jesus Christ!

Owing to the suddenly bursting and rapidly succeeding calamities and untoward experiences that have befallen us, we have been somewhat tardy, we think, in giving our attention to the subjects of dispute in your community, beloved. We mean that execrable and godless schism so utterly foreign to the elect of God. And it is only a few rash and headstrong individuals that have inflamed it to such a degree of madness that your venerable, widely-renowned, and universally and deservedly cherished name has been greatly defamed. Indeed, was there ever a visitor in your midst that did not approve your excellent and steadfast faith? Or did not admire your discreet and thoughtful Christian piety? Or did not proclaim the magnificent character of your hospitality? Or did not congratulate you on your perfect and secure fund of knowledge? You certainly did everything without an eye to rank or station in life, and regulated your conduct by God's commandments. You were submissive to your officials and paid the older men among you the respect due them. The young you trained to habits of self-restraint and sedateness. . . . Moreover, you were all in a humble frame of mind, in no way arrogant, practicing obedience rather than demanding it, happier in giving than in receiving. . . . Guileless and sincere you were, and bore one another no malice. The very thought of insubordination and schism was an abomination to you. Over the failings of your neighbors you mourned; their shortcomings you judged to be your own. . . .

All splendor and scope for expansion were bestowed upon you, and then the Scripture was fulfilled: *The*

beloved ate and drank, and he waxed large and fat, and then he kicked out [Deut 32:15]. **From this sprang jealousy and envy, strife and sedition, persecution and anarchy, war and captivity. Then the dishonored rose up against the honored, the ignoble against the highly esteemed, the foolish against the wise, the young against their elders. For this reason piety and peace are far removed, because everyone has abandoned the fear of God and lost the clear vision which faith affords, and nobody regulates his conduct by the norms of His commandments, or tries to make his life worthy of Christ. On the contrary, everyone follows the appetites of his depraved heart, for they have absorbed that unjust and unholy jealousy through which death came into the world.**[53]

At this point Clement vividly sketches out many Old Testament examples, both of jealousy and rebellion (Cain, Esau, and so on) and also of submission and faith (Abraham, Lot, Rahab). He then paints a charming picture of the orderly submissiveness of nature, where stars and planets "**obedient to His arrangement, roll on in harmony**", and the four seasons "**make room for one another in peaceful succession**".[54] Yet surely every Christian, then as well as now, would be willing at least to pay lip service to "harmony" and "submission". How were believers supposed to turn these ideals into something more than platitudes? Harmony with what, for example? Submission to whom? For Clement, the answers are plain and clear:

---

[53] Clement, *Epistle to the Corinthians*, prologue; chap. 1, nos. 1–2; chap. 2, nos. 1, 5–6; chap. 3, nos. 1–4, ACW 1:9–11.

[54] Ibid., chap. 20, nos. 3, 9, ACW 1:22.

> **The Apostles preached to us the Gospel received from Jesus Christ, and Jesus Christ was God's Ambassador. Christ, in other words, comes with a message from God, and the Apostles with a message from Christ. Both these orderly arrangements, therefore, originate from the will of God. And so, after receiving their instructions and being fully assured through the Resurrection of our Lord Jesus Christ, as well as confirmed in faith by the word of God, they went forth, equipped with the fullness of the Holy Spirit, to preach the good news that the Kingdom of God was close at hand. From land to land, accordingly, and from city to city, they preached, and from among their earliest converts appointed men whom they had tested by the Spirit to act as bishops and deacons for future believers. And this was no innovation, for, a long time before the Scripture had spoken about bishops and deacons; for somewhere it says: "*I will establish their overseers in observance of the law and their ministers in fidelity*"** [Is 60:17].[55]

Recounting the story of Korah's rebellion in Numbers 16, Clement tells how Moses, **"when the priesthood had become an object of jealousy and the tribes were quarrelling as to which of them had been honored with that glorious dignity",**[56] produced Aaron's miraculously budding rod as proof of God's sanction on the house of Levi.

> **He acted in this manner** [continues Clement] **to prevent any insubordination in Israel, so that the name of the**

[55] Ibid., chap. 42, nos. 1–5, ACW 1:34–35.
[56] Ibid., chap. 43, no. 2, ACW 1:35.

> **true and only God might be glorified. . . . Our Apostles, too, were given to understand by our Lord Jesus Christ that the office of the bishop would give rise to intrigues. For this reason, equipped as they were with perfect foreknowledge, they appointed the men mentioned before, and afterwards laid down a rule once and for all to this effect: when these men die, other approved men shall succeed to their sacred ministry. Consequently, we deem it an injustice to eject from the sacred ministry the persons who were appointed by them, or later, with the consent of the whole Church, by other men in high repute and have ministered to the flock of Christ faultlessly, humbly, quietly and unselfishly, and have moreover, over a long period of time, earned the esteem of all.**[57]

Here is Clement's own life experience translated into action! Rival gurus jockeying for position, smoke-filled rooms where this week's version of truth is decided by committee—these things belong, not to the Household of God, but to the pagan world of insanity Clement had left behind. The budding staff belongs to Jesus' Twelve Apostles and to their chosen disciples! And from this point on, Clement will write with every ounce of his considerable skill to beg, cajole, and warn the straying usurpers of Corinth back into harmony with God's plan:

> **Why are [these] quarrels and outbursts of passion and divisions and schisms and war in your midst? Or, do we not have one God and one Christ and one Spirit of grace,**

[57] Ibid., no. 6; chap. 43, no. 6; chap. 44, nos. 1–3, ACW 1:36.

a Spirit that was poured out upon us? And is there not one calling in Christ? Why do we tear apart and disjoint the members of Christ and revolt against our own body, and go to such extremes of madness as to forget that we are mutually dependent members? Remember the words of Jesus our Lord. For He said, "*Utterly wretched is that man; it would be better for him not to have been born than to be an occasion of sin to one of my elect; it would be better for him to lie at the bottom of the sea with a millstone hung round his neck than to pervert one of my elect*" [Mt 26:24; Lk 17:1–2; Mk 9:42]. Your schism has perverted many; many it has thrown into discouragement, many it has bewildered, and to all of us it has brought sorrow. And your schism persists!

Take up the epistle of the blessed Apostle Paul. What is the most important thing he wrote to you in the early days of gospel preaching? He was truly inspired when he wrote to you regarding himself and Cephas and Apollos, because already at that time you had engaged in factious agitation. But that display of factiousness involved you in less guilt, for [then, at least] you took the part of Apostles, men of attested merit, and of a man in good repute with them. But now consider who those are who have perverted you and vilified the venerable character of your celebrated fraternal charity. Disgraceful, beloved, indeed, exceedingly disgraceful and unworthy of your training in Christ, is the report that the well-established and ancient Church of the Corinthians is, thanks to one or two individuals, in revolt against the presbyters. And this report has reached not only us, but also people that differ from us in religion, with the result that, owing to your folly, you heap blasphemy upon the name of the Lord and withal create a danger to yourselves.

Let us, then, quickly blot out this blemish and fall on our knees before the Master, and with tears implore Him to have mercy on us and be reconciled to us and to restore us to the venerable and holy practice of brotherly love.[58]

Let us, then, ask pardon for our waywardness and for what we have done yielding to any wiles of the adversary; but those, too, who were the ringleaders in this quarrel and sedition, ought, for their part, to ponder on the common nature of our hope. Surely, those who live in fear and love prefer that they themselves should suffer indignities rather than their neighbors; they prefer to have reproach cast on themselves rather than on that traditional concord so well and justly established among us. It is better for a man to make a clean breast of his failings than to harden his heart in imitation of those who, after rebelling against God's servant Moses, hardened their hearts, and whose condemnation was brought to light: "*alive they went down to Hades, where death shall be their shepherd*" [Ps 48:15].[59]

Now, then, who among you is noble, who compassionate, who full of charity? Let him say: "If I am the cause of sedition and strife and schism, then I depart; I go wherever you wish; I do whatever the majority enjoins: only let the flock of Christ have peace with the

[58] Ibid., chap. 46, no. 5—chap. 48, no. 1, ACW 1:37–39.

[59] Ibid., chap. 51, nos. 1–4, ACW 1:40–41.

appointed presbyters." He who acts thus will win great glory for himself in Christ, and every place will welcome him; for the earth and all that is in it are the Lord's. Those who live as citizens of God's Kingdom —a life that never brings regrets—have acted thus and will act thus.[60]

Let us, too, therefore, pray for those who are guilty of some fault, that meekness and humility may be granted them, and incline them to submit—not to us—but to the will of God; thus our compassionate remembrance of them before God and the saints will bear perfect fruit for them. . . .[61]

You, therefore, the prime movers of the schism, submit to the presbyters, and, bending the knees of your hearts, accept correction and change your minds. Learn submissiveness, and rid yourselves of your boastful and proud incorrigibility of tongue. Surely, it is better for you to be little and honorable within the flock of Christ than to be esteemed above your deserts and forfeit the hope which He holds out.[62]

Accept our counsel, and you shall have nothing to regret. For, as truly as God lives, as truly as the Lord Jesus Christ and the Holy Spirit live, and the faith and hope of the elect, so truly will he who in a humble frame of mind, with eagerness to yield, and unregretfully carries out the commandments and precepts given by God, be enrolled and be in good standing among the number

[60] Ibid., chap. 54, ACW 1:42.
[61] Ibid., chap. 56, no. 1, ACW 1:43.
[62] Ibid., chap. 57, nos. 1–2, ACW 1:44.

of those who are on the way to salvation through Jesus Christ, through whom is to Him the glory forever and evermore. Amen.

But should any disobey what has been said by Him through us, let them understand that they will entangle themselves in transgression and no small danger.[63]

[Contrariwise] you will certainly give us the keenest pleasure if you prove obedient to what we have written through the Holy Spirit, and extirpate the lawless passion of your jealousy in accordance with the pleas we have made in this letter for peace and concord. We are sending trustworthy and prudent men, who have led blameless lives among us from youth to old age, that they may be witnesses between you and us. We do this to make you feel that our whole care has been, and is, directed toward establishing speedy peace in your midst.

And now may the all-seeing God and Master of spirits and Lord of all flesh, who chose the Lord Jesus Christ and us through Him to be a people set apart for Himself, grant to every soul that invokes His transcendent and holy name—faith, fear, peace, patient endurance and long-suffering, self-control, holiness, and sobriety, so that they may be well-pleasing to His Majesty through our High Priest and Ruler, Jesus Christ, through whom be to Him glory and greatness, power and honor, both now and forever and evermore. Amen.

As for our representatives Claudius Ephebus and Valerius Bito, accompanied by Fortunatus, send them back to us at an early convenience, full of peace and joy, that

[63] Ibid., chaps. 58, no. 2—59, no. 1, ACW 1:45.

they may without delay bring tidings of peace and concord — the object of our most ardent desires — and that we in turn may without delay rejoice in your tranquillity.

May the grace of our Lord Jesus Christ be with you and with all that have anywhere in the world been called by God and through Him, through whom be to Him glory and honor and power and majesty and everlasting dominion, from eternity to eternity. Amen.[64]

The Unfading Crown of Glory

Did Clement's letter restore order at Corinth? He himself may never have known for sure. Eusebius tells us that **"In the third year of Trajan's reign** [A.D. 101], **Clement departed this life, yielding his office to Evarestus."**[65] Our noble bishop, then, had less than six years to live when he wrote to Corinth, and the situation there may not have had time to resolve itself fully before his passing. The facts concerning the place and manner of his death have not survived. A few confused and unsatisfactory legends would have him a martyr, but in another place he is said to have died at Rome surrounded by his loved ones; a rare blessing in those days. However it happened, when Clement of Rome finally laid down his earthly burden, the Church was still in her infancy, and he will be remembered by believers forever, as he has been these nineteen hundred years, as one of her most beloved midwives.

How, in fact, *did* the church of Corinth fare? It would have gratified Clement's soul, surely, to look into the future and

---

[64] Ibid., chap. 63, no. 2—chap. 65, no. 2, ACW 1:48–49.

[65] Eusebius, *History of the Church*, bk. 3, chap. 34, in EHC 97.

read this account from Hegesippus, a traveling Christian scholar, who stopped briefly with the brethren at Corinth about A.D. 170:

> **The Church of the Corinthians has continued in the correct doctrine to the time of Primus, who has become bishop in Corinth, and with whom I conversed at length on my way to Rome, when I spent some days with the Corinthians, during which time we were mutually refreshed in the correct doctrine. When I had come to Rome, I made a succession up to Anicetus, whose deacon was Eleutherus. . . . In each succession and in each city there is a continuance of that which is proclaimed by the Law, the Prophets, and the Lord.**[66]

Here is a final, beautiful passage from Clement's *Epistle*, a prayer for the little lost sheep of Christ throughout the world:

> **We beg Thee, O Master, to be our Helper and Protector: deliver those of us who are in distress, raise up the fallen, show Thy face to those in need, heal the infirm, bring back the erring of Thy people, feed the hungry, ransom our prisoners, set the infirm upon their feet, comfort the fainthearted: let all the nations know that Thou art the only God, that Jesus Christ is Thy Son, that we are Thy people and the sheep of Thy pasture.**[67]

---

[66] Hegesippus, "Fragment in Eusebius, *History of the Church*, Bk. 4, Ch. 22", no. 1, in FEF 1:80, no. 188.

[67] Clement, *Epistle to the Corinthians*, chap. 59, no. 4, ACW 1:46.

Ignatius of Antioch

Today is December 20, A.D. 107. At least two hours before sunrise, they begin to arrive for work; the groundskeepers and the gardeners, the maintenance men and the concessionaires, the animal trainers and the acrobats. Sleepy-eyed and silent, they pass through the designated employee entrances and then "clock-in" (however that might have been done early in the second century) before moving to fill every corner of the enormous structure with a mounting buzz of activity. At the various streetside service docks dozens of lorries wait in impatient lines to deliver their miscellaneous cargoes, the massive stock of goods that will be needed to supply the fifty thousand or so spectators anticipated here today. Long queues soon begin to form at the public entries as well, though the gates will not open for hours. Yet, as any citizen of Rome would be quick to tell you, a good seat at the Flavian Amphitheater on a holiday is worth the wait. Yes, the Flavian Amphitheater: that fabulous sports and entertainment complex that will be better known in ages to come as simply *The Coliseum*.

Before long, the sun comes up over the city, revealing a sharp azure sky and the high, thin clouds of early winter. Temperatures here in Rome today will rise perhaps into the upper fifties; a beautiful clear day for sport and a certain guarantee of big box-office. Though nearing its thirtieth birthday now, the Coliseum still seems new to most, and it remains the pride of the city and the admiration of the world. Situated between the Esquiline and Palatine hills, in what used to be a swampy abandoned fish pond, the vast edifice is also a wonder of urban renewal, drawing tourism (and the money that accompanies it) from all over the Empire. Its sheer physical beauty retains the ability to impress also. Elliptical in shape—564 feet long, 467 feet wide, standing 157 feet high with four distinct stories—the Coliseum's architecture has been described as *faux Egyptian*: deliberately exotic and artificial, designed to startle and impress, like a Disneyland ride pavilion or a 1920s movie palace. The exterior walls, encrusted with marble and decorated with statues, are constructed of a creamy calcium carbonate material called travertine, which seems to glow a ravishing rose color from within in the light of this morning's dawn. Inside, the appointments are Greek in style and piled on for luxury.

When the designated hour arrives and the gates are finally unlocked, each of the excited onlookers rushes quickly, via a highly sophisticated set of ramps and staircases, to one of the sixty or eighty rows of marble seats covered with comfortable cushions. Taking their places, the growing crowd looks down in anticipation onto the arena proper—the wide wooden floor on which the spectacle will take place. *Arena* is simply the Latin word for *sand*, and this broad space is covered with the very finest, trucked in pure and white from the beaches of the Mediterranean. The grounds crews are raking and smoothing it now, taking pride in their work. At the center of the arena stands a famous and enormous statue of Jupiter, father of the gods. There is a seating chart, of course; the various levels are partitioned out according to social standing. The front row seats—"Field Level," as it were—are reserved for senators and other VIPs. The fourteen rows immediately above are set apart for other wealthy

Romans and visiting foreign dignitaries. Above this is the "Club Level"—luxury boxes for the emperor himself, should he choose to attend, and the Vestal Virgins, among others. Still higher, the middle class has a large section reserved. And at the very top—the "nosebleed" section—there are cheap wooden seats for the poor; yes, the bleachers, where the rowdy *hoi polloi* will drink and holler to their hearts' content.

Quite a different sound begins to be heard, however, *down below*, in the cavernous basement spaces beneath the public area. Though ingeniously lit by a fantastic array of oil lamps, skylight shafts, and mirrors, this huge labyrinth of hellish service cellars still has the look and feel of a storybook dungeon. And in fact, though it also contains elaborate mechanical appliances—elevators and trap-door systems and drainage works of almost impossible complexity—a *dungeon* is exactly what it is. Everywhere within the substructure are cells and dens and holding areas for men and for beasts. Along one corridor perhaps seventy great cats—tigers, lions, and leopards—are penned individually into iron cages arranged in double rows. Their last meal has been nearly three days ago now. In preparation for today's show, a team of experienced handlers walks methodically down the corridor in between, stopping at each cage to poke and goad and even injure each captive into a state of frenzy. Carefully evading the grasping talons that swipe at them from between the bars, they work until satisfied . . . and then move on. In another part of the basement, elephants are being dressed in costume armor, in readiness for a routine based on Hannibal's crossing of the Alps. But mainly, there are cellblocks full of captive humans—foreigners, for the most part, disobedient slaves, prisoners of war, with a few domestic criminals mixed in, too. Knowing the part that *they* will play in today's entertainment, these also are worked up into their own brand of frenzy. Some pray loudly, with tears and outstretched arms, to whatever heathen and barbaric deity out of Africa or Germany or the East seems most likely to deliver. Others, less religious, curse and threaten and rage impotently, fighting among themselves. Many sit alone, shivering and weeping, thinking about home and mother.

What happens here at the Coliseum is, of course, well known to everyone. Horrible, horrible scenes will be played out within these walls today; the Romans expect them, and would be disappointed if they failed to materialize. It would, however, be an important mistake to say that this jaded generation has become *hardened* to the shock of violence. No, indeed—that shock is precisely what they are after, what they have paid to experience, the whole reason for their coming out today. Like the rollicking, squealing crowds at the newest gory horror movie, like the long lines of vacationers queuing up for the latest and scariest roller coaster, the Romans *want* to be shocked. They *want* to dare themselves to look, challenge themselves not to throw up, laugh and hoot and cover their eyes . . . and then go safely home with the warm satisfaction of having *survived* the ordeal. Yes, this is just exactly what they want and what they expect.

What they do not expect, however, is that by the time the sun sets tonight—December 20, A.D. 107—they will also have witnessed one of the most beautiful miracles in history, an event that will instantaneously transform their sick, gilded charnel house into one of the most sacred spots in Christendom.

A Man of Apostolic Character

Simon Peter had another successor. **"When Trajan, not long since, succeeded to the empire of the Romans, Ignatius, the disciple of John the apostle, a man in all respects of an apostolic character, governed the Church of the Antiochians with great care. . ."**[1] Antioch, as may be remembered, was the location of Peter's first church, established before his journey to Rome, at the city (according to the book of Acts) where believers were first called *Christians*. And this man Ignatius, described by Eusebius as a man **"whose fame is still celebrated by a great many"**, is also identified by the great Church historian as the one **"chosen bishop of Antioch, second in succession to Peter"**.[2] Like his contemporary Clement, Ignatius, too, is believed to have been ordained by Peter himself, and his rise to the pastorate (upon the death of someone called Evodius, of whom nothing is known) is thought to have happened in the year 69.

About A.D. 399, the great "golden-throated" preacher of Antioch, John Chrysostom,[3] gave a sermon in honor of Ignatius, the city's most famous native son. That sermon has been preserved and is worth quoting at length for the insight it gives into our subject's character and the scope of the task he faced:

---

[1] *The Martyrdom of Ignatius*, chap. 1, trans. Alexander Roberts and James Donaldson, in ANF 1:129.

[2] Eusebius, *Church History*, bk. 3, chap. 36, no. 2, trans. Arthur Cushman McGiffert, in NPNF2 1:166.

[3] John of Antioch (347?–407), perhaps the greatest of the Eastern Fathers, was given the surname Chrysostom ("golden-throat" or "golden-mouth") by later generations in remembrance of his brilliant and persuasive preaching.

[Ignatius of Antioch] held true converse with the apostles and drank of spiritual fountains. What kind of person then is it likely that he was who had been reared, and who had everywhere held converse with them, and had shared with them truths both lawful and unlawful to utter, and who seemed to them worthy of so great a dignity? . . . He obtained this office from those saints, and . . . the hands of the blessed apostles touched his sacred head. . . . [By this] they bore witness that every virtue possessed by man was in him. . . .

Let us consider the time at which he obtained this dignity. For it is not the same thing to administer the Church now as then, just as it is not the same thing to travel along a road well trodden, and prepared, after many wayfarers; and along one about to be cut for the first time, and containing ruts, and stones, and full of wild beasts, and which has never yet received any traveller. For now, by the grace of God, there is no danger for bishops, but deep peace on all sides, and we all enjoy a calm, since the Word of piety has been extended to the ends of the world, and our rulers keep the faith with strictness. But then there was nothing of this, but wherever any one might look, precipices and pitfalls, and wars, and fightings, and dangers; both rulers, and kings, and people and cities and nations, and men at home and abroad, laid snares for the faithful. And this was not the only serious thing, but also the fact that many of the believers themselves, inasmuch as they tasted for the first time strange doctrines, stood in need of great indulgence, and were still in a somewhat feeble condition and were often upset. And this was a thing which used to grieve the teachers, no less than the fightings without, nay rather much more. For the fightings without, and the plottings, afforded much pleasure to them on account of the hope of the rewards awaiting them. On this account the apostles returned from the presence of the Sanhedrin rejoicing because they had been beaten; and Paul cries out, saying: "I rejoice in my sufferings," and he glories in his afflictions everywhere. But the wounds of those at home, and the falls of the brethren, do not suffer [the bishops] to breathe again, but always, like some most heavy yoke, continually oppress and afflict the neck of their soul. . . .

Just as then we admire the pilot, not when he is able to bring those who are on board safe to shore when the sea is calm, and the ship is borne along by favourable winds, but when the deep is raging and the waves contending, and the passengers themselves within in revolt, and a great storm within and without besets those who are on board, and he is able to steer the ship with all security; so we ought to wonder at, and admire those who then had the Church committed to their hands, much more than those who now have the management of it; when there was a great war without and within, when the plant of the faith was more tender, and needed much care when, as a newly-born babe, the multitude in the church required much forethought, and the greatest wisdom in any soul destined to nurse it.[4]

---

[4] John Chrysostom, *Eulogy*, nos. 1–3, trans. W. R. W. Stephens and T. P. Brandram, in NPNF1 9:136–37.

Ignatius, by most accounts, piloted his church in this heroic way for over thirty years—but his last battle was his greatest. The seven priceless epistles that survive from his pen were generated during that final conflict, and an eyewitness record of its furious climax may just be our oldest fragment of Church history outside the New Testament.[5] From these ancient documents a spellbinding tale emerges; the story of a man of God who, for the sake of his flock, voluntarily positioned himself as a living lightning rod for practically every type of fiery dart being hurled at the Church during those crucial formative years.

Bishop Ignatius, we are told, by **"prayer and fasting, by the earnestness of his teaching, and by his [constant] spiritual labour",**[6] brought the Antiochians safely through Domitian's persecution and enjoyed with them (as we observed Clement doing with the Romans) the peace that came with the heartless emperor's death in the year 96. And though he **"rejoiced over the tranquil state of the Church, when the persecution ceased for a little time"**, Ignatius was, nevertheless, **"grieved as to himself, that he had not yet attained to a true love of Christ, nor reached the perfect rank of a disciple"**.[7] Recalling, no doubt, the many brave members of his church who had shed their blood during the test, **"he inwardly reflected, that the confession which is**

---

[5] The only existing copies of *The Martyrdom of Ignatius* are, it is true, marred by later interpolations. This has led many recent scholars to reject the document's historicity outright; but this seems (at least to me) to throw the baby out with the bath water. Most likely it represents in its current form a late (though still very ancient) gloss on an authentic contemporary report.

[6] *The Martyrdom of Ignatius*, chap. 1, in ANF 1:129.

[7] Ibid.

made by martyrdom, would bring him into a yet more intimate relation to the Lord. Wherefore, continuing a few years longer with the Church, and, like a divine lamp, enlightening every one's understanding by his expositions of the Scriptures, [Ignatius at length] attained the object of his desire."[8]

Make-Believe Christianity

Our ancient documents also tell us that there was another church in Antioch at this time—under another shepherd than Ignatius. Most likely this other congregation looked, for all practical purposes, exactly like his; indeed, its members probably took some little trouble to ensure that this remained the case. The same hymns were probably sung, the same prayers were likely said, and in a meeting place chosen precisely for its homey resemblance to that used by the "old school". The faces were quite similar, too. As a matter of fact, this new church was almost certainly filled with former members of Ignatius' own flock, and with the brothers, daughters, wives, and other relations of his current parishioners. Pagan outsiders looking on probably saw very little difference between the two congregations—a response, it may be noticed, not dissimilar to that of the previous generation when confronted with two bearded Simons out of Palestine.

Yet quite unlike the situation in the days of the Magus, the similarities between these two churches at Antioch, circa A.D. 100, were more than just skin deep. Though they cer-

[8] Ibid.

tainly styled themselves followers of Jesus, Simon's pure-bred Gnostics taught a theology as wild and extravagant as that of Brigham Young, full of multiple gods and weird heavenly hierarchies, denying either implicitly or explicitly pretty much the entire Christian schema. But this new congregation at Antioch was, on nine points out of ten, completely orthodox—and proud of it. They allowed themselves only two distinctives: first, a slight difference of opinion on what some might call a rather fine point of Christology; and second, the sovereign democratic right to disagree on that point with Ignatius.

Called *Docetists* by Church historians, these "alternative" Christians were part of a recognized semi-Gnostic sect that flourished for a season during these early decades. The term is derived from the Greek word *dokesis*, meaning an "appearance" or even a "make-believe". What was the make-believe? Simply this: the Docetists denied that the eternal Son of God had actually become a real human being in Jesus Christ. Rather, they maintained that He had only taken on the appearance of a man in order more easily to interface with His fallen creatures. In other words, though Jesus the Messiah had indeed been "God with us", He was not actually "God-in-the-flesh". His *apparent* humanity—and by extension His suffering on the Cross—was, in truth, nothing but a divine bit of playacting.

This notion, of course, contrasts strongly with what Ignatius would have learned from the Apostles. It was, after all, Ignatius' own mentor, the Apostle John, who wrote in his Gospel about **"the Word [who] became flesh and dwelt among us"** (Jn 1:14). In fact, this is one of the central themes in all of John's writing, and at several points he seems to be going to bat himself against something like Docetism. In his first epistle, for example, the Apostle sends out these strong words of admonition:

> **Beloved, do not believe every spirit, but test the spirits to see whether they are of God; for many false prophets have gone out into the world. By this you know the Spirit of God: every spirit which confesses that Jesus Christ has come in the flesh is of God, and every spirit which does not confess Jesus is not of God. . . . They [who teach otherwise] are of the world, therefore what they say is of the world, and the world listens to them. We are of God. Whoever knows God listens to us, and he who is not of God does not listen to us. By this we know the spirit of truth and the spirit of error.** (1 Jn 4:1–2, 5–6)

Here we see clearly that if Ignatius was indeed John's disciple, then he knew this particular falsehood well and battling it was a job for which he came uniquely qualified.

Now, the Gnostic element in all this is plain enough: in each of its many forms Gnosticism insists on identifying flesh itself—sheer created *matter*—with evil. Spirit only can be good. This being the case, if Jesus of Nazareth was going to find any place at all in their systems He would need to be radically reinterpreted. And, sure enough, most Gnostic teachers turned our Lord into little more than an angelic messenger from on high—as do today's Jehovah's Witnesses and other cults. But how did these "strange doctrines" begin to worm their way into the churches? What would motivate wavering Christians to dabble in this kind of thing? What possible temptation could such a heresy offer to believers so close in time to the real Jesus and so easily able to consult His true disciples about the nature of His message?

Sadly, the more things change, the more they stay the same. As John intimated in the passage above, first-century believers faced the same deadly tug we Christians face today: *the temptation to compromise with the world.* To put it briefly, Docetism allowed its adherents to remain ostensibly Christian while yet avoiding what has been aptly called "the Scandal of the Incarnation".

As we noted in the previous chapter, a Jesus who was merely *a* god—rather than *the* Almighty God—would present no problem to the pagan mind at all. And, to tell the truth, even the real God would not be much trouble so long as He was kept similarly *subjective*, a mere heavenly phantom rumored once to have haunted the hills of Judea. But to an empire schooled in the elegant pieties of Plato and Epicurus, the very idea that the actual *Creator of the Universe* had become a baby in a manger (a real baby, who might have needed his diaper changed from time to time) was simply grotesque or puerile. More offensive still was the use to which this outrageous conception was being put by the Christians. The gooey, amorphous "spirituality" of paganism allowed people to do their own thing in matters of religion. Sing, shout, prophesy, pray, go into a trance . . . nobody gave a fig, so long as you did not attempt to impose any of your high-falutin' opinions on anyone else.[9] But

---

[9] The one exception to this, of course, was the obligation to honor ritually the divinity of Caesar, along with the official gods of the city. This act was seen as a guarantor of shared values in an increasingly fragmented culture, a necessary societal "glue" that the Romans probably required for much the same reason that the United States government requires citizen-

these Christians, since they claimed that the one and only God Himself had come to earth to be their tutor, expected their teachings to be received as the voice of God. They wanted what they said to be accepted as literal truth. And worst of all, they had the effrontery to promote their particular brand of rather quixotic morality with nothing less than threats of eternal damnation!

This, obviously, was . . . well, *rude*. It left a man no wiggle room. It had an intolerable "take it or leave it" quality that no true believer in liberty or tolerance could possibly accept. And so the pagans instinctively realized that any new society talking in *that* way would have to be either completely accepted or completely destroyed.

The Christians knew this, too. And consequently, most of them were not surprised when the storms began to break. They had seen Peter go, and Paul; and they knew, just as the Apostles had, that the servant is not greater than his Master. But by this time a new generation of churchgoers had arisen, the first crop of cradle Christians in history. Their parents had accepted the Christian life (and all that it entailed in those difficult days) for themselves, with eyes wide open. They, on the other hand, had been carried off into this wilderness without their consent. This is not to say that most of them regretted having come to the knowledge of Christ; and we need not insist that it was chiefly the physical persecutions they feared. No, what they seem to have wanted (and some of their weaker elders along with them,

---

ship exams for immigrants. And this, of course, was the law that doomed so many innocent Christians in those days, with their notoriously rigid beliefs about the sin of idolatry.

no doubt) was something all of us are still tempted to want today. They just wanted to *belong* a bit better.

The Docetists did not want to drop their faith, they simply wondered whether it would really do all that much harm just to *tweak* it a little. After all, think of it: with just this one tiny adjustment to just one of the more obscure inferences of the new Christian gospel, all this horrible war between the Faith and the Empire could simply be *called off*. All the crosses and crucibles and hot irons and gibbets—all of it gone at one blow, like some hideous nightmare. And who knows? If Christians, merely by making this single modest concession, were then allowed to take their rightful place in Roman society, who could say what great victories for Christ might be won? The Church might be able to shed her frightful reactionary image (still lingering from the days of Nero) and work to change the culture from *within*. Of course, it is true that there *were* certain passages in the writings of the Apostles that might be seen as problematical to such a course; but after all, are there not always going to be "difficult passages"? And anyway, who really is bold enough to say that he truly *understands* the nature of God-in-Christ? Whether Jesus had a Body of true flesh or a Body of some unknown divine essence appearing to the senses as flesh—isn't it all rather like arguing over how many angels can dance on the head of a pin? What sensible person, having it within his power to do differently, would willingly choose to leave the Church in torment for the sake of a hair-splitting theological scruple like that?

At Antioch, that sensible person was Ignatius. As we shall see in his epistles, the bishop of the church in Syria saw very clearly what the Docetists wanted: they wanted nothing less than a *synthesis* of Christianity and paganism. And Ignatius also saw that if Jesus had shed His blood to give the world nothing more than *that*, then surely we are all still in our sins.

With Ignatius, then, just as with Clement of Rome, we find that it is the man left in charge by the Apostles who is blocking the path to "progress". At Corinth the assault had come in the form of a brazen bid to hijack the existing church founded by Paul. But when, thanks to Clement (and probably others elsewhere), that particular tack failed, we begin to see the innovators experimenting with another methodology. Yes, we all know that up until now churches have been founded by the men appointed by Jesus; and after that, by the "other approved men who succeeded to their sacred ministry". And yes, we know that those same Apostles commanded believers (as, for example, in Hebrews 13:17) to **"Obey your leaders and submit to them; for they are keeping watch over your souls, as men who will have to give account."** But just supposing: What if the *people* of the church—or the intelligent, progressive ones, at any rate—were to get together and choose *new leaders* for themselves? Responsive leaders. Leaders more in touch with the times. Leaders *worthy* of obedience. Might not such intelligent people go peaceably off to themselves and follow Jesus in their own way—leaving the extremists and the die-hards to bloody their fool heads against the might of Rome to their hearts' content?

After all, what is Ignatius? Or Clement? Or Peter, or Paul—or any other mere man, for that matter? Is it not true, as Korah said to Moses and Aaron, that **"all the congregation are holy, every one of them, and the LORD is**

among them" (Num 16:3)? Why should any man, or set of men, be allowed to **"exalt [themselves] above the assembly"** (Num 16:3)? Did Christ not come to make us free? Should not the Christian be at liberty to worship God as he sees fit?

Does a man not have the right, each and every Sunday, to "attend the church of his choice"?

Theophorus before Trajan

The story of Ignatius proper (as related in the *Martyrium Ignatii*—that eyewitness account quoted earlier) begins late in the 106th year of the Christian era; a year known to the Romans as "the ninth of the emperor Trajan". It was in that year, after concluding a series of glorious military triumphs on the borders of civilization, that Trajan, **"being lifted up"** with pride, began to reason in his heart that only **"the religious body of the Christians were yet wanting to complete the subjugation of all things to himself."**[10] Hitherto, this obstinate tribe had stubbornly resisted every effort directed by his illustrious predecessors toward their rehabilitation. What better way to make a name for himself on the pages of history than to succeed where the other emperors had failed? Therefore, **"threatening them with persecution unless they should agree to worship daemons, as did all other nations, [Trajan] thus compelled all who were living godly lives either to sacrifice or die. Wherefore the noble soldier of Christ [Ignatius], being in fear for the Church of the Antiochians, was, in accordance with his own desire,**

[10] *Martyrdom of Ignatius*, chap. 2, in ANF 1:129.

brought before Trajan, who was at that time staying at Antioch."[11]

It is a very remarkable scene. As Chrysostom said, Ignatius' first thought is for *the little lambs*, for "the Church of the Antiochians". He fears most, of course, for the new believers, for recent converts, for those in the church "needing great indulgence". Having lived through at least one such holocaust already, the bishop knows that as the axes are sharpened, when the scream of the cats sounds from behind the door, the danger of falling away—even for mature Christians—becomes all too real. Yet how much more perilous still the situation had now become! When the Apostles suffered under Nero, when he and Clement had suffered under Domitian, the choice had been so much clearer, so much cleaner. It was Christ or nothing; it was victory or everlasting shame. But now something new had been added; this so-called *alternative*, this numbing "third way" to sap their strength and confuse their terror-stricken hearts. Now there was another church, another bishop—someone as learned as he or more learned, someone who could quote you the law and the prophets, look you in the face and tell you that so long as the spirit remains willing it would matter nothing if the flesh were weak. After all, it is the soul that belongs to God, not the body. Not lips, not voice—these things will be left behind in the grave, along with any meaningless mumbo-jumbo they might have been forced to spout in moments of duress. *Lord God!* How enticing it all might sound even to Ignatius, were he looking, even now, on the racks and the ropes and the red-hot pokers!

---

[11] Ibid.

We know today from the writings of the Fathers that many Gnostics and semi-Gnostic Christians did, in fact, offer just this pernicious option to early believers struggling under persecution. Irenaeus tells us that **"the Church does in every place, because of that love which she cherishes towards God, send forward, throughout all time, a multitude of martyrs to the Father; while others [the heretics] not only have nothing of this kind to point to among themselves, but even maintain that such witness-bearing**[12] **is not at all necessary, for that their system of doctrines is the true witness"**[13] And Eusebius records that one early teacher taught, in the name of a more "spiritual" religion, **"that there was no objection to eating meat offered to idols, or to cheerfully forswearing the Faith in times of persecution".**[14] In such a brave new world as this, guileless, valiant shepherds like Ignatius must truly have borne their responsibilities "like some most heavy yoke" afflicting the neck of their souls.

And so Ignatius determines to mount a preemptive strike. Perhaps he departs from his congregation under their tearful protests; possibly he keeps his brave plan to himself, leaving only a "good-bye note"—a few final words of solace and exhortation to the family he loves so well. At any rate, what

---

[12] The Christian term "martyr" is derived from the Greek word *martus*, meaning "a witness"—as Stephen, for example, in Acts 7, seals with his blood his testimony of Christ. Thus, when Irenaeus writes the phrase translated here as "witness-bearing", he is actually using the Greek word for martyrdom.

[13] Irenaeus of Lyons, *Against Heresies*, bk. 4, chap. 33, no. 9, trans. Alexander Roberts and James Donaldson, in ANF 1:508.

[14] Eusebius Pamphilus, *History of the Church*, bk. 4, chap. 7, in EHC 109.

he certainly does do is to walk directly and deliberately into the spider's web. In accordance with his own desire, Ignatius seeks an audience with the antichrist.

It may be that Ignatius' intention (like that of Justin, who will write to the emperor a few years later) is to mount an apology for the faith, an attempt to persuade the dictator to change his mind. More likely his thought is to offer himself as a ransom; the chief of the Christians in Syria in exchange for peace to his flock. But whatever his thought may have been, the *Martyrium* soon has the bishop of Antioch standing before the emperor of the Romans: *Imperator Rex, Pontifex Maximus*, the Master of the Universe himself. Here if anywhere would Christ's words to his disciples at their commissioning be fulfilled: **"You will be dragged before governors and kings for my sake, to bear testimony before them and the Gentiles. When they deliver you up, do not be anxious how you are to speak or what you are to say; for what you are to say will be given to you in that hour; for it is not you who speak, but the Spirit of your Father speaking through you"** (Mt 10:18–20).

Being the head and promoter of Christianity in Antioch, Ignatius was undoubtedly treated by the pagans as a prize catch—though they themselves had done nothing to reel him in. The arrest was announced to the monarch, a presentation of the prisoner arranged. Probably the usual charges were read: atheist, traitor, conspirator, deceiver of the people. Finally, Trajan himself decides to cross-examine the captive, and, in one of the most remarkable scenes preserved in all of ancient literature, he opens his mouth to speak:

"Who art thou, wicked wretch, who settest thyself to transgress our commands, and persuadest others to do the same, so that they [also] should miserably perish?"

Ignatius replied, "No one ought to call Theophorus wicked; for all evil spirits have departed from the servants of God."[15]

Theophorus, a Greek word meaning "God-bearing", was apparently a nickname for Ignatius used in the churches—and the aged bishop employs it here to open a unique dialogue with the emperor; in fact, we might even say that Ignatius, far from cowering before his captor, begins right away to witness the gospel to him!

Trajan answered, "And who is Theophorus?"

Ignatius replied, "He who has Christ within his breast."

Trajan said, "Do *we* not then seem to you to have the gods in our minds, whose assistance we enjoy in fighting against our enemies?"

Ignatius answered, "Thou art in error when thou callest the daemons of the nations gods. For there is but one God, who made heaven, and earth, and the sea, and all that are in them; and one Jesus Christ, the only-begotten Son of God, whose kingdom may I enjoy."

Trajan said, "Do you mean Him who was crucified under Pontius Pilate?"

Ignatius replied, "I mean Him who crucified my sin, with him who was the inventor of it, and who has con-

[15] *Martyrdom of Ignatius*, chap. 2, in ANF 1:129.

demned all the deceit and malice of the devil under the feet of those who carry Him in their heart."

Trajan said, "Dost thou then carry within thee Him that was crucified?"

Ignatius replied, "Truly so; for it is written, 'I will dwell in them, and walk in them'" [2 Cor 6:16].[16]

One imagines that the emperor sat silently for a moment or two. Some historians believe that Trajan was less bloodthirsty than the other Caesars up to that time and that he persecuted Christians mainly for political advantage, a pandering to popular opinion calculated to "win votes", so to speak. Nevertheless, if the emperor had any personal qualms about condemning a man so obviously innocent as Ignatius, he kept them to himself. He would hear no more. Following in the footsteps of the accursed Judean procurator whose name he had just invoked, Trajan rose to deliver what he knew in his heart to be an unjust sentence:

"We command that Ignatius, who affirms that he carries about within him Him that was crucified, be bound by soldiers, and carried to the great [city] Rome, there to be devoured by the beasts, for the gratification of the people."[17]

When Ignatius heard this decree he instantly dropped to his knees on the palace floor. Stretching his arms toward heaven, he cried out in a loud voice:

"I thank thee, O Lord, that Thou hast vouchsafed to honour me with a perfect love towards Thee, and hast

---

[16] Ibid., in ANF 1:129–30.

[17] Ibid., in ANF 1:130; [brackets in the original].

made me to be bound with iron chains, like Thy Apostle Paul!"

Having spoken thus, he then, with delight, clasped the chains about him; and when he had first prayed for the Church, and commended it with tears to the Lord, he was hurried away by the savage cruelty of the soldiers, like a distinguished ram, the leader of a goodly flock, that he might be carried to Rome, there to furnish food to the bloodthirsty beasts.[18]

Through the Land of Revelation

Word of Ignatius' arrest and condemnation spread quickly through the churches, by word of mouth and by the impulse of the Holy Spirit. As an important prisoner, a noted insurgent whose public execution would be a valuable propaganda victory, the transport of Theophorus to Rome was assigned to a detachment of soldiers; **"ten leopards"**, as he would call them in one of the epistles, **"who prove themselves more malevolent for kindnesses shown them"**.[19] The route they took to the Imperial City carried them always westward; first to Seleucia (closest seaport to Antioch) and from there across the eastern Mediterranean for a probable landfall at Tarsus in Asia Minor. John Chrysostom, in his sermon, says that the devil made **"the course [of the journey] twice as long, expecting to depress his mind both by the length of the way and the number of the days, and not knowing that**

---

[18] Ibid.

[19] Ignatius of Antioch, *Epistle to the Romans*, chap. 5, no. 1, in *The Epistles of St. Clement of Rome and St. Ignatius of Antioch*, trans. James A. Kleist, ACW, vol. 1 (Mahwah, N.J.: Paulist Press, 1948), p. 82.

having Jesus with him, as a fellow traveller, and fellow exile on so long a journey, he rather became the stronger, and afforded more proof of the power that was with him, and to a greater degree knit the Churches together."[20]

Satan meant it for evil, but God meant it for good. News of the bishop's destination, and also his probable itinerary, went swiftly before him, and all along the way the travelers found little knots of pilgrims waiting to receive him—to offer their prayers, their tears, their holy kisses. In fact, the overland journey through what is today modern Turkey became, for Ignatius, something of a triumphal tour. Though chained to an armed guard twenty-four hours a day, the prisoner was nevertheless afforded the opportunity to meet with local believers in a fairly unrestricted way; possibly the "ten leopards" learned to enjoy exploiting the company of these "traitors"—whose treason took the form of loving their enemies and being "much given to hospitality" toward them.

Asia Minor is very far from Syria by the standards of the ancient world. Yet Ignatius of Antioch would have been well acquainted with the churches there, just as modern students of the Bible will find their names familiar: Ephesus, Philadelphia, Pergamos, Thyatira—this was the Apostle John's old stomping ground! He ministered to these churches himself and the majestic book of Revelation (which he brought back from his cell on Patmos) contains, for each of them, a personalized message from the risen Christ in glory. According to reliable traditions, John (following in the footsteps of Paul, who passed through this region on his third missionary journey), made Ephesus his permanent base of operations

[20] John Chrysostom, *Eulogy*, no. 4, in NPNF1 9:138.

for the evangelization of the entire area.[21] And that great work, though temporarily interrupted by exile, was nevertheless resumed upon his release, which came also with the passing of Domitian in 96. Returning to his adopted city, the Apostle then spent the remaining days of his life there, up until his own death about the year 100. So it seems quite likely that Ignatius had been to Asia before; in fact, it is probable he worked out his apprenticeship to John in these surroundings, making this new visit into something of a bittersweet homecoming. He was certainly received, at any rate, like an old friend: **"The cities which were on the road,"** we are told by John Chrysostom, **"encouraged the athlete, and sped him on his way with many supplies, sharing in his conflict by their prayers, and intercessions."**[22]

The entourage seems to have turned northward at Laodicea, following the river Lycus through the very heart of John's country. They passed through Sardis, through Philadelphia, and came finally to Smyrna on the Aegean, which is called today Izmir. Here they stayed for quite some time, perhaps as much as six months. Though we do not know the specific reason for this lengthy delay, we do know that travel in those days was always an adventure. It would not have been considered at all unusual in ancient times for

---

[21] Writing about A.D. 200, Clement of Alexandria has this to say: **"After the death of the tyrant [Domitian] the [Apostle John] came back again to Ephesus from the Island of Patmos; and, upon being invited, he went even to the neighboring cities of the pagans, here to appoint bishops, there to set in order whole Churches, and there to ordain to the clerical estate such as were designated by the Spirit"** (*Who Is the Rich Man That Is Saved?*, chap. 42, no. 2, in FEF 1:187, no. 438).

[22] *Eulogy*, no. 4, in NPNF1 9:138–39.

a journey from Antioch to Rome to exhaust (as seems to have been the case here) the better part of a year or more.

At Smyrna, Ignatius was greeted by what must have been an almost inexpressibly welcome sight: the face of **"the holy Polycarp, his fellow-disciple, and [now] bishop of Smyrna. For they had both, in old times, been disciples of St. John the Apostle."**[23] Born about the year 70, Polycarp was a much younger man than Ignatius and was destined to outlive him by many years. They did, nevertheless, think of themselves as brothers, it seems—though the Antiochian's training must have come early in John's career and that of Polycarp very late. As pastor of this church at the time, Polycarp is believed by most scholars to be "the angel" (or "messenger") whose work is commended by Jesus in Revelation 2:8–10: **"And to the angel of the church in Smyrna write . . . I know your tribulation and your poverty (but you are rich). . . . Be faithful unto death, and I will give you the crown of life."** How Polycarp eventually redeemed this promise we will learn later in our story. But for now he appears as the great encourager of Ignatius; who will, in return, receive all of his encouragement back tenfold.

Polycarp's house becomes a kind of shrine during the time of Ignatius' stay. The high drama and profound meaning of the prisoner's sacrifice is not being lost on the churches, and they begin to send representatives from miles around to hear his last words and to offer their gratitude. It may seem surprising that these meetings were allowed to take place without interference from the soldiers or other authorities; it is probable that Trajan's persecution had not yet been put fully

[23] *Martyrdom of Ignatius*, chap. 3, in ANF 1:130.

into effect in this part of the world. We know, too, from evidence within the epistles and elsewhere, that believers were not at all above raising a collection for the express purpose of *bribery* under such circumstances. In fact, it is probable that great financial sacrifices were made for this purpose—Christians willingly surrendering their earthly treasures to buy one more precious hour with a man who was practically a martyr already.

Bishop Onesimus, John's own successor, comes at the head of a delegation from Ephesus. From Magnesia, Bishop Damas arrives with a group of envoys, and Bishop Polybius from Tralles. Doubtless there were many memorable nights of prayer and praise here in Polycarp's house; and it seems certain that the visitors must have cherished the memory of them for the rest of their lives. In exchange for their love and affection, Ignatius sends the bishops back to their home churches bearing gifts: three short, powerful epistles more valuable than gold. They contain not only his exhortations and farewells, but also some of the most important glimpses of the early Church to have survived the wreck of the ages.

The following excerpts (nearly nineteen hundred years old now), are taken from these three letters—to the *Ephesians*, the *Magnesians*, and the *Trallians*.

Letters from Smyrna

Ignatius, also called Theophorus, sends heartiest good wishes for unalloyed joy in Jesus Christ to the Church at Ephesus in Asia; a church deserving of felicitation, blessed, as she is, with greatness through the fullness of God the Father; predestined, before time was, to be

—to her abiding and unchanging glory—forever united and chosen, through real suffering, by the will of the Father and Jesus Christ our God.

With joy in God I welcomed your community, which possesses its dearly beloved name because of a right disposition, enhanced by faith and love through Christ Jesus our Savior. Being imitators of God, you have, once restored to new life in the Blood of God,[24] perfectly accomplished the task so natural to you. Indeed, as soon as you heard that I was coming from Syria in chains for our common Name and hope—hoping I might, thanks to your prayer, obtain the favor of fighting wild beasts at Rome and through this favor be able to prove myself a disciple—you hastened to see me. In the name of God, then, I have received your numerous community in the person of Onesimus, a man of indescribable charity and your bishop here on earth. I pray you in the spirit of Jesus Christ to love him, and wish all of you to resemble him. Blessed, indeed, is He whose grace made you worthy to possess such a bishop.[25]

Our English word *bishop*, it may be worthwhile to note, is derived from the New Testament term *episkopos*, meaning an "overseer" and carrying with it the implication of authority. When the Apostles, after Pentecost, went out to plant the first churches, they referred to themselves as their bish-

---

[24] This very striking phrase—"the Blood of God"—would seem sufficient to remove all doubt concerning the early Church's belief in the doctrine of the Incarnation.

[25] Ignatius, *Epistle to the Ephesians*, prologue and chap. 1, in *Epistles*, ACW 1:60.

ops.[26] Then, as the work continued, they deputized other men to assist them and called these *presbyters*, or the "elders" of the church. When the number of churches became great and their locations widespread, twelve men would, of course, not have been able to guide them all personally; and, as in the case of Paul's disciple Timothy, some of the presbyters were themselves raised to the role of pastor, or bishop.[27] We see in the pages of the *Didache* that once the twelve Apostles were gone there did come to be an element of democracy in this process: **"Elect for yourselves bishops"** the Didachist writes, **"men who are an honor to the Lord".**[28] But it is equally clear, as we saw in Clement's letter and elsewhere, that the key element—the *active ingredient*, so to speak—in making these candidates legitimate was their approval and ordination by either an Apostle or one of his chosen successors. This is how the Household of God maintained "quality control" in her teachers—and how she passed on, by discipleship, the authority to speak in Jesus' name.

Ignatius of Antioch knows these things—and knows also

---

[26] This fact is seen not only in the writings of the Fathers but in the New Testament; as for example, in Acts 1:20, where Peter, referring to the defection of Judas Iscariot, declares "his bishoprick [*episkipous*] let another take" (KJV). The "other" spoken of by Peter would be Matthias, who was soon chosen to fill the traitor's vacated position.

[27] Something of the spirit of this action may be seen in Paul's words to Titus (2:15): **"Declare these things; exhort and reprove with all authority. Let no one disregard you."**

[28] The *Didache*, chap. 15, no. 1, in *The Didache, The Epistle of Barnabas, The Epistles and The Martyrdom of St. Polycarp, The Fragments of Papias, The Epistle to Diognetus*, trans. James A. Kleist, ACW, vol. 6 (Mahwah, N.J.: Paulist Press, 1948), p. 24.

that these are the critical facts in his crusade to save his flock from Docetism.

"It is therefore proper in every way", Ignatius continues, **"to glorify Jesus Christ who has glorified you, so that you, fully trained in unanimous submission, may be submissive to the bishop and the presbytery, and thus be sanctified in every respect."**[29] These words seem strange to modern ears; especially in America, where we assign authority to our rulers from the bottom up, in a Jeffersonian "social contract". We expect our political leaders to be submissive to us, not the other way around—and with good historical justification, no doubt. But according to our witnesses, things were to be different in the early Church. Here, all authority comes from Jesus, and His Truth is intended to be passed down, not voted up—or voted down. And so Ignatius, while making it clear that the bishop's authority is not to be lorded over the people, nevertheless goes on to insist upon it strongly as God's own plan for the Church:

> **I give you no orders as though I were somebody. For, even though I am in chains for the sake of the Name, I am not yet perfected in Jesus Christ. Indeed, I am now but being initiated into discipleship, and I address you as my fellow disciples. Yes, I ought to be anointed by you with faith, encouragement, patient endurance, and steadfastness. However, since affection does not permit me to be silent where you are concerned, I am at once taking this opportunity to exhort you to live in harmony with the mind of God. Surely, Jesus Christ, our inseparable life, for His part is the mind of the Father, just**

---

[29] Ignatius, *Epistle to the Ephesians*, chap. 2, no. 2, ACW 1:61.

as the bishops, though appointed throughout the vast, wide earth, represent for their part the mind of Jesus Christ.[30]

Hence it is proper for you to act in agreement with the mind of the bishop; and this you do. Certain it is that your presbytery, which is a credit to its name, is a credit to God; for it harmonizes with the bishop as completely as the strings with a harp. This is why in the symphony of your concord and love the praises of Jesus Christ are sung. But you, the rank and file, should also form a choir, so that, joining the symphony by your concord, and by your unity taking your key note from God, you may with one voice through Jesus Christ sing a song to the Father. Thus He will both listen to you and by reason of your good life recognize in you the melodies of His Son. It profits you, therefore, to continue in your flawless unity, that you may at all times have a share in God.[31]

A memorable passage from the *Didache* seems to be echoed in Ignatius' next exhortation: **"Obviously, anyone whom the Master of the household puts in charge of His domestic affairs, ought to be received by us in the same spirit as He who has charged him with this duty. Plainly, then, one should look upon the bishop as upon the Lord Himself."**[32]

That these words are, in fact, directed against the errors of the Docetists and other Gnostic innovators becomes plain as Ignatius continues: **"Some there are, you know, accus-**

---

[30] Ibid., chap. 3, nos. 1–2, ACW 1:61.
[31] Ibid., chap. 4, nos. 1–2, ACW 1:61–62.
[32] Ibid., chap. 6, no. 1, ACW 1:62.

tomed with vicious guile to go about with the Name on their lips, while they indulge in certain practices at variance with it and an insult to God. These you must shun as you would wild beasts: they are rabid dogs that bite in secret; you must beware of them, for they are hard to cure."[33] Is there any hope at all, one might ask, for these victims of "spiritual rabies"? Yes, one hope only—but His true nature is the very thing being denied by those who need His help: **"There is only one Physician, both carnal and spiritual, born and unborn, God become man, true life in death; sprung both from Mary and from God, first subject to suffering and then incapable of it—Jesus Christ Our Lord."**[34]

All of these themes are restated—with variations—in Ignatius' other letters from Smyrna as well. To the Magnesians, for example, the heroic bishop wrote these words:

> **When I learned of your well-ordered God-inspired love, I was jubilant and decided to have a chat with you in the spirit of the faith in Jesus Christ. I am privileged to bear a name radiant with divine splendor, and so in the chains which I carry about on me, I sing the praises of the Churches and pray for union in their midst, a union based on the flesh and the spirit of Jesus Christ, our enduring life. . . .**
>
> **It has been my privilege to have a glimpse of you all in the person of Damas, your bishop and a man of God, and in the persons of your worthy presbyters Bassus and Apollonius, and of my fellow servant, the deacon Zotion.**

[33] Ibid., chap. 7, no. 1, ACW 1:63.
[34] Ibid., no. 2, ACW 1:63.

Would that I might enjoy the latter's company! He is obedient to the bishop as to the grace of God, and to the presbyters as to the law of Jesus Christ.[35]

In this important passage, we see plainly the three separate types of Church officers in existence at the time of Ignatius: the *bishop*, ordained as pastor in succession to one of the Apostles; the elders, or *presbytery*, who follow his leadership and assist him in his work; and the *deacons* (*diakonos*, or servants) who work under and obey the presbyters. Starting from this point, Ignatius proceeds to illustrate the nature of these roles, spelling out the parts they are intended to play in the life of the Church:

It is fitting not to take advantage of the bishop's youth, but rather, because he embodies the authority of God the Father, to show him every mark of respect—and your presbyters, so I learn, are doing just that: they do not seek to profit by his youthfulness, which strikes the bodily eye; no, they are wise in God and therefore defer to him—or, rather, not to him but to the Father of Jesus Christ, the bishop of all men. . . . I exhort you to strive to do all things in harmony with God: the bishop is to preside in the place of God, while the presbyters are to function as the council of the Apostles, and the deacons, who are most dear to me, are entrusted with the ministry of Jesus Christ. . . .[36] **Let there be nothing**

[35] Ignatius, *Epistle to the Magnesians*, chaps. 1–2, in *Epistles*, ACW 1:69.

[36] Ignatius is possibly alluding to Clement's epistle here: **"Christ, in other words, comes with a message from God, and the Apostles with a message from Christ"** (Clement, *Epistle to the Corinthians*, chap. 42, no. 2, in *Epistles*, ACW 1:34). In his analogy, then, Theophorus puts the bishop symbolically

among you tending to divide you, but be united with the bishop and those who preside—serving at once as a pattern and as a lesson of incorruptibility.[37]

The Docetists knew this arrangement quite well—and ignored it. But for Ignatius, "free-lance" Christianity was simply not a valid option for Christians. He makes this unmistakably clear as he continues:

Just as the Lord, therefore, being one with the Father, did nothing without Him, either by Himself, or through the Apostles, so neither must you undertake anything without the bishop and the presbyters; nor must you attempt to convince yourselves that anything you do on your own account is acceptable. No; at your meetings there must be one prayer, one supplication, one mind, one hope in love, in joy that is flawless, that is, Jesus Christ, who stands supreme. Come together, all of you, as to one temple and one altar, to one Jesus Christ—to Him who came forth from one Father and yet remained with, and returned to, one. . . .[38]

Be zealous, therefore, to stand squarely on the decrees of the Lord and the Apostles, that in all things whatsoever you may prosper, in body and soul, in faith and in love, in the Son and the Father and the Spirit, in the beginning and the end, together with your most

into the role of the Good Shepherd, the presbyters into the role of His Apostles or chosen messengers, and the deacons, like the seven picked in Acts 6, into the role of their day-to-day helpers.

[37] Ignatius, *Epistle to the Magnesians*, chap. 3, no. 1; chap. 6, nos. 1b, 2b, ACW 1:69–71.

[38] Ibid., chap. 7, nos. 1–2, ACW 1:71.

> **reverend bishop and with your presbytery—that fittingly woven spiritual crown!—and with your deacons, men of God. Submit to the bishop and to each other's rights, just as did Jesus Christ in the flesh to the Father, and as the Apostles did to Christ and the Father and the Spirit, so that there may be oneness both of flesh and spirit.**[39]

Finally, in his third letter from Smyrna, Theophorus speaks most emphatically yet. There is some reason to believe that of all the congregations he wrote to, the church of the Trallians stood in greatest danger from Docetism. Consequently, his words to them, though filled with compassion, are words of strong, fatherly counsel. They still speak powerfully today:

> **Ignatius, also called Theophorus, to the holy Church at Tralles in Asia, loved by God the Father of Jesus Christ. . . .**
>
> **[After conferring with Polybius] I burst into thanks and praise, finding that you, as I learned, were patterning yourselves after God.**
>
> **Surely, when you submit to the bishop as representing Jesus Christ, it is clear to me that you are not living the life of men, but that of Jesus Christ, who died for us, that through faith in His death you might escape dying. It is needful, then—and such is your practice—that you do nothing without your bishop; but be subject also to the presbytery as representing the Apostles of Jesus Christ, our hope, in whom we are expected to live forever. It is further necessary that the deacons, the dis-**

---

[39] Ibid., chap. 13, nos. 1–2, ACW 1:73.

pensers of the mysteries of Jesus Christ,[40] should win approval in every way; for they are not dispensers of food and drink, but ministers of a church of God. . . .

Let all respect the deacons as representing Jesus Christ, the bishop as a type of the Father, and the presbyters as God's high council and as the Apostolic college. Apart from these, no church deserves the name. . . .

I exhort you therefore — no, not I, but the love of Jesus Christ: partake of Christian food exclusively; abstain from plants of alien growth, that is, heresy. Heretics weave Jesus Christ into their web — to win our confidence, just like persons who administer a deadly drug mixed with honeyed wine, which the unsuspecting gladly take — and with baneful relish they swallow death!

So, then, beware of such! And you will do so if you are not puffed up and [if you] cling inseparably to God Jesus Christ, to the bishop, and to the precepts of the Apostles. He that is inside the sanctuary is pure; he that is outside the sanctuary is not pure. In other words: he that does anything apart from bishop, presbytery, or deacon has no pure conscience. . . .

Stop your ears therefore when anyone speaks to you that stands apart from Jesus Christ, from David's scion and Mary's Son, who was really born and ate and drank, really persecuted by Pontius Pilate, really crucified and died while heaven and earth and the underworld looked on; who also really rose from the dead, since His

[40] This is a reference to the Lord's Supper, which the deacons carried to shut-ins and others who could not attend the service in person. The word "mysteries" (in Greek, *mysterion*) was usually translated in Latin as *sacramentum* and is thus the source of our English word "sacraments".

Father raised Him up—His Father, who will likewise raise us also who believe in Him through Jesus Christ, apart from whom we have no real life.

But if, as some atheists, that is, unbelievers, say,[41] His suffering was but a make-believe—when, in reality, they themselves are make-believes—then why am I in chains? Why do I even pray that I may fight wild beasts? In vain, then, do I die! My testimony is, after all, but a lie about the Lord! . . .

Surely, such persons are not the planting of the Father.[42] For if they were, they would appear as branches of the Cross, and their fruit would be imperishable—the Cross through which by His Passion He calls you to Him, being members of His body. . . .

Remember in your prayers the Church in Syria, to which I do not deserve to belong, being the least of her members. Farewell in the name of Jesus Christ. . . . May you in union with Him be found above reproach.[43]

The Letters from Troas

When, in the late autumn of 107, the welcome delay with Polycarp came to an end, Ignatius laced up his sandals and stepped again onto the Calvary Road.

---

[41] The Docetists did not, of course, deny the existence of God per se; but by denying the God revealed by the Apostles and substituting in His place a nonexistent God tailored to their own imaginations, they did become atheists for all practical purposes.

[42] Cf. Mt 15:13.

[43] Ignatius, *Epistle to the Trallians*, prologue, chaps. 1–3, 6–7, 9–11, 13 in *Epistles*, ACW 1:75–79.

"Setting sail from Smyrna (for Christophorus[44] was pressed by the soldiers to hasten to the public spectacles in the mighty [city] Rome, that, being given up to the wild beasts in the sight of the Roman people, he might attain to the crown for which he strove), he [next] landed at Troas."[45]

The stop here was much briefer than at Smyrna, though Ignatius did find time to compose at least three more letters. The first of these, the *Epistle to the Philadelphians*, gives us a window into the state of our holy bishop's soul as the hour grows late and the end of the trail draws near:

> **Ignatius, also called Theophorus, to the Church of God the Father and the Lord Jesus Christ, which is at Philadelphia in Asia; a church which has found mercy and is irrevocably of one mind with God; which unwaveringly exults in the Passion of Our Lord, and firmly believes in His resurrection through sheer mercy. This Church I salute in the Blood of Jesus Christ. She is a source of everlasting joy, especially when the members are at one with the bishop and his assistants, the presbyters and deacons, that have been appointed in accordance with the wish of Jesus Christ, and whom He has, by His own will, through the operation of His Holy Spirit, confirmed in loyalty.[46]**

Notice that all the same themes are here—but the references to death and resurrection are becoming more cen-

[44] A variation of Ignatius' appellation, of course—meaning, this time, "Christ-bearer".

[45] *Martyrdom of Ignatius*, chap. 5, in ANF 1:130; [brackets in original].

[46] Ignatius, *Epistle to the Philadelphians*, prologue, in *Epistles*, ACW 1:85.

tral, the invocations of Christ's suffering more urgent and frequent. Theophorus clearly has something on his mind, and that something is much more than merely his own impending demise.

The Docetists, remember, denied that God could suffer at all; since, as they taught, He is pure spirit and wholly unwilling to entangle Himself in filthy flesh. This denial—their "modest little concession"—they quickly began following to its logical, ghastly conclusion. Before long, the story of the Passion was being referred to among them as "the mystical fiction of the Cross". The Resurrection they began to deny altogether, since Jesus had never truly had a Body to raise in the first place. This novelty in turn led them naturally to the next: disbelief in the bodily resurrection of the individual believer. Finally, worst of all, the rubber of their errors hit the road. While one might expect a group so hostile to the flesh to be found practicing asceticism and self-denial, historians tell us that the Docetists, quite to the contrary, were enthusiastically given over to license and immorality. After all, what does it matter what this sack of dung called the body might happen to have been doing last Saturday night? **"Salvation belongs to the soul alone,"** according to the Gnostics Irenaeus knew, **"for the body is by nature subject to corruption."**[47]

> **[And] just as it is impossible that material substance should partake of salvation (since, indeed, they maintain that it is incapable of receiving it), so again it is impossible that spiritual substance (by which they mean themselves) should ever come under the power of corruption,**

---

[47] Irenaeus, *Against Heresies*, bk. 1, chap. 24, no. 5, in ANF 1:350.

> **whatever sort of actions in which they indulged. . . . Wherefore also it comes to pass, that the "most perfect" among them addict themselves without fear to all those kinds of forbidden deeds of which the Scriptures assure us that "they who do such things shall not inherit the kingdom of God"** [Gal 5:21].[48]

So simple . . . and yet so deadly. The Docetists, who began by refusing to worry themselves over the angels on a pinhead, end up turning the entire Christian life into a meaningless mirage, a spiritual house of mirrors without any exit. No sin can distance us from their disembodied Christ, no act of obedience can draw us one inch closer. And there is certainly no need to take up—as the willful Ignatius seemed bent on doing—any crude, physical crosses. Not when even Jesus Himself had refused to do so. **"For this reason,"** concludes Irenaeus, **"persons of such a persuasion are also ready to recant; yea, rather, it is impossible that they should suffer on account of a mere name."**[49]

It was this horrible spectacle—and his fears that it might spread to the apostolic churches—that inspired Theophorus to continue in these words:

> **Being born, then, of the light of truth, shun division and bad doctrines. Where the shepherd is, there you, being sheep, must follow. For many wolves there are, apparently worthy of confidence, who with the bait of baneful pleasure seek to capture the runners in God's race; but if you stand united they will have no success. . . .**

---

[48] Ibid., chap. 6, nos. 2–3, in ANF 1:324.

[49] Ibid., chap. 24, no. 6, in ANF 1:350.

Surely, all those that belong to God and Jesus Christ are the very ones that side with the bishop; and all those that may yet change their mind and return to the unity of the Church, will likewise belong to God, and thus lead a life acceptable to Jesus Christ. Do not be deceived, my brethren: if a man runs after a schismatic, he will not inherit the kingdom of God; if a man chooses to be a dissenter, he severs all connection with the Passion.[50]

Ignatius also sent from Troas a second letter; this time back to his grieving friends at Smyrna. In it, the Antiochian expresses his joy that they have thus far kept themselves apart from this new schism, before emphasizing the ongoing need to remain vigilant:

I extol Jesus Christ, the God who has granted you such wisdom. For I have observed that you are thoroughly trained in unshaken faith, being nailed, as it were, to the Cross of the Lord Jesus both in body and in soul, and that you are well established in love through the Blood of Christ and firmly believe in Our Lord: He is really of the line of David according to the flesh, and the Son of God by the will and power of God; was really born of a virgin, and baptized by John in order to comply with every ordinance. Under Pontius Pilate and the tetrarch Herod He was really nailed to the cross in the flesh for our sake—of whose fruit we are, in virtue of His most blessed Passion. And thus, through the Resurrection, He raised a banner for all times for His saints and faithful followers, whether among the Jews or the

[50] Ignatius, *Epistle to the Philadelphians*, chaps. 2–3, ACW 1:85–86.

Gentiles, that they might be united in a single body, that is, the Church. All these sufferings, assuredly, He underwent for our sake, that we might be saved. . . .

Let no one be deceived! Even the heavenly powers and the angels in their splendor and the principalities, both visible and invisible, must either believe in the Blood of Christ or else face damnation. . . .

You must all follow the lead of the bishop, as Jesus Christ followed that of the Father; follow the presbytery as you would the Apostles; reverence the deacons as you would God's [own] commandment. Let no one do anything touching the Church apart from the bishop. . . . Where the bishop appears, there let the people be, just as where Jesus Christ is, there is the Catholic Church.[51]

This is the first recorded use of the term "the Catholic Church"—though Ignatius seems to employ it here as an expression already familiar to his readers. What does it mean in this context? It is not, obviously, being used as a denominational label, since the bishop's whole intent is to repudiate denominationalism. The word itself—catholic, or *katholikē* in Greek—means *universal*, in the sense of "appearing everywhere" or "subsisting throughout the whole". And, sure enough, Ignatius himself told us earlier that the Church in his day had already spread her bishops "throughout the vast, wide earth". It would seem, then, that up until about this time the one true Church founded by Jesus had been alone. Renegades like Simon Magus had carried away the stray lambs, surely, but no one had as yet established, with any

[51] Ignatius, *Epistle to the Smyrnaeans*, chaps. 1–2, 6, 8, in *Epistles*, ACW 1:90, 92–93.

degree of success, a rival body significant enough to confuse the issue. But as this did begin to happen, as the waters—thanks to the Docetists and others—began to muddy again on a larger scale, it became necessary to distinguish the genuine article from the imitations. And thus the name *Katholikē Ekklēsia* begins to be used, as it is here, to mean "the original Church known everywhere". And that original Church, Theophorus insists, is always recognizable as the one that "clings inseparably" to a bishop appointed by the Apostles.[52]

Ignatius wrote one last letter along the road to Rome: an epistle sent also back to Smyrna but chiefly addressed to his old friend Polycarp. Here the tone is warm and personal rather than official, filled not with commands but with man-to-man advice; like a dying soldier who, having been behind enemy lines, briefs his comrades for the fight he will never see finished. Time is running very, very short—but Theophorus pauses to write a letter as full of the spirit of Jesus as any in existence:

Ignatius, also called Theophorus, sends heartiest greetings to Polycarp, who is bishop of the Church of Smyrna, or rather has for his bishop God the Father and the Lord Jesus Christ.

---

[52] Early Church historian J. N. D. Kelly, a Protestant, has this helpful note to offer: "As regards 'Catholic' . . . in the latter half of the second century at latest, we find it conveying the suggestion that the Catholic is the true Church as distinct from heretical congregations. . . . What these early Fathers were envisaging was almost always the empirical, visible society; they had little or no inkling of the distinction which was later to become important between a visible and an invisible Church" (*Early Christian Doctrines*, rev. ed. [San Francisco: HarperSanFrancisco, 1978], pp. 190–91).

I am so well pleased with your God-mindedness, firmly built, as it were, upon an immovable rock, that I am exceedingly grateful for the privilege I had of seeing your saintly face. May it, please God, be a constant joy to me! I exhort you, clothed as you are with the garment of grace, to speed on your course and exhort all others to attend to their salvation. Do justice to your office with the utmost solicitude, both physical and spiritual. Be concerned about unity, the greatest blessing. Bear with all, just as the Lord does with you. Have patience with all in charity, as indeed you do. To prayer give yourself unceasingly; beg for an increase in understanding; watch without letting your spirit flag. Speak to each one singly in imitation of God's way. Bear the infirmities of all, like a master athlete. The greater the toil, the greater the reward. . . .

As God's athlete, be sober; the stake is immortality and eternal life. . . .

Men that seem worthy of confidence, yet teach strange doctrines, must not upset you. Stand firm, like an anvil under the hammer. It is like a great athlete to take blows and yet win the fight. For God's sake above all we must endure everything, so that God, in turn, may endure us.[53]

One section of this letter stands out from the rest. In written words that were among his last on earth, the great champion turns his thoughts back to the little lambs. He commends his flock in Syria to the care of Polycarp, asking

---

[53] Ignatius, *Epistle to Polycarp*, prologue, chap. 1, chap. 2, no. 3, chap. 3, in *Epistles*, ACW 1:96–97.

him to assist in the choosing of a successor there. Then, in what may be the crowning passage in all of his letters, Theophorus speaks his final peace to the sheep themselves:

> **Heed the bishop, that God may heed you, too. My life is a ransom for those who are obedient to the bishop, presbyters, and deacons; and in their company may I obtain my portion! Toil together, wrestle together, run together, suffer together, rest together, rise together—since you are stewards in God's house, members of His household, and His servants. . . . May you be my joy always![54]**

The Bread of God

Today is December 20, A.D. 107. The sun is falling quickly toward the western horizon; the brief rain showers that delayed the games earlier have left nothing but a spectacular crimson sunset that now hangs over the city like the twilight of the gods. That unmistakable "party's over" feeling is in the air—with this being, of course, the last day of *Signillaria*, and the games coming to an end for the season. And though the virtually non-stop entertainment is now entering its ninth consecutive hour, very few Romans have yet headed for the exits. Everyone knows that the best events at the Coliseum are always scheduled for last and that there still remains, if things go according to tradition, a grand finale that will keep the city talking straight through the long winter off-season until next year.

---

[54] Ibid., chap. 6, nos. 1–2, ACW 1:98.

As a matter of fact, today's has already been a memorable performance. Everyone agrees that the early morning acts were among the most charming yet, with the clowns and mimes and "vaudeville" players really outdoing themselves—much better than last year, certainly. And the drunken elephants! Never, perhaps, have fifty thousand people laughed so hard at once. Yet clearly it would be a shame to let the riotous comedy overshadow the great things that were done in the way of tragedy and sentiment. Rome would not soon forget, surely, the ruddy Gallic slave who had assayed the role of Orpheus. Even the impressive mechanical special effects—the forest of trees, for example, that sprang suddenly from the sand in imitation of the Garden of the Hesperides—did not detract from his simple beauty and innocence. It seemed almost a shame, in fact, to watch him devoured finally by the bears . . . though that is, of course, how the traditional story must end. But how fine it all was! And every parent in the city, no doubt, will now be telling his children about the carefully trained lion seen here today. How gorgeous he was, spangled with gold and precious jewels! How much skill and patience must have gone into his raising! And what a noble conception: the most ferocious of beasts made to represent the virtue of clemency. It brought a genuine tear to the eye to see him take that frightened little rabbit into his mouth, to lick and caress it, and play with it like one of his own cubs. Knowing the businessmen of Rome (who never miss a trick) it is a safe bet that stuffed toys made in the brute's image will be choking the shelves of Trajan's Market in time for Saturnalia.

The more adult entertainments began about midday. Croton, the champion gladiator, successfully defended his title against all comers—leaving behind him as usual plenty of work for the *Charons*; those men who, dressed as demons of the underworld, carry the vanquished off the field to the Spoliarium, or "dead house". After that, dozens of gladiators fought at once in an epic recreation of one of the emperor's recent triumphs against the barbarians—a rousing second-century "action movie" with enough blood and patriotism to satisfy the most jaded of fans. Then, about the ninth hour of the day, the *vivarium* was practically emptied against a group of POWs from Scythia—*vivarium*, of course, being the Latin word for the animal house.

Love of country was a common theme in many of the arena's spectacles, with capital punishment against her enemies a perennial favorite. Perhaps the most splendid example of this impulse came just before the afternoon break: an astonishing Roman sea battle staged full-scale, in person. The arena itself was cleared and the Coliseum's legendary tanks were emptied, turning the wide stadium floor into an enormous indoor lake. Then two gigantic oaken doors rumbled apart allowing two authentic slave galleys to emerge, replete with full complements of genuine living slaves at the oars. The groaning ships sidled into position; boarding parties readied themselves. One vessel flew the flags of Rome, the other the banner of some hated foreign enemy. At the climactic moment, the grappling hooks were hurled and scores of armed men collided with each other across the gap between, a gap now filled with splintering and shattering oars. Torches were flung, and soon both vessels were on fire. The two teams fought each other as if the fate of the Empire were at stake—knowing, as they did, that the victors would be released at the end of the day and any surviving losers would be saved for the lions. The cards, naturally, were stacked in favor of the Roman ship. About halfway through the contest a secret system of pulleys and levers caused the "enemy" vessel to start breaking apart—much to the delight of the whistling, cheering crowd. In a moment, the sea was filled with drowning men, and the air with their miserable cries. More such noises issued from within the foundering craft—the sound of the galley slaves still chained at their posts. At last, with the battle successfully concluded, a thunderous hurrah was accorded to the "winners", who sailed immediately to shore to receive their laurel wreaths. Good had triumphed over evil. Rome would stand another day.[55]

The massive ovation lasted ten full minutes; no one had ever seen entertainment on such a grand scale. And then, as the flooded arena began to be drained and the accompanying orchestra segued smoothly into the *entr'acte* (signifying the start of the final intermission), the citizens filing out for refreshments could not help but wonder: How could the producers of the games possibly top *that*? Where would they go from here? And what more could the gods have in store for an audience in just one afternoon?

Had Rome now, at last, finally *seen it all?*

As the shadows lengthened, another group of Romans had assembled as well—the Body of Christ met elsewhere in the city for worship. This was Clement's old church, some eleven years since our last visit and now under the leadership

---

[55] All of the entertainments described in this section actually took place at the Coliseum and were recorded during the reign of Domitian by the Roman poet Martial.

of his second successor, Alexander. Her members knew that the hateful games were in progress; they often assembled for prayer at such times, to beg God's mercy for both victims and spectators, and for "Babylon" herself, just as Abraham prayed for Sodom and Gomorrah. But there was something more specific on the agenda today. Word had come in from the suburbs: Ignatius of Antioch had reached his destination at last.

He had been seen earlier in the day. A group of Christians had recognized him as he debarked—along with his "ten leopards"—from a ship at the port of Rome. **"The brethren [were] full of fear and joy"**, it was reported, **"rejoicing indeed because they were thought worthy to meet with Theophorus, but struck with fear because so eminent a man was being led to death."**[56] In spite of the danger, these believers approached the prisoner of Christ. They offered to accompany him to the Coliseum, in hopes of beseeching the mobs along the way for mercy. Ignatius dissuaded them from doing so, **"since he was in haste as soon as possible to leave this world, that he might attain to the Lord whom he loved."** Therefore, with **"the unhallowed sports being just about to close, the soldiers began to be annoyed at [their] slowness, but the bishop rejoicingly yielded to their urgency."**[57]

At times like these, the early Church was accustomed to read aloud. As we mentioned before, printed Bibles as we know them today did not exist; and so the bishops, or anyone else who was able, were enlisted to interpret the Word

---

[56] *Martyrdom of Ignatius*, chap. 6, in ANF 1:131.

[57] Ibid., chap. 5, in ANF 1:130.

of God out of the original Greek into the language of the people, in this case Latin. The Greek Old Testament had already been long familiar, and gradually the Greek writings of the Apostles had also made the rounds and been incorporated (as was God's intention) into the collection of sacred scrolls. But in this particular instance there was another important piece of writing to be read to the congregation as well. We mentioned at the start that there have survived seven epistles of Ignatius, and thus far we have cited only six. The last was addressed, from Polycarp's house, to the Romans: and surely those Romans read it over and over again with tears as Ignatius came ever closer to his destiny within the walls of their own hometown.

And so we imagine Alexander taking the parchment gingerly from a safe place and sharing its words again with his flock; like a father reading to his assembled family a cherished letter from a distant loved one in danger:

Ignatius, also called Theophorus, to the Church that has found mercy in the transcendent Majesty of the Most High Father of Jesus Christ, His only Son; the church by the will of Him who willed that all things exist, beloved and illuminated through the faith and love of Jesus Christ our God; which also presides in the chief place of the Roman territory; a church worthy of God, worthy of honor, worthy of felicitation, worthy of praise, worthy of success, worthy of sanctification, and presiding in love, maintaining the law of Christ, and bearer of the Father's name: her do I therefore salute in the name of Jesus Christ, the Son of the Father. . . .

By prayer to God . . . I have been pleading for [a great]

> **favor: as a prisoner in Christ Jesus I hope to embrace you [there at Rome], provided it is His will that I should be privileged to reach the goal. An auspicious beginning has certainly been made—if only I obtain the grace of taking due possession of my inheritance without hindrance. The truth is, I am afraid it is your love that will do me wrong. For you, of course, it is easy to achieve your object; but for me it is difficult to win my way to God, should you be wanting in consideration for me.**[58]

What is this "lack of consideration" that Ignatius fears? Apparently, the bishop is actually worried that the Christians in Rome might succeed in gaining his freedom for him! We know from history that even at this early date there were secret believers in high places throughout pagan society; generals and centurions and perhaps even senators. Most writers believe Theophorus was concerned that "strings might be pulled" on his behalf at Rome, gaining him a cheap, meaningless pseudo-victory. And though he obviously rejected this strategy in the end, it is no slander to Ignatius to imagine that he might have struggled with the decision. It was, after all, the old temptation again; success without the struggle, Christianity without the Cross, the servant greater than his Master. Would Theophorus try and win, by cleverness and influence, goals that his Lord had not been able to win without the shedding of real blood, real sweat, and physical tears? Would Ignatius come home to Antioch, to his little lambs in the Lord, and tell them that the Docetists had been right, that "witness-bearing" is not really necessary after all? After already coming so far?

---

[58] Ignatius, *Epistle to the Romans*, prologue, chap. 1, ACW 1:81.

Surely, I do not want you to court the good pleasure of men, but to please God, as indeed you do please Him. Yes, I shall never again have such an opportunity of winning my way to God, nor can you, if you remain quiet, ever have your name inscribed on a more glorious achievement. For if you quietly ignore me, I am the word of God; but if you fall in love with my human nature, I shall, on the contrary, be a mere sound. Grant me no more than that you let my blood be spilled in sacrifice to God, while yet there is an altar ready [cf. Phil 2:17; 2 Tim 4:6].

I am writing to all the Churches and state emphatically to all that I die willingly for God, provided you do not interfere. I beg you, do not show me unseasonable kindness. Suffer me to be the food of wild beasts, which are the means of making my way to God. God's wheat I am, and by the teeth of wild beasts I am to be ground that I may prove Christ's pure bread. Better still, coax the wild beasts to become my tomb and to leave no part of my person behind: once I have fallen asleep, I do not wish to be a burden to anyone. Then only shall I be a genuine disciple of Jesus Christ when the world will not see even my body. . . .

Of no use to me would be the farthest reaches of the universe or the kingdoms of this world. I would rather die and come to Jesus Christ than to be king over the entire earth. Him I seek who died for us; Him I love who rose again because of us. The birth pangs are upon me. Forgive me, brethren; do not obstruct my coming to life. . . . Permit me to be an imitator of my suffering God. If anyone holds Him in his heart, let him under-

stand what I am aspiring to; and then let him sympathize with me, knowing in what distress I am. . . .

Pray for me that I may succeed. What I write to you does not please the appetites of the flesh, but it pleases the mind of God. If I suffer you have loved me; if I am rejected, you have hated me! . . .

Remember in your prayers the Church in Syria, which now has God for her Shepherd in my stead. . . . For myself, I am ashamed to be counted as one of her members. I certainly do not deserve to be one, being the least of them and one that came to birth unexpectedly. However, if I but make my way to God, then by His mercy I shall be someone. . . .

Farewell to the end in the patient endurance of Jesus Christ![59]

From this point we again pick up the story in the words of the ancient *Martyrium Ignatii—The Martyrdom of Ignatius*: **"Having therefore, by means of this Epistle, settled, as he wished, those of the brethren at Rome who were unwilling . . . [Ignatius of Antioch] was led with all haste into the amphitheatre."**[60]

The last scheduled events of the day have now played themselves out—leaving the formerly white sands of the arena looking like Omaha Beach. The howling, drunken mob cries out in an agony of bloodlust, a lust that has not grown a notch less furious for being thoroughly sated. A con-

[59] Ibid., chap. 2, nos. 1–2a; chap. 4, nos. 1–2; chap. 6, nos. 1–3; chap. 8, no. 3—chap. 9, no. 2; chap. 10, no. 3, ACW 1:81–84.

[60] *Martyrdom of Ignatius*, chaps. 5–6, in ANF 1:130.

temporary pagan author captured the flavor of these frenzies in a guilty account of one of his own visits to the Coliseum:

> **When one man fell another would immediately take his place. And this went on and on till none were left, and even the last was killed. You may say, "but that one committed a robbery." So what? Does he deserve to be crucified? "He committed a murder." Even so, does he deserve to die like this? What sort of punishment do you deserve for watching him? All day long the crowd cries, "kill him, flog him, burn him!" "Why does he run on the sword so timidly? Why is he so unwilling to die?"[61]**

Here is paganism writhing in its death throes. Every ounce of Roman anger, Roman despair, Roman helplessness pours out upon her chosen scapegoats, and still Rome is filled with terror and self-loathing.

Then comes the word that there is to be an *encore* tonight; a curtain call, so to speak. It spreads by word of mouth, in waves across the surface of the vast throng, and the word is met with a mighty cheer. *Ignatius is here*—and without a moment to spare. Ignatius the Christian, the spreader and fomenter of Christianity. Ignatius, who reproaches us—oh, not with words, always—but who continually reproaches us, for our adulteries, for our lies, for our hypocrisies, for our fourth and fifth wives, for all the hideous inhuman things we do to shut out that still, small voice! Ignatius, who claims that he carries God within his breast—when everyone knows

---

[61] This pagan writer was Seneca, a famous Roman man of letters and one of the emperor Nero's reluctant confidants: *Letters of a Stoic* 7, trans. Robin Campbell (London: Penguin Books, 1969), p. 139.

that God is just somebody's stupid opinion, like all of our stupid hopeless opinions. He must die. He must die today —like his predecessors who burned the city, like his co-conspirator Peter, like the miserable naked Jew who started the whole filthy business in the first place. Ignatius must die —because, like them, he tells us the Truth.

And then the crowd goes dead quiet. The eastern gate rises and a group of soldiers appears, hustling a feeble old man out into the open. His appearance startles the assembly. There is no fear. There is no pleading, no attempt to escape. His step is firm, his face seems . . . peaceful. Joyful, in fact. He smiles. His eyes, it is true, are filled with tears—but these tears are not like any other tears seen here today. The astonishing creature almost seems . . . *God help us!* . . . happy to be here.

An old tradition maintains that the martyr was given an opportunity to speak a word or two to the crowd and that the incredulous mass actually listened. He opened his mouth and simply reiterated, to no one in particular, the words of his earlier epistle: **"I am God's wheat, and I am being ground by the teeth of wild beasts to make a pure loaf for Christ."**[62]

The soldiers withdraw. The elderly gentleman drops to one knee, then both knees. Over in the corner a scarred wooden slab is slowly raised. From behind it, two tawny female lions—bloodstained themselves from their own torments at the hands of the keepers—bound swiftly into the arena. They take only a moment to orient themselves

---

[62] Ignatius of Antioch, *Letter to the Romans*, in *Early Christian Fathers*, ed. Cyril C. Richardson (New York: Collier Books, 1970), 104.

before racing purposefully across the open expanse, kicking up great plumes of the bloodstained sand as they go. Still the mob makes no sound; every eye is transfixed, every ear alert. Ignatius bows his head, clasps his fists together in prayer, and waits calmly for God's good pleasure.

And then finally—*victory* at last.

"[Thus did the pagans] cast [him] to the wild beasts, . . . that so by them the desire of the holy martyr Ignatius should be fulfilled, according to that which is written, 'The desire of the righteous is acceptable [to God]' " [Prov 10:24].[63] And indeed, the desire of Ignatius was fulfilled completely, down to the last detail. **"For only the harder portions of his holy remains were left, which were conveyed to Antioch and wrapped in linen, as an inestimable treasure left to the holy Church by the grace which was in the martyr."**[64]

Eusebius finishes the story curtly: **"There we must leave Ignatius. As Bishop of Antioch he was succeeded by Heros."**[65]

Nearly three hundred years later, John Chrysostom preached his sermon on the martyrdom of Ignatius—and the bones of Ignatius were still there at Antioch, wrapped in linen, resting in the church with him as he spoke. In that sermon, the Antiochian bishop explains for the ages the miracle that consecrated the bloody Coliseum forever as a holy place of remembrance:

[63] *Martyrdom of Ignatius*, chap. 6, in ANF 1:131.

[64] Ibid.

[65] Eusebius, *History of the Church*, bk. 3, chap. 36, in EHC 100.

> God permitted [Ignatius] there to end his life, so that this man's death might be instructive to all who dwell in Rome. For *we* by the grace of God need henceforward no evidence, being rooted in the faith. But they who dwelt in Rome, inasmuch as there was great impiety there, required more help. On this account both Peter and Paul, and this man after them, were all slain there—partly, indeed, in order that they might purify with their own blood, the city which had been defiled with blood of idols, but partly in order that they might by their works afford a proof of the resurrection of the crucified Christ, persuading those who dwell in Rome, that [Christians] would not with so much pleasure disdain this present life, did they not firmly persuade themselves that they were about to ascend to the crucified Jesus, and to see him in the heavens. For in reality it is the greatest proof of the resurrection that the slain Christ should show forth so great power after death, as to persuade living men to despise both country and home and friends, and acquaintance and life itself, for the sake of confessing him, and to choose in place of present pleasures, both stripes and dangers and death. For these are not the achievements of any dead man, nor of one remaining in the tomb but of one risen and living.[66]

Ignatius Triumphant

Two groups of church members, we believe, observed the martyrdom of Ignatius. The first was a trio of deacons,

[66] John Chrysostom, *Eulogy*, no. 4, in NPNF1 9:139.

Carus, Philon, and Agathophus, who secretly but officially witnessed the event on behalf of the *Katholikē Ekklēsia*. We know this because they became the eyewitnesses whose testimony is included in the *Martyrdom*. For the second group, however, we must speculate a bit, though according, once again, to Irenaeus there are sound reasons to believe that our guess is well founded: **"At every heathen festival celebrated in honour of the idols, these men are the first to assemble"** writes the great expert on Gnosticism. **"And to such a pitch do they go, that some of them do not even keep away from that bloody spectacle hateful both to God and men, in which gladiators either fight with wild beasts, or singly encounter one another."** These "alternative" Christians, he writes, **"yield themselves up to the lusts of the flesh with the utmost greediness, maintaining that carnal things should be allowed to the carnal nature, while spiritual things are provided for the spiritual."**[67]

Yes, the Docetists saw the end of Ignatius. But the Church Ignatius fortified with his blood would see the end of Docetism. Scarcely a century went by before the sect became completely extinct; an obscure page in a forgotten chapter of the ancient history of discredited heresies. But the Household of God goes on. The little lambs turned away from the brink. They rejected the temptations of Gnosticism, with its bodiless, ghostly Christ. They rejected the friendship of the world, which is enmity with God. And they did cling to the bishop, the presbyters, and the deacons. And before long, they were not little lambs anymore, but strong, goodly rams like their spiritual father Ignatius. They followed him

[67] Irenaeus, *Against Heresies*, bk. 1, chap. 6, no. 3, in ANF 1:324.

in true discipleship; just as Ignatius followed Peter; just as Peter followed Christ. And they remembered always, as had Theophorus himself, the sweet promises of Jesus to all martyrs throughout time: **"To him that overcometh will I grant to sit with me in my throne, even as I also overcame, and am set down with my Father in his throne"** (Rev 3:21). **"He that loveth his life shall lose it; and he that hateth his life in this world shall keep it unto life eternal"** (Jn 12:25).[68]

Of Ignatius Theophorus, second successor of Peter in the bishopric of Antioch, let the great Golden-Throat, Chrysostom, have the last word: **"He presided over the Church among us nobly, and with such carefulness as Christ desires. For that which Christ declared to be the highest standard and rule of the Episcopal office, did this man display by his deeds. For having heard Christ saying, the good shepherd layeth down his life for the sheep, with all courage he did lay it down for the sheep."**[69]

---

[68] Both these citations have been taken, for beauty's sake, from the King James Version.

[69] *Eulogy*, no. 1, in NPNF1 9:135–36.

Justin Martyr

Five hundred years before the Romans executed Ignatius for treason, the city fathers of Athens in Greece had brought another eccentric old man to trial on charges nearly identical: sedition, "atheism", subverting the youth of the nation. His name was Socrates, and his crime was nothing less than the rejection of pagan idolatry and the search for the one true God. The birth of Jesus Christ—God's ultimate act of self-revelation—was still four centuries in the future; and so Socrates was forced, in the words of the Apostle Paul, to rely solely upon **"what can be known about God . . . his eternal power and deity . . . in the things that have been made"** (Rom 1:19–20). Nevertheless, by this method alone (and by the conscientious practice of virtue) this learned Greek attained to a conception of God that is startlingly close to that revealed by God to the Hebrews. It was for walking this lonely path, and teaching others to do the same, that Socrates of Athens was condemned and sentenced to drink a poisonous cup of hemlock. His final words to his judges are preserved for us in Plato's *Apology*: "The hour of my departure has arrived, and we go our ways—I to die, and you to live. Which is better only God knows."[1]

When Paul himself reached Athens about A.D. 52, he found that Socrates had left his mark on the city. Though there were still idols and pagan shrines everywhere, one altar

[1] Plato, *The Apology of Socrates*, trans. Benjamin Jowett, in *Dialogues of Plato* (New York: Charles Scribner's Sons, 1871), p. 171.

at least was dedicated "To the Unknown God"—that God perhaps who had been glimpsed by Socrates but whom even Socrates had died without truly knowing. Yet we must hasten to say that the ancient Athenian did accomplish one thing; he provided the Apostle with an excellent "foot in the door" to his latter-day philosophical brethren on Mars Hill. **"What you therefore worship as unknown,"** Paul told the scholars assembled there, **"this I proclaim to you"** (Acts 17:23). The brief sermon that followed is a masterpiece of apologetics. In it, the Apostle proves not only that Socrates had been right, but even uses the words of one of their own heathen poets to teach them the truths of the Christian gospel (17:28). Sadly, however, only a few believed and joined him that day. In fact, many of them mocked—illustrating just how very singular Socrates' journey really had been. In a world where only those who become like little children may enter the kingdom of heaven, the path of philosophical inquiry is too fraught with pitfalls—pride, self-importance, and pedantry—to be successfully traveled by many.

Clement of Rome found this to be the case. His stay among the proud philosophers brought him mainly pain, and he had already despaired of finding the truth with them before he heard the message of Jesus. But one of our four witnesses found Christ *before* giving up on philosophy. Indeed, **"Justin of Neapolis, a man who was not far separated from the apostles either in age or excellence"**,[2] found

[2] Methodius of Olympus, *On the Resurrection*, no. 5, quoted in "Other Fragments from the Lost Writings of Justin", trans. Alexander Roberts, in ANF 1:300.

Christ while still a philosopher and remained a philosopher to the end. For Justin, the good news about Jesus was *the missing piece of Socrates' puzzle*—and philosophy turned out to be the schoolmaster that brought him to Christ. He took up the ministry pioneered by Paul at Mars Hill, and **"wearing the garb of a philosopher he proclaimed the divine message, and contended by means of his writings on behalf of the Faith."**[3] Not surprisingly, this mission eventually cost Justin his life and earned him that glorious title which popular usage has affixed to his own forever as a kind of surname.

Yet Justin Martyr's career on earth had not been in vain; he was God's man in the right place at the right time. When the mysterious workings of Fate placed one of his brother philosophers on the throne of the Caesars itself, Justin was there. Marcus Aurelius Antoninus, the greatest of the Stoics, continued to wear the distinctive *pallium* of the itinerant philosopher even after he became emperor in A.D. 161, even as Justin continued to wear it as a Christian. And when it pleased God to bring these two mighty philosophers together—Justin as Christian Apologist, Marcus as Lord High Persecutor of the Christians—the result was a clash of the titans destined to echo through the ages, right down to our own generation.

[3] Eusebius Pamphilus, *History of the Church*, bk. 4, chap. 11, in EHC 114.

> **The Christians are men of a desperate, lawless, reckless faction, who collect together out of the lowest rabble the thoughtless portion, and credulous women seduced by the weakness of their sex, and form a mob of impure conspirators, whose bond of union is nocturnal assemblies and solemn fastings and unnatural food. A tribe lurking and light-hating, dumb for the public, talkative in corners, they despise our temples as if graves, spit at our gods, deride our religious forms; pitiable themselves, they pity, forsooth, our priests; half-naked themselves, they despise our honors and purple; monstrous folly and incredible impudence! Day after day their abandoned morals wind their serpentine course; over the whole world are those most hideous rites of an impious association growing into shape. They recognize each other by marks and signs, and love each other almost before they recognize each other; promiscuous lust is their religion. Thus does their vain and mad superstition glory in crimes.[4]**

These are the words of a pagan lawyer named Caecilius Natalis from early in the third century A.D., and they pretty much sum up all the accusations made against the Church by the Romans in those days. Because they kept aloof from the debauchery that had become the norm in Rome by that time, Christians were despised as narrow-minded bigots. Be-

---

[4] This passage is included in the *Octavius* of Marcus Minucius Felix, trans. John Henry Newman and quoted in *Church History*, by John Laux (Rockford, Ill.: TAN Books and Publishers, 1989), p. 45.

cause they held their meetings behind closed doors and in private homes, they were accused—paradoxically enough—of immorality and perversion. What sketchy details did filter out of their church services were twisted into horror stories; since they were said to eat the Flesh of Jesus in their Lord's Supper, they were called cannibals; because they drank the cup of His Blood, they were held to practice vampirism. The miracles of healing and deliverance that followed them everywhere were obviously the work of sorcerers. Their notorious refusal to worship Caesar was unmistakable proof of a secret conspiracy to overthrow the government.

Happily, we know that at least one bright young Roman was clearheaded enough to question this conventional wisdom. **"For I myself,"** Justin recalled years later, **"when I was delighting in the doctrines of Plato, and heard the Christians slandered, and saw them fearless of death, and of all other things which are counted fearful, perceived that it was impossible that they could be living in wickedness and pleasure. For what sensual or intemperate man, or who that counts it good to feast on human flesh, could welcome death that he might be deprived of his enjoyments, and would not rather continue always the present life, and attempt to escape the observation of the rulers?"** This, we must say, is an excellent bit of Socratic reasoning; and though his training in the discipline of logic alone may not have been enough to save Justin's soul, it had apparently done a good job of teaching him to recognize baloney when he smelled it . . . and perhaps this, too, is ultimately a work of the Spirit. **"When I discovered [therefore] the wicked disguise which the evil spirits had thrown around the divine doctrines of the Christians, to turn aside others**

from joining them, [I] laughed both at those who framed these falsehoods, and at the disguise itself, and at popular opinion."[5]

Our Lord Jesus, recall, had special promises for people like this: **"Ask, and it will be given you"**, he said. **"Seek, and you will find; knock, and it will be opened to you. For every one who asks receives, and he who seeks finds, and to him who knocks it will be opened"** (Mt 7:7–8). And Justin, clearly, had been knocking for some time already by this stage of the game. Born to pagan Greek parents, at the Roman city of Neapolis in colonized Samaria, his philosophical bent showed itself early in life. From his writings we learn that he spent time with the Stoics, the Peripatetics, and the Pythagoreans, before finally settling upon the study of Plato as the most promising road to Truth—Plato, and Plato's great master, Socrates. This study Justin found to be deeply enriching and, in some ways, satisfying. It is true that he still had many unanswered questions (he had learned, for example, very little about Socrates' tantalizing Unknown God), but he seems to have reasoned that with enough patience and diligence these difficulties would surely be resolved one by one. Our friend Clement, had he been there, might have warned this kindred spirit otherwise, might have predicted for him an inevitable and heartbreaking dead-end farther down the road. But Clement's all-merciful Lord chose instead to reward Justin's brave, pagan tenacity with a miracle. The philosopher knocked faithfully—and the door, at last, was opened.

[5] Justin Martyr, *Second Apology*, chap. 12, trans. Alexander Roberts and James Donaldson, in ANF 1:192.

Justin tells the story himself in his *Dialogue with Trypho*. This passage is also, incidentally, the earliest known example of that cherished Christian tradition, the old-fashioned "salvation testimony":

> **"While I was thus disposed, when I wished at one period to be filled with great quietness, and to shun the path of men, I used to go into a certain field not far from the sea. And when I was near that spot one day, which having reached I purposed to be by myself, a certain old man, by no means contemptible in appearance, exhibiting meek and venerable manners, followed me at a little distance. And when I turned round to him, having halted, I fixed my eyes rather keenly on him.**
>
> **"[Finally] he said, 'Do you know me?'**
>
> **"I replied in the negative.**
>
> **" 'Why, then,' said he to me, 'do you so look at me?'**
>
> **" 'I am astonished,' I said, 'because you have chanced to be in my company in the same place; for I had not expected to see any man here.'**
>
> **"And he says to me, 'I am concerned about some of my household. These are gone away from me; and therefore have I come to make personal search for them, if, perhaps, they shall make their appearance somewhere. But why are you here?' said he to me.**
>
> **" 'I delight,' said I, 'in such walks, where my attention is not distracted, for [here] converse with myself is uninterrupted; and such places are most fit for philology.' "[6]**

---

[6] Justin Martyr, *Dialogue with Trypho, A Jew*, chap. 3, trans. Alexander Roberts and James Donaldson, in ANF 1:195.

Philology, of course, is the study of words and their meanings—and Justin's choice of this particular branch of inquiry on this particular day turns out to be providential. It leaves him vulnerable to a stinging "opening shot", as it were; it serves as the summons to what will be, though he does not know it yet, the most important debate of his career:

> **" 'Are you, then, a philologian,' said [the Old Man], 'but no lover of deeds or of truth? and do you not aim at being a practical man so much as being a sophist?' "[7]**

One can almost feel Justin bristle. No taunt was more galling to the genuine Greek philosopher than to be called a mere sophist—that is, a "pop" philosopher, a man playing long-winded intellectual word games, usually for money. And it was a barb absolutely guaranteed to get a rise out of Justin Martyr—a fact that this mysterious stranger seems to have known all too well:

> **" 'What greater work,' said I, 'could one accomplish than this, to show the reason which governs all, and having laid hold of it, and being mounted upon it, to look down on the errors of others, and their pursuits? But without philosophy and right reason, prudence would not be possible to any man. Wherefore it is necessary for every man to philosophize, and to esteem this the greatest and most honourable work; but other things only of second-rate or third-rate importance, though, indeed, if they be made to depend on philosophy, they are of moderate value, and worthy of acceptance. . . .'**

[7] Ibid., 195–96.

"'Does philosophy, then, make happiness?' said he, interrupting.

"'Assuredly,' I said, 'and it alone.'

"'What, then, is philosophy?' he says; 'and what is happiness? Pray tell me, unless something hinders you from saying.'

"'Philosophy,' then, said I, 'is the knowledge of that which really exists, and a clear perception of the truth; and happiness is the reward of such knowledge and wisdom.'"[8]

So far Justin has answered well, and the old gentleman seems to recognize it. But he wants to take Justin farther, to push him beyond the truths he already knows into uncharted waters—waters that, up until now, our earnest young Platonist has only glimpsed from afar:

"'But what do you call God?'" asks the Old Man.[9] Justin seems to pause momentarily. Here was the great unknown mystery, the unspoken Subject at the back of every philosophical dispute. Socrates himself did little more than humbly recognize his own ignorance at this colossal frontier. And yet Justin does finally collect himself and hesitantly puts forward the best that his own Platonic school has to offer on the topic:

"'That which always maintains the same nature, and in the same manner, and is the cause of all other things—that, indeed, is God.' So I answered him; and he listened to me with pleasure, and thus again interrogated me."[10]

---

[8] Ibid., 196.

[9] Ibid.

[10] Ibid.

From here, Justin's Old Man leads him on quite a merry chase. Though he honors Justin's Greek methods (and indeed, employs some of them himself), the stranger forces the young Samaritan up one philosophical blind alley after another, into corners and against brick walls, right up to the very limits of what reason alone can do, and then leaves him wriggling there on the hook. Finally, he confronts Justin directly with philosophy's greatest failing: the inescapable fact that, however fine and perfect your proofs, however polished and pleasing your syllogisms, at the end of the day all your pretty theories are still just that . . . *theories*:

> **" 'How then,' [the Old Man] said, 'should the philosophers judge correctly about God, or speak any truth, when they have no knowledge of Him, having neither seen Him at any time, nor heard Him?' "**[11]

Unmistakably, Justin feels the bite, just as the Old Man intends that he should. He stutters and stammers, before finally allowing his true heart to speak:

" 'Did [these facts] escape the observation of Plato and Pythagoras," he asks plaintively, **"those wise men . . . who have been as a wall and fortress of philosophy to us?' "**[12] What hope is there, Justin cries out, if even giants like these had ultimately failed to reach their goal? **" 'Should any one, then, employ a teacher? . . . or whence may any one be helped, if not even in them there is truth?' "**[13]

---

[11] Ibid.

[12] Ibid., chap. 5, in ANF 1:197–98.

[13] Ibid., chap. 7, in ANF 1:198.

The trap springs remorselessly shut. Justin now knows the question to which Jesus Christ is the only answer. When man has done all that he can do in the search for God, the only possible hope that remains is in a God who has taken up the search for man. This God, hitherto unknown to Justin, the strange Old Man now proclaims:

> " 'There existed, long before [our] time, certain men more ancient than all those who are esteemed philosophers, both righteous and beloved by God, who spoke by the Divine Spirit, and foretold events which would take place, and which are now taking place. They are called prophets. These alone both saw and announced the truth to men, neither reverencing nor fearing any man, not influenced by a desire for glory, but speaking those things alone which they saw and which they heard, being filled with the Holy Spirit. Their writings are still extant, and he who has read them is very much helped in his knowledge of the beginning and end of things, and of those matters which the philosopher ought to know, provided he has believed them. For they did not use demonstration in their treatises, seeing that they were witnesses to the truth above all demonstration, and worthy of belief; and those events which have happened, and those which are happening, compel you to assent to the utterances made by them, although, indeed, they were entitled to credit on account of the miracles which they performed, since they both glorified the Creator, the God and Father of all things, and proclaimed His Son, the Christ [sent] by Him. . . . Pray that, above all things, the gates of light may be opened to you; for these things

cannot be perceived or understood by all, but only by the man to whom God and His Christ have imparted wisdom.'

"When he had spoken these and many other things, which there is no time for mentioning at present, he went away, bidding me attend to them; and I have not seen him since. But straightway a flame was kindled in my soul; and a love of the prophets, and of those men who are friends of Christ, possessed me; and whilst revolving his words in my mind, I found this philosophy alone to be safe and profitable. Thus, and for this reason, I am a philosopher. Moreover, I would wish that all, making a resolution similar to my own, do not keep themselves away from the words of the Saviour. For they possess a terrible power in themselves, and are sufficient to inspire those who turn aside from the path of rectitude with awe; while the sweetest rest is afforded those who make a diligent practice of them. If, then, you have any concern for yourself, and if you are eagerly looking for salvation, and if you believe in God, you may—since you are not indifferent to the matter—become acquainted with the Christ of God, and, after being initiated, live a happy life."[14]

The Philosopher-Kings

Marcus Aurelius, like Justin across the sea, was by nature a dreamy and contemplative young man; and he also was much concerned with the philosophical pursuit of happi-

[14] Ibid., chaps. 7–8, in ANF 1:198.

ness. Born at Rome on April 26, A.D. 121, Marcus was orphaned as a boy and then adopted by his grandfather, one Annius Verus. Verus, as it happened, was a prominent Roman citizen, a personal friend of Emperor Hadrian himself; and before long the former orphan Marcus found himself with the Lord of the World as his patron. Hadrian, we are told, took a personal interest in the boy and also in his more vigorous half-brother Lucius. They were both sent by him to the best schools in the Empire, taught rhetoric and riding, mathematics and military tactics, and afforded every honor and privilege. This fabulous run of good fortune culminated spectacularly in an unexpected Imperial command —that Marcus and his brother were to be adopted in turn by Hadrian's chosen successor, Antoninus Pius, ensuring that the two favored youths would eventually get their own shot at godhood and immortality.

When Hadrian died on July 10, 138, Antoninus did indeed succeed him as emperor of Rome; and in Antoninus the luck of the dying Empire seemed at last to have turned. Though he was no great thinker himself, Antoninus Pius was an avid reader and a man of high ideals, and he particularly admired the writings of Zeno, founder of a dignified school of thought called Stoicism. As a matter of fact, Stoicism under Antoninus—with its insistence on patience, resignation, and virtue—totally transformed the Imperial Court. Suddenly, Caesar was observed to fill his entire palace with its sober, puritanical teachers; and he banished completely the orgies, the intrigue, and the excess of earlier years. Correspondingly, the health of the Empire as a whole improved dramatically; and most historians consider the reign of Antoninus Pius to have been one of the most peaceful and prosperous in Roman history. More importantly for our purposes, however, Antoninus saw to it that his two adopted sons—now tall, handsome young men—were also schooled in the Stoic way of life. Lucius Verus, though he later became soldier and statesman rather than philosopher, did adhere to this upbringing faithfully. But Marcus!—Marcus Aurelius became not only an ardent Stoic, but a Stoic of the Stoics; and, even today, he is remembered as the greatest exponent of that hard, austere creed. In fact, it might almost be said that during these forty years or so (A.D. 138 to 180, when Antoninus and then his two sons occupied the throne) old Plato's highest dream for human government had at last come true, and, in the words of his *Republic*, the rulership of the world had been put into the hands of a race of "*philosopher-kings*."

In later years, Marcus would sing the praises of Emperor Antoninus and spell out the noble qualities of the man whom he himself had tried to emulate:

> **In my father I observed his meekness; his constancy without wavering in those things which, after due examination, he had determined. How free from all vanity he carried himself in matters of honor and dignity. . . . [How ready] to hear any man that had aught to say tending to the common good! . . . Remember Antoninus Pius' constancy in things that were done by him in accordance with reason, his equability in all things; how he would never give over a matter until he understood the whole state of it fully and plainly . . . how he would never be overhasty in anything, nor give ear to slanders or false accusations, but examine and observe with**

the best diligence the several actions and dispositions of men. He would easily be content with a few things —mere lodgings, bedding, the ordinary food and attendance. He bore with those who opposed his opinions and even rejoiced if any man could better advise him, and finally he was exceedingly religious without superstition. . . . A man, in short, might have applied to him what is recorded of Socrates.[15]

Reading all this, the question of the hour seems clear: What will the gracious philosopher-kings (successors, after all, to Nero and Domitian) do with their growing minority of *Christian* subjects?

Even Trajan, after the murder of Ignatius, had been forced to back down somewhat, when his general persecution threatened to take on all the qualities of a witch-hunt. Anyone in Rome who carried a grudge, it seems, or owed money he was disinclined to pay, found that he had only to make the accusation of "Christian" under such circumstances, and the object of his animus would be quickly carried off to the arena. Later, Hadrian, illustrious patron of Antoninus and his royal sons, had gone farther; insisting upon a fair, impartial trial for anyone accused of Christianity, with strict rules of evidence. But even Hadrian had elected to leave in place Nero's sixty-year-old edict on the subject: "*Christiani non sint*" (Christians must be exterminated). After all, to be a Christian was to recognize an authority higher than that of the Empire—to take an oath of

[15] Marcus Aurelius, *Meditations*, bk. 1, from *Readings in Ancient History: Illustrative Extracts from the Sources*, ed. William Stearns Davis (Boston, Mass.: Allyn and Bacon, 1912–1913), 2:214.

allegiance, in effect, to a foreign government. And this was something that Rome had never yet been capable of tolerating in anyone.

Public opinion also weighed heavily against any change in policy; day by day, the pagans at large grew more hostile to Christianity. Lynch mobs were common; and "citizens' arrests"—in which some hapless Christian girl, or incautious elderly person, would be dragged bodily before the local authorities for summary condemnation. An unpleasant mix of jingoism and superstition seems to have been responsible for most of it: the old gods were offended, many believed, at being abandoned by the Christian "atheists" and were therefore withdrawing the heavenly favors that had made Rome what she is today. This process reached a memorable pitch in Tertullian's era. In one of the most famous passages in all of patristic literature, he records for posterity something of the spirit of those terrifying times:

> **They consider the Christians to be the cause of every public disaster and of every misfortune which has befallen the people from the earliest times. If the Tiber rises to the city walls, if the Nile does not rise to the fields, if the weather continues without change, if there is an earthquake, if famine, if pestilence, immediately, "Christians to the lion!" [*Christianos ad leonem!*].**[16]

So, once again, we cannot help but watch this scene with intense curiosity: What will Antoninus do under such circumstances? What of Marcus and Lucius—this new and very different breed of Roman emperor, still sitting, never-

[16] Tertullian, *Apology*, chap. 40, no. 1, in FEF 1:117, no. 282.

theless, in the traditional seat of tyrants? The question seems to cry out for an answer.

The Property of Christians

Justin's conversion to Christianity is thought to have happened at the city of Ephesus, around A.D. 130, when our inquisitive young Samaritan was roughly thirty years of age. And though he was undoubtedly given a warm reception into the Christian congregation there in Asia—that venerable church founded by John, written to by Ignatius from the house of Polycarp—Justin, to tell the truth, may have raised a few eyebrows by his conduct as a new believer. For the fact is that he continued to frequent his old haunts. He kept all his old friendships and ran with the same unregenerate crowd he had associated with as a heathen. In short, Justin of Neapolis became known, much like his Lord before him, as "the friend of publicans and sinners"—only in Justin's case, the publicans and sinners were not prostitutes or winebibbers, but mystic Pythagorean mathematicians and long-faced logicians studiously following Xenophon and Parmenides. In other words, Justin became an *apologist*—a defender of the faith, a philosophical evangelist—and from the day of his redemption he seems to have been possessed by one burning desire: to see his own people, his brother philosophers, come to the knowledge of the truth.

The *Dialogue with Trypho*, which took place at Ephesus during this period,[17] gives us a window into Justin's

[17] Though the debate itself is believed to have taken place just after the Bar Cocheba uprising in A.D. 132, the final written form of the *Dialogue* dates from later—probably about 160.

methods. As it opens, we find him, wearing his pallium, walking among the colonnades of a great temple (possibly the same great temple of Diana where earlier Paul had raised the ire of the silversmiths [Acts 19]). Such places were where the philosophers of the day plied their trade, and little groups of them could always be found arguing, from sun up to sun down, on the steps of every pagan shrine in the Empire. On this particular day, Justin drew the attention of Trypho, the Hellenized rabbi, famous as one of the most learned Jews in the East. Yet it might just as well have been the representative of any of a hundred different world views who chose to debate him that day, for they all met here on equal terms, all contending (though they little knew it at the time) for the intellectual fate of Europe and the world.

In the case of Trypho, the conversation turns quickly to Old Testament prophecy and its alleged fulfillment in Jesus of Nazareth. But even with pagan opponents Justin was known to declare his Christianity boldly—and this in spite of the popular mania against the Faith that swirled around him like a tempest. While this is certainly brave, it is not *quite* reckless. Justin knows, and is consciously depending upon, an unwritten code of honor current among Greek philosophers. Socrates' great motto had been to "follow the argument wherever it leads"—and, as a result, his successors held the keeping of an open mind to be among the highest of virtues. They prided themselves upon the fact that just about any viewpoint could gain a respectful hearing among them—at least until they felt that it had been conclusively disproved. Therefore, to surrender their old comrade to the authorities solely because he had altered his opinions would have been seen as a serious violation of their liberal traditions.

And so Justin walks a tightrope. His beliefs are outlawed, and he knows that there is not another public platform in the Empire open to his message. Yet he also knows that one false step will send him to the lions. His chosen strategy, then, is precarious in the extreme, and strangely poignant; Justin will count, prayerfully and trustingly, on the intellectual integrity of his old friends. He will speak, as only a man in his unique position could, to the one group of Roman citizens on earth who are committed *not* to turn him in for treason.

What is his approach? In the true spirit of discipleship, Justin resolves to walk in the footsteps of his own spiritual father—a certain nameless Old Man, the gentle but tough-minded Christian Socrates who once beat him at his own game. Justin will practice logic with the logicians; he will use philosophy on the philosophers. To the Platonists, he will remain a Platonist; to the Stoics, he will talk Stoicism —and talk it *better* than they can, and more ruthlessly. He will become all things to all men, that he might by all means save some.

The best example of Justin's apologetic, perhaps, comes in his answer to their most serious and common objection. The single greatest stumbling block for pagan academics, it seems, was Christianity's *exclusivity*—its claim to be the one true religion, the one sure way to God, established *by* God. Were the Christians really saying that the whole world had been stumbling hopelessly in the dark until a mere one hundred years ago? Was Justin now asking his friends to deny all the priceless insights they had learned together by their study of philosophy? Would a man not have to commit something like *intellectual suicide* to do that? And had Justin himself managed such a feat? Did their respected colleague now consider himself a mere Christian sectary—just another mystery cultist, making, as the skies blackened over Rome, just one more religious leap in the dark?

Justin answered—and in his answer Jerusalem and Athens speak together for the first time; the new City of God, set on a hill forever: **"[Yes,] I confess that I both pray and with all my strength strive to be found a Christian; not because the teachings of Plato are different from those of Christ, but because they are not in every respect equal."** Certainly Plato spoke the truth, responds Justin. So did all the poets and philosophers and historians!

> **For each person spoke well, according to the part present in him of the divine logos, the Sower. . . . We [Christians, on the other hand,] worship and love the Logos, who is from the unbegotten and ineffable God, since He became man for our sakes; so that, by becoming a partaker of our sufferings, He might also bring us healing. All the writers were able to see realities darkly** [cf. 1 Cor 13:12], **through the presence in them of an implanted seed of logos. For the seed and imitation of something, imparted according to capacity, is one thing, and another is the thing itself.**[18]

---

[18] Justin Martyr, *First Apology*, chap. 13, trans. Leslie William Barnard, in St. Justin Martyr, *The First and Second Apologies*, ACW, vol. 56 (New York: Paulist Press, 1997), pp. 83–84.

> **What we have, then, appears to be greater than all human teaching, because *the whole rational principle became Christ*, who appeared for our sake, body, and reason, and soul.[19]**

> **Therefore, whatever things were rightly said among all people are the property of us Christians.[20]**

What an astonishing set of words! The whole glorious history of Christian thought is prefigured here, from Augustine to Aquinas to C. S. Lewis! And—more to our own point—what a magnificent obstacle God has raised up in the path of Marcus Aurelius: iron to sharpen iron, mind to answer mind, fashioned by the Spirit to save the soul of an emperor!

Justin and Marcus

About A.D. 140, Justin moved his base of operations from Ephesus to the city of Rome. Antoninus Pius still ruled the Empire from his palace there, while the leadership of the church at Rome had passed to another man called Pius, the first Roman bishop of that name and the ninth successor to the Apostle Peter. Exactly why Justin left Asia for the Imperial City is not known. We do know that the persecution of Christians was especially fierce in the East, and much less so in the capital itself—where, as befitting sophisticated urbanites, the patriotic cult of emperor-worship was looked on a bit more cynically. So it may be that our subject came

[19] Ibid., chap. 10, ACW 56:80, emphasis added.
[20] Ibid., chap. 13, ACW 56:84.

to Rome in search of more freedom, a safer spot from which to fish, as it were.

At any rate, we find, before long, that Justin had established something like a school of Christian philosophy at Rome!—though it may have been small, more like a home Bible study, perhaps, or a discipleship group. It met regularly, we know, in the house of a man called Martinus, and the men and women enrolled there under Justin's tutelage grew close and developed a profound love for their teacher. One of these students "graduated" to become famous in his own right; his name was Tatian the Syrian, and he composed an important book called the *Diatessaron*, which is the first known attempt at a harmony of the Gospels.[21] Of all our four witnesses, Justin Martyr was the only layman. Though he worked, no doubt, in close association with the leadership at Rome, there is no evidence that he was ever ordained himself as one of their company. Yet we see him taking a strong, vigorous role in teaching and in the training of ministers; evidence, surely, that the laity in the early Church was active and involved, and expected to be so.

Unfortunately, other teachers were, once again, at work in Rome as well. The chief Gnostics of the day were Valentine, an Egyptian who had once been a faithful member of the Church catholic; and Cerdo, the predecessor and mentor of

[21] Tatian's full story, alas, is a sad one. After Justin's death, he reacted so violently against the hedonism of Roman society that he strayed into non-Christian thought-forms; repudiating even married love as "depravity and fornication", imposing extreme forms of discipline on himself and his followers, and finally ending up as the founder of another semi-gnostic sect. His fate is a reminder that even the best-taught student can allow strong emotion to overcome reason and faith.

Marcion.[22] These and others like them kept Satan's strategy for these early decades alive and well: confuse the issue, make uncertain the sound, muddy the waters. And, sadly, this strategy seems to have been quite effective; for though the various pagan calumnies against the *Katholikē Ekklēsia* were unfounded, these same charges—everything from orgies to infant sacrifice—were often true of the Gnostics, and the suspicions thoroughly merited.

A Greek named Fronto, for example, was the paid tutor of young Marcus Aurelius himself, his lifelong bosom friend and one of his strongest influences. Fronto, around this time, actually composed a formal philosophical denunciation of Christianity—except that most of it was directed at Gnostic practices instead. Just as we saw in the days of Clement, the pagans could not consistently tell the difference, nor could they reasonably be expected to. And how heartbreaking this knowledge must have been to Justin of Neapolis! Justin, early on, must have recognized a fellow traveler in the emperor's adopted son. Marcus was a Stoic; Justin had once studied Stoicism, and he still admired much of its teaching. Marcus, by all accounts, had read all the same books that Justin loved and could recite all his favorite poets. How Justin must have longed, then, to spend one single hour with his more famous counterpart—perhaps walking near the seashore, where the attention is not distracted, and converse uninterrupted. How he must have ached to answer Fronto's lies (however inadvertent) and to force the future

[22] Marcion was among the most successful of the second-century Gnostics. In a passage not included here, Justin seems to regard him as the most formidable heretic of his era.

emperor, by God's grace, to the end of his rope—just as his beloved Old Man had once forced him to the end of his!

Such an interview was never likely to occur. If Justin ever stood before Marcus Aurelius it would be, almost certainly, as Theophorus had stood before Trajan—to hear his own death sentence. And yet, just possibly, there was another way. A letter might be written. A letter to set the record straight, to refute the slanders and spell out the case for Christianity. A letter assuring the emperor that he had nothing to fear from the followers of Jesus and appealing for peace. And why not? Yes, Antoninus and his sons were undoubtedly surrounded by a whole troupe of meddling "handlers", as they say; but with their well-known interest in all things philosophical, such a letter might get through—especially if it were well written, in the customary rhetorical Greek. Of course, he knew it was a long shot; Justin did not *really* imagine that anything might actually change in response. But no . . . no, that is not true. It is the flesh that speaks that way, not the Spirit. Is not our God still the God of miracles, who holds the hearts of kings in His hand?

And so, sometime between A.D. 153 and 155, Justin Martyr composed the work that is known to us today as his *Apologia*—his First Apology. He addressed it **"To the Emperor Titus: Ælius Adrianus Antoninus Pius Augustus Caesar, and to his son Verissimus the Philosopher [Marcus Aurelius], and to Lucius the Philosopher . . . and to the sacred Senate, with the whole People of the Romans."** Introducing himself, he wrote: **"I, Justin, the son of Priscus and grandson of Bacchius, natives of Flavia Neapolis in Palestine, present this address and petition in behalf of those**

of all nations who are unjustly hated and wantonly abused, myself being one of them."[23] He sent the finished epistle, crafted with all the skill he could muster, to the Imperial palace; probably by means of a paid courier. And then he committed the rest, with prayer, to the Father of Lights.

After that, Justin's thoughts were only with Marcus.

Justin for the Defense

Reason directs those who are truly pious and philosophical to honour and love only what is true, declining to follow traditional opinions, if these be worthless. For not only does sound reason direct us to refuse the guidance of those who did or taught anything wrong, but it is incumbent on the lover of truth, by all means, and if death be threatened, even before his own life, to choose to do and say what is right.[24]

So you, then [continues Justin, as the great letter begins], **since you are called pious and philosophers and guardians of justice and lovers of culture, [must] listen in every way; and it will be shown if you are such. For we have come into your company not to flatter you by this writing, nor please you by our address, but to ask that you give judgment, after an exact and searching inquiry, not moved by prejudice or by a wish to please superstitious people, nor by irrational impulse or long prevalent**

[23] Justin Martyr, *First Apology*, chap. 1, trans. Alexander Roberts and James Donaldson, in ANF 1:163.

[24] Ibid., chap. 2, in ANF 1:163.

rumors, so as to give a decision which will prove to be against yourselves. For we indeed reckon that no evil can be done us, unless we are proved to be evildoers or shown to be wicked. You are able to kill us, but not to hurt us. . . .

We ask that the charges against us be investigated, and that, if they are substantiated let us be punished as is fitting. But if nobody can prove anything against us, true reason forbids you, because of an evil rumor, to wrong innocent people. . . . It is then our task to offer to all an opportunity of inspecting our life and teachings, lest, on account of those who do not really know of our affairs, we should incur the penalty due to them for mental blindness. But it is for you, as reason demands, to listen [to us] and to be found good judges. For if, having learned the truth, you fail to do what is righteous, you have no defense before God. . . .[25]

It is in our power when we are examined to deny [our Christianity]; but we would not live by telling a lie. For, impelled by the desire for the eternal and pure life, we seek to dwell with God, the Father and [Creator] of all things, and hasten to confess [our faith], being persuaded and convinced that those who have shown to God by their works that they follow Him, and long to dwell with Him where there is no evil to cause disturbance, are able to obtain these things. This, then, to

[25] Ibid., chaps. 2–3, ACW 56:23–24.

speak briefly, is what we look for and have learned from Christ, and teach.[26]

What the Christians taught in Justin's time, outlined with considerable fullness, is precisely the subject of the remainder of his *Apologia*; and the document gives us our clearest and most detailed picture of that fascinating subject. The pagans had lied, first, about the beliefs of Christians (calling them atheists, magicians, and so on); so Justin, with a good deal of gusto, begins his rejoinder with an outline of *true* Christian theology, as it was held here in the mid-second century A.D.:

We [have been] called atheists. And we confess that we are atheists with reference to gods [of the pagan sort], but not with reference to the most true God, the Father of righteousness and temperance and the other virtues, who is unmixed with evil. . . . And neither do we honor with many sacrifices and garlands of flowers the objects that people have formed and set in temples and named gods; since we know that they are lifeless and dead. . . .

But we have received [from tradition] that God does not need the material offerings from people, seeing, that He Himself is the provider of all things. . . . And we have been taught that in the beginning He of His goodness, for people's sakes, formed all things; and if they, by their actions, show themselves worthy of His design, they are accounted worthy, so we have received, of

---

[26] Ibid., chap. 8, ACW 56:27.

reigning with Him, being delivered from corruption and suffering. . . .[27]

Our teacher of these things is Jesus Christ, who was also born for this purpose, and was crucified under Pontius Pilate, procurator of Judaea, in the time of Tiberius Caesar. . . . [Therefore] we follow the only unbegotten God through His Son. Those who formerly delighted in fornication, now embrace chastity alone; those who formerly made use of magical arts have dedicated themselves to the good and unbegotten God; we who once valued above everything the gaining of wealth and possessions now bring what we have into a common stock, and share with everyone in need; we who hated and destroyed one another, and would not share the same hearth with people of a different tribe on account of their different customs, now since the coming of Christ, live familiarly with them, and pray for our enemies, and try to persuade those who unjustly hate us to live according to the good advice of Christ, to the end that they may share with us of the same joyful hope of a reward from God the Master of all.[28]

Just possibly, Antoninus will not appreciate hearing about some "master of all" other than himself. And so Justin pauses to reveal the true nature of Christ's reign on earth—and the foolishness of charging His followers with conspiracy and treason:

[27] Ibid., chaps. 9–10, ACW 56:26–28.
[28] Ibid., chaps. 13–14, ACW 56:30.

> **When you hear that we look for a kingdom, you uncritically suppose that we speak of a human one; whereas we speak of that with God, as appears also from the confession of their faith made by those who are charged with being Christians, although they know that death is the penalty meted out to him who so confesses. For if we looked for a human kingdom, we would deny it, that we might not be slain; and we would try to escape detection, that we might obtain the things we look for. But since we do not have our hope set on the present, we do not heed our executioners since death is in any case the debt of nature.[29]**

From here, Justin goes on—much as the *Didache* had done years earlier when instructing pagans—to encapsulate in a brief digest all the beautiful moral precepts of Jesus. Then, he launches directly into a brilliant defense of the faith, beginning with the argument from prophecy, tracing from the time of Moses how everything concerning Jesus and His coming had been revealed by God beforehand.

But the most important section of the *Apologia*, for our purposes today, is its defense against all the various smears and slanders, against all the wild distortions of Christian rites and practices that were making the rounds in those days. For the best way to refute these rumors, Justin knows, is simply to give the emperor and his sons an "insider's account"—the straight dope, straight from the horse's mouth. If Christians do not practice cannibalism at their secret meetings, what *do* they do? If they do not join this mysterious *Ekklēsia*

[29] Ibid., chap. 11, ACW 56:29.

by blood baths and weird initiations, how do they join it? The result is that this remaining section reads like the minutes of a church meeting—like a play-by-play account of a Sunday morning church service in A.D. 153.

And this is where Justin Martyr shows himself to be, of all our four witnesses, perhaps the most valuable of all.

Justin on Baptism

Justin starts off where the Christian life itself begins—with baptism:

> **I will also explain the manner in which we dedicated ourselves to God when we were made new through Christ, since if we left this out in our exposition we would seem to falsify something. As many as are persuaded and believe that the things we teach and say are true, and undertake to live accordingly, are instructed to pray and ask God with fasting for the remission of their past sins, while we pray and fast with them. Then they are brought by us where there is water, and are born again, for in the same manner of rebirth by which we ourselves were born again, they then receive washing in water in the name of God the Father and Master of all, and of our Savior Jesus Christ, and of the Holy Spirit** [cf. Mt 28:19]. **For Christ also said, "Except you are born again, you will not enter into the Kingdom of heaven"** [Jn 3:3]. **Now it is clear to all that it is impossible for those who have once come into being to enter into their mother's wombs. And it is said through Isaiah the prophet . . . in what manner those who have sinned and repented shall**

escape from their sins. He thus spoke:[30] "Wash, become clean, put away evil doings from your souls, learn to do good, judge the orphan and plead for the widow, and come and let us reason together, says the Lord. And though your sins be as scarlet, I will make them white as wool and though they be crimson, I will make them white as snow. But if you will not listen to me, a sword will devour you; for the mouth of the Lord has spoken these things" [Is 1:16–20].[31]

---

[30] In his *Dialogue with Trypho*, Justin makes an additional reference to this passage from Isaiah: **"It is necessary to hasten to learn in what way forgiveness of sins and a hope of the inheritance of the promised good things may be yours. There is no other way than this: acknowledge this Christ, be washed in the washing announced by Isaias for the forgiveness of sins; and henceforth live sinlessly"** (*Dialogue with Trypho the Jew*, chap. 44, in FEF 1:60, no. 135a).

[31] Ibid., chap. 61, ACW 56:66. Though many of us might want to challenge Justin's interpretation of these verses, his understanding was by no means merely his own; indeed, we can say without fear of contradiction that he represents here the universal opinion of the early Church. As an example, Irenaeus wrote: **"'And dipped himself,' says [2 Kings 5:13], 'seven times in Jordan.' It was not for nothing that Naaman of old, when suffering from leprosy, was purified upon his being baptized, but [it served] as an indication to us. For as we are lepers in sin, we are made clean, by means of the sacred water and the invocation of the Lord, from our old transgressions; being spiritually regenerated as new-born babes, even as the Lord has declared: 'Except a man be born again through water and the Spirit, he shall not enter into the kingdom of heaven'"** ("Fragments from the Lost Writings of Irenaeus", no. 34, trans. Alexander Roberts and James Donaldson, in ANF 1:574). Tertullian speaks more forcefully still; writing about A.D. 200, he says: **"It is in fact prescribed that no one can attain to salvation without Baptism, especially in view of that declaration of the Lord, who says: 'Unless a man shall be born of water, he shall not have life'"** (*Baptism*, chap. 12, no. 1, in FEF 1:127, no. 306).

We see here that at this early date no one had yet drawn any distinction between actual water baptism and the interior regeneration of the soul that makes a person a Christian. Indeed, since the two things normally went together there had not been any immediate need to do so. The cry of the early Church remains identical with that of the Apostles: **"Rise and be baptized, and wash away your sins, calling on his name"** (Acts 22:16). Later, as the number of converts steadily increased, new and unforeseen questions began to arise. Sometimes pagan students of Christianity, for example, and people who were preparing to receive baptism but had not yet done so were interrupted in their journey by *death*—often as martyrs to the faith of Christ. Surely such persons were not lost, were they? And what about the Good Thief on the cross—he who had not been baptized but to whom Jesus had nevertheless said, **"Today you will be with me in Paradise"** (Lk 23:43)?

Eventually, during the time of Augustine, the Church will begin to address these questions. She will come to speak of a "baptism of blood" (in which God applies the normal effects of baptism to the soul of a person dying for Christ without it) and of a "baptism of desire" (in which these effects are bestowed on someone who is looking to Christ for salvation, but who, through either ignorance or circumstance, has been prevented from receiving water baptism itself). Even so, the Church will be careful to maintain Justin's early reluctance to sever the tie between the exterior act and the interior result. After all, it was the *Gnostics* who taught that regeneration involves nothing more than the interior acceptance of a theology. Irenaeus, for example, tells us that while some of them had their own mock baptisms in imitation of the

Church, most Gnostics held **"that the knowledge of the unspeakable Greatness is itself perfect redemption".**[32] In their eyes, nothing so crude and physical as a bath of water could possibly serve as a vehicle for divine grace. Their so-called "God"—ever effete, fastidious, and disdainful of the material world—was always to be approached by the naked mind alone.

Justin, on the other hand, patiently explains to the emperor the true Christian understanding of baptism as he knows it:

> **We have learned from the Apostles the reason for this [rite]. Since at our first birth we were born of necessity without our knowledge, from moist seed by the intercourse of our parents with each other, and were brought up in bad habits and wicked behavior; in order that we should not remain children of necessity and ignorance, but of free choice and knowledge, and obtain remission of the sins formerly committed,[33] there is named at the water over him who has chosen to be born again, and has repented of his sinful acts, the name of God the Father and Master of all.**[34]

Here, Justin is outlining what will later be called the doctrine of "original sin"—that primordial curse Paul referred to when he spoke of the unregenerate man as being "in

[32] *Against Heresies*, bk. 1, chap. 21, no. 4, trans. Alexander Roberts and James Donaldson, in ANF 1:346.

[33] Compare this phrase to Peter's words in Acts 2:38: **"Repent, and be baptized every one of you in the name of Jesus Christ for the forgiveness of your sins."**

[34] Justin Martyr, *First Apology*, chap. 61, ACW 56:66.

Adam" and the Christian "in Christ". Without something to wash away this inherited stain—some completely gratuitous act of God—a man must, of necessity, remain **"dead in trespasses and sins"** (Eph 2:1, KJV).[35] Gnostics notwithstanding, then, Justin Martyr, in company with the whole early Church, teaches that this cleansing, flowing like a fountain from the wounds of Christ, is accomplished by water baptism. In the words of Tertullian, writing a few years later:

> **The Spirit who in the beginning hovered over the waters would continue to linger as an influence upon the waters. . . . All waters, therefore, by reason of the original sign at their beginning, are suitable, after God has been invoked, for the sacrament of sanctification. The Spirit immediately comes from heaven upon the waters, and rests upon them, making them holy of Himself; and having been thus sanctified they absorb at the same time the power of sanctifying. Even so, there is a similitude well-adapted to the simple act: that since we are defiled by sins, as if by dirt, we are washed in water.**[36]

---

[35] This gratuitous quality is well illustrated by the fact that the early Church undoubtedly practiced infant baptism. Two good proofs are these passages; first, from Irenaeus, then from Origen: **"For He came to save all through means of Himself—all, I say, who through Him are born again to God—infants, and children, and boys, and youths, and old men"** (ca. A.D. 180, Irenaeus, *Against Heresies*, bk. 2, chap. 22, no. 4, in ANF 1:391). **"The Church received from the Apostles the tradition of giving Baptism even to infants. For the Apostles, to whom were committed the secrets of divine mysteries, knew that there is in everyone the innate stains of sin, which must be washed away through water and the Spirit"** (ca. A.D. 244, Origen, *Commentaries on Romans*, chap. 5, no. 9, in FEF 1:209, no. 501).

[36] Tertullian, *Baptism*, chap. 4, nos. 1, 4–5, in FEF 1:126, no. 303.

Tertullian also preserves some interesting details that Justin omits—about an anointing at the conclusion of the baptismal service:

> **After coming from the place of washing we are thoroughly anointed with a blessed unction, from the ancient discipline by which in the [Levitical] priesthood they were accustomed to be anointed with a horn of oil, ever since Aaron was anointed by Moses. . . . So also with us, the unction runs on the body but profits us spiritually, in the same way that Baptism is itself a corporal act by which we are plunged in water, while its effect is spiritual, in that we are freed from sins.[37] After this, the hand is imposed for a blessing, invoking and inviting the Holy Spirit.[38]**

Justin concludes his account of early Christian baptism with these words:

> **And this washing is called illumination,[39] as those who learn these things are illuminated in the mind. And he**

---

[37] Compare this sentence to 1 Peter 3:21: **"Baptism, which corresponds to this [Noah's flood], now saves you, not as a removal of dirt from the body but as an appeal to God for a clear conscience, through the resurrection of Jesus Christ."**

[38] Tertullian, *Baptism*, chap. 7, no. 1—chap. 8, no. 1, in FEF 1:127, no. 304.

[39] Writing about A.D. 200, Clement of Alexandria supplements this information: **"When we are baptized, we are enlightened. Being enlightened, we are adopted as sons. Adopted as sons, we are made perfect. Made perfect, we are become immortal. . . . This work is variously called grace, illumination, perfection, and washing. It is a washing by which we are cleansed of sins; a gift of grace by which the punishments due our sins are remitted"** (*The Instructor of Children*, bk. 1, chap. 6, no. 26, 1, in FEF 1:178, no. 407). Knowing that the early Church used these terms as syn-

who is illuminated [has been] washed in the name of Jesus Christ, who was crucified under Pontius Pilate, and in the name of the Holy Spirit, who through the prophets foretold all things about Jesus. . . .[40] [After the washing] we lead him to those who are called brethren, where they are assembled; and we offer prayers in common for ourselves and for the one who has been illuminated and for all others everywhere, that we may be accounted worthy, having learned the truth, by our deeds also to be found good citizens and guardians of what is commanded, so that we may be saved with eternal salvation. Having ended the prayers we greet one another with a kiss.[41]

Justin on the Lord's Supper

From here, Justin moves directly into his account of the ordinary weekly meetings: **"And on the day called Sunday all who live in cities or in the country gather together in one place, and the memoirs of the Apostles or the writings of the prophets are read, as long as time permits"** [cf. 2 Cor 13:12; 1 Thess 5:26; 1 Pet 5:14].[42]

Notice that the Gospels are still new enough to be referred to, rather charmingly, as "the memoirs of the Apostles", and that even the Old Testament books are still a loose

onyms for baptism is helpful in interpreting various passages of Scripture, such as Romans 5:2; 5:15; Ephesians 5:26; Titus 3:5; Hebrews 6:4; 7:11; 10:32; and James 1:17.

[40] Justin Martyr, *First Apology*, chap. 61, ACW 56:66.

[41] Ibid., chap. 65, ACW 56:70.

[42] Ibid., chap. 67, ACW 56:71.

collection of sacred scrolls. Yes, even in Justin's time, a final authoritative Christian Bible was nearly 250 years in the future. Nevertheless, the Scriptures still play a vital part here in Justin's church service; interpreted aloud at length to a congregation most of whom may not have understood any Greek at all themselves.

"Then when the reader has finished, the Ruler [of the Brethren] in a discourse instructs and exhorts to the imitation of these good things. Then we all stand up together and offer prayers."[43] This title, "Ruler of the Brethren"—or *proestos ton adelphon* in Greek—does not appear to have been the Church's own name for her leaders, but rather Justin's way of expressing, in language Antoninus and his sons will understand, the authority granted to the Christian bishop: that same authority we saw insisted upon so strongly by Ignatius.

> **Then there is brought to the Ruler of the Brethren bread and a cup of water and [a cup of] wine mixed with water, and he taking them sends up praise and glory to the Father of the Universe through the name of the Son and the Holy Spirit, and offers thanksgiving at some length for our being accounted worthy to receive these things from Him.**[44]

Exactly what were these prayers like? Though Justin himself gives us few details, we can perhaps glean something of their content from a supplementary source, an account provided by another of the Fathers, Hippolytus of Rome, writing a bit later (around A.D. 215):

[43] Ibid.

[44] Justin Martyr, *First Apology*, chap. 65, ACW 56:70.

The deacons shall then bring the offering to [the bishop]; and he, imposing his hand on it, along with all the presbytery, shall give thanks, saying: "The Lord be with you." And all shall respond, "And with your spirit." "Hearts aloft!" "We keep them with the Lord." "Let us give thanks to the Lord." "It is right and just." And then he shall continue immediately:

"We give you thanks, O God, through your beloved Son Jesus Christ, whom in these last days you have sent to us as Savior and Redeemer and as the angel [messenger] of your will; He that is your inseparable Word, through whom you made all things, and who is well-pleasing to you; whom you sent from heaven into the womb of a Virgin, and who, dwelling within her, was made flesh and was manifested as your Son, born of the Holy Spirit and of the Virgin; who, fulfilling your will and winning for Himself a holy people, extended His hands when it was time for Him to suffer, so that by His suffering He might set free those who believed in you; who also, when He was betrayed to His voluntary suffering, in order that He might destroy death and break the bonds of the devil and trample hell underfoot and enlighten the just and set a boundary and show forth His resurrection, took bread and gave thanks to you, saying: 'Take, eat: this is My Body, which is broken for you.' Likewise with the cup too, saying: 'This is My Blood, which is poured out for you. Whenever you do this, you do it in my memory' [cf. 1 Cor 11:23–26].

"Remembering, therefore, His death and resurrection, we offer to you the bread and the cup, giving thanks to you, because of your having accounted us wor-

thy to stand before you and minister to you. And we pray that you might send your Holy Spirit upon the offering of the holy Church. Gather as one in the fullness of the Holy Spirit your saints who participate; and confirm their faith in truth so that we may praise and glorify you through your Son Jesus Christ, through whom be glory and honor to you, to the Father and the Son with the Holy Spirit, in your holy Church, both now and through the ages of ages. Amen."[45]

Referring to the Lord's Supper as an "offering" is not common in many churches today; indeed, the thought that the Lord's Table represents an *altar* or that communion itself can be thought of as a *sacrifice* is believed by many to conflict with the doctrine of the one, final sacrifice of Christ; who sacrificed for sins **"once for all when he offered up himself"** on the Cross (Heb 7:27). Yet, the fact that Justin did, along with the whole early Church,[46] consider it to be so is established by his own writings. When disputing, for example, with Rabbi Trypho, Justin offered these arguments based on the Hebrew Scriptures:

---

[45] Hippolytus of Rome, *The Apostolic Tradition*, no. 4, in FEF 1:167, no. 394a.

[46] As testimony to this, Protestant Church historian Phillip Schaff wrote these words: "The Lord's Supper was universally regarded not only as a sacrament, but also as a sacrifice, the true and eternal sacrifice of the new covenant, superceding all the provisional and typical sacrifices of the old; taking the place particularly of the passover, or the feast of the typical redemption from Egypt" (*History of the Christian Church* [Grand Rapids, Mich.: Wm. B. Eerdmans Publishing, 1994], 2:245).

> **The offering of fine wheat flour which was prescribed to be offered on behalf of those cleansed from leprosy was a type of the Bread of the Eucharist,**[47] **the celebration of which our Lord Jesus Christ prescribed in memory of the passion He suffered on [our] behalf. . . . [But] concerning the sacrifices which you at that time offered, God speaks through Malachias, one of the twelve [prophets], as follows: "I have no pleasure in you, says the Lord; and I will not accept your sacrifices from your hands; for from the rising of the sun until its setting, my name has been glorified among the gentiles; and in every place incense is offered to my name, and a clean offering: for great is my name among the gentiles, says the Lord; but you profane it"** [Mal 1:10–12]. **It is of the sacrifices offered to Him in every place by us, the gentiles, that is, of the Bread of the Eucharist and likewise of the cup of the Eucharist, that He speaks at that time; and He says that we glorify His name, while you profane it.**[48]

Writing just a few years after Justin (ca. 180), Irenaeus adds some additional testimony. He says plainly that Jesus **"taught the new sacrifice of the new covenant, . . . [which] in every place . . . will be offered to Him."**[49] **"Sacrifice as such has not been reprobated. There were sacrifices then, sacrifices among the [Jewish] people; and there are sacri-**

[47] This word Eucharist—or *Eucharistia* in Greek, meaning literally "a thanksgiving"—was the most common name for the Lord's Supper used by the early Church.

[48] Justin Martyr, *Dialogue with Trypho*, chap. 41, in FEF 1:60, no. 135.

[49] Irenaeus, *Against Heresies*, bk. 4, chap. 17, no. 5, in FEF 1:95, no. 232.

fices now, sacrifices in the Church. Only the kind has been changed; for now the sacrifice is offered not by slaves but by free men."[50] To begin to understand this apparent contradiction, we will have to push ahead and gain a more complete picture of this ancient rite.

Justin himself continues now, from the *First Apology*:

> **When [the Ruler] has concluded the prayers and the thanksgiving, all the people assent by saying, *Amen. Amen* in the Hebrew language signifies, "so be it."**
>
> **And when the Ruler has given thanks and all the people have assented, those who are called by us deacons give to each of those present a portion of the eucharistized[51] bread and wine and water, and they carry it away to those who are absent. And this food is called among us Eucharist, of which no one is allowed to partake except one who believes that the things which we teach are true, and has received the washing that is for remission of sins and for rebirth, and who so lives as Christ handed down. For we do not receive these things as common bread or common drink; but in like manner as Jesus Christ our Savior having been incarnate by God's logos took both flesh and blood for our salvation, so also we have been taught that the food eucharistized through the word of prayer that is from Him, from which our blood and flesh are nourished by transformation, is the**

---

[50] Ibid., chap. 18, no. 2, in FEF 1:95, no. 233.

[51] This translation of the verb *eucharistein* is perhaps ungainly but serves a useful purpose—indicating that Justin wishes to show that something that *was not* considered Eucharist (i.e., the bread and wine prior to the prayers) has now been *changed into* Eucharist.

flesh and blood of that Jesus who became incarnate. For the Apostles in the memoirs composed by them, which are called Gospels, thus handed down what was commanded them: that Jesus took bread and having given thanks said: "Do this for my memorial, this is my body." [1 Cor 11:24]; **and likewise He took the chalice and having given thanks said: "This is my blood"** [cf. 1 Cor 11:25]; **and gave it to them alone.**[52]

Here is the solution to our problem of sacrifice—and what a solution! No, the Lord's Supper does not constitute *another* sacrifice . . . because the Church believed it to be the *same* sacrifice: Jesus' actual Body and Blood, broken and spilled on Calvary, really made present on her altars until He comes again. Not broken and spilled *again*, mind you, but *once for all*—yet communicated forever to the individual believer by means of a sacred memorial meal. Just as the ancient Hebrew Passover was not considered complete until everyone had actually *eaten the Lamb*, so Justin and the early Christians took the Lord's words to Peter literally: **"He who eats my flesh and drinks my blood abides in me, and I in him. As the living Father sent me, and I live because of the Father, so he who eats me will live because of me"** (Jn 6:56–57).[53]

---

[52] Justin Martyr, *First Apology*, chap. 65, ACW 56:70–71.

[53] Gregory of Nyssa, one of the great Eastern Fathers, wrote this in A.D. 382: **"He offered Himself for us, Victim and Sacrifice, and Priest as well, and 'Lamb of God, who takes away the sin of the world.' When did He do this? When He made His own Body food and His own Blood drink for His disciples; for this much is clear enough to anyone, that a sheep cannot be eaten by a man unless its being eaten be preceded by its being slaughtered. This giving of His own Body to His disciples for eating**

That this was, in fact, the teaching of the Apostles and the early Church is abundantly clear from the writings of any of a dozen different authors. It was, significantly, denied *only by the Gnostics*, who, after all, held that Jesus Himself had been little more than a symbol. Our beloved Ignatius, for instance, in his *Epistle to the Philadelphians*, wrote these words: **"Take care, then, to partake of one Eucharist; for, one is the Flesh of Our Lord Jesus Christ, and one the cup to unite us with His Blood, and one altar, just as there is one bishop assisted by the presbytery and the deacons, my fellow servants."**[54] Elsewhere, he speaks of the Eucharist as **"the Bread of God . . . the medicine of immortality, the antidote against death."**[55] Concerning the Gnostic doubters, Theophorus wrote this to the Smyrnaeans:

> **Observe those who hold erroneous opinions concerning the grace of Jesus Christ which has come to us, and see how they run counter to the mind of God! They concern themselves with neither works of charity, nor widows, nor orphans, nor the distressed, nor those in prison or out of it, nor the hungry or thirsty.**
>
> **From Eucharist and prayer they hold aloof, because they do not confess that the Eucharist is the Flesh of our Savior Jesus Christ, which suffered for our sins, and**

---

clearly indicates that the sacrifice of the Lamb has now been completed" (*Sermon One on the Resurrection of Christ*, in FEF 2:59, no. 1063).

[54] Ignatius of Antioch, *Epistle to the Philadelphians*, chap. 4, in *The Epistles of St. Clement of Rome and St. Ignatius of Antioch*, trans. James A. Kleist, ACW, vol. 1 (Mahwah, N.J.: Paulist Press, 1948), p. 86.

[55] Ignatius of Antioch, *Epistle to the Ephesians*, chaps. 5 and 20, in *Epistles*, ACW 1:62, 68.

> **which the Father in His loving-kindness raised from the dead.**[56]

Irenaeus, speaking also of the Gnostics, writes that,

> **these men reject the commixture of the heavenly wine, and wish it to be water of the world only, not receiving God so as to have union with Him. . . . [They] despise the entire dispensation of God, and disallow the salvation of the flesh, and treat with contempt its regeneration, maintaining that it is not capable of incorruption. But if [flesh] indeed [does] not attain salvation, then neither did the Lord redeem us with His blood, nor is the cup of the Eucharist His blood, nor the bread which we break the communion**[57] **of His body.**[58]

But the true Church, continues Irenaeus, has no such disdain for God's created world:

> **As we are His members, so too are we nourished by means of created things. . . . He has declared the cup, a part of creation, to be His own Blood, from which He causes our blood to flow; and the bread, a part of creation, He has established as His own Body, from which He gives increase to our bodies. [Since,] therefore, the**

---

[56] Ignatius of Antioch, *Epistle to the Smyrnaeans*, chap. 6, no. 2, chap. 7, no. 12, in *Epistles*, ACW 1:92.

[57] Compare this phrase to 1 Cor 10:15–17: **"I speak as to wise men; judge ye what I say. The cup of blessing which we bless, is it not the communion of the blood of Christ? The bread which we break, is it not the communion of the body of Christ? For we being many are one bread, and one body: for we are all partakers of that one bread"** (KJV).

[58] Irenaeus, *Against Heresies*, bk. 5, chap. 1, no. 3, and chap. 2, no. 2, in ANF 1:527–28.

mixed cup and the baked bread receives the Word of God and becomes Eucharist, the Body of Christ . . . how can they say that the flesh is not capable of receiving the gift of God, which is eternal life—flesh which is nourished by the Body and Blood of the Lord, and is in fact a member of Him?[59]

Believing in such a gift, then, is it any wonder that Justin knows nothing of any church service that does not include the Eucharist? Indeed, everything we know of early Christianity confirms this fact: that the celebration of the Lord's Supper was the central event in the life of the Church in those days. Everywhere, all across the known world and in every scrap of evidence that has survived from those ages, she calls out with one voice—summed up in the famous cry of John Chrysostom: **"Reverence, therefore, reverence this table, of which we are all communicants! Christ, slain for us, the Sacrificial Victim who is placed thereon!"**[60]

Concluding his outline of the eucharistic service, Hippolytus instructs that:

Breaking the Bread into individual particles which he then distributes, [the bishop] shall say: "Heavenly Bread in Christ Jesus!" And he that receives shall answer: "Amen!"[61]

---

[59] Ibid., bk. 5, chap. 2, nos. 2–3, in FEF 1:99, no. 249.

[60] John Chrysostom, *Homilies on the Epistle to the Romans* 8, 8, in FEF 2:114, no. 1183.

[61] Hippolytus of Rome, *The Apostolic Tradition*, no. 23, in FEF 1:170, no. 394i.

Then, after everyone has eaten, Justin draws his account to a close:

> **And those who prosper, and so wish, contribute what each thinks fit; and what is collected is deposited with the Ruler, who takes care of the orphans and widows, and those who, on account of sickness or any other cause, are in want, and those who are in bonds, and the strangers who are sojourners among us, and in a word [He] is the guardian of all those in need. . . . We all hold this common gathering on Sunday, since it is the first day, on which God transforming darkness and matter made the Universe, and Jesus Christ our Savior on the same day rose from the dead. For they crucified Him on the day before Saturday, and on the day after Saturday He appeared to His Apostles and disciples and taught them these things which we have passed on to you for your consideration.**[62]

Cup of Blood, Cup of Hemlock

Antoninus Pius died on the seventh day of March, A.D. 161: six or eight years after receiving the *First Apology* of Justin Martyr. His son Marcus Aurelius was immediately acknowledged by the Senate as sole emperor of Rome. Marcus, however, acting entirely on his own initiative, chose to promote his adopted brother Lucius Verus to the position of colleague, with co-equal rights as *Imperator Rex*. Together, then, the two brothers set out to reign as worthy successors

[62] Justin Martyr, *First Apology*, chap. 67, ACW 56:71.

of their venerable father, a man whom the citizens of the Empire began immediately to think of as a saint.

How had Justin's letter been received by the saintly Antoninus? For years, we felt we had some idea; in his *Church History* Eusebius quotes a decree that supposedly went out from the emperor to the cities of Asia Minor forbidding any further "tumultuous outbreaks against the Christians". Unfortunately, later scholarship seems to have proven this document untrustworthy. Probably Antoninus did continue, at the very least, the careful policies of Hadrian. Anything more, however, is speculation.

About Marcus himself, however, a good deal more is known.

The death of his father, ironically, appears to have triggered a wave of nostalgia for the "good old days"—both in the new emperor himself and in his subjects. Paganism's stock was up, so to speak, in response to Antoninus' good example—and especially the stock of the emperor's own chosen philosophical system. Marcus Aurelius, therefore, is in no mood to have his thinking challenged. His desire is to live up to his father's legacy, to stick by the traditions of his family. Perhaps he *had* read a word or two, some years back, that had troubled his complacency about the Christians. But, after all, one is always reading something . . . and, of course, as every philosopher knows, anything can be made to sound plausible by a skilled rhetorician. What was completely *unthinkable* was the notion of actually forsaking Stoicism at such an hour. And for what? For some detested oriental sect? The very idea was almost inconceivable. A Christian emperor! The mind rebelled. It was a sheer impossibility. In fact, it was probably illegal . . . or, at the very least, an excellent way to get assassinated or to have one's throne taken away. Not that Marcus was afraid of death. Everything we know of the son of Antoninus assures us that he was a sincere Stoic, who would have faced any reasonable calamity with dignity. But when he thought of the *scandal* such news would create, the heartbreak of his mother, of his brother Lucius. His whole being revolted against the prospect.

No, with a little effort one might easily forget that strange letter from that strange man, that man who had claimed to be both Christian *and* philosopher, as if such a thing were possible. Yet admittedly, his words had worked a curious spell. In fact, Marcus would have liked, under different circumstances, to have questioned that strange man a bit, to have walked with him for an hour or so; perhaps by the seashore, where the attention is not distracted, and converse uninterrupted. But he could not allow himself to think in such a way. He was *emperor* now, with responsibilities to the people. As a matter of fact, it was these very mystery cults that had worked so much harm lately—dividing the population into factions, enticing them away from the traditions of Rome into fads and manias, filling their hearts with so many inconsolable longings.

No. The very last thing the Empire needed right now was more religious chaos—and in high places, no less. Marcus Aurelius had been accused of flightiness before—of being dreamy, preoccupied, more suited to the halls of academy than to the corridors of power. And here, clearly, was an opportunity for firmness and decisive action. Stoicism had been good enough for his father; it would be good enough for him. If he had his way, it would be good enough for the whole Empire some day. And as far as these nagging doubts and uncertainties were concerned . . . well, Marcus would simply do his best, by the lights of his own conscience, and leave the rest up to the gods.

One of the first official acts, then, of Emperor Marcus Aurelius Antoninus was to issue the following edict: **"Whoever introduces new sects or religions whose true nature is unknown, and thereby excites the people, he shall be banished if he be of noble birth, and killed by the sword if he be of mean extraction."**[63]

Though Marcus was no Nero, though in his heart he may have meant well for the Roman Empire, this sad decree was the signal for a new round of general persecution against the *Katholikē Ekklēsia*—the fourth such in her history—which was to last until Marcus' own death in the year 180. And the most famous victim of it would be Justin Martyr himself.

Justin did his best to avert the tragedy. His *Second Apology*, many scholars believe, was written immediately after the opening of this new campaign. And the title of it is somewhat misleading; for the second, much shorter, seems to have been an appendix to the first, or a follow-up if you will, rather than a separate, independent work. Justin addresses his apology, this time, to the Roman Senate, in protest of **"the things which have recently happened in your city under Urbicus [Prefect at that time], and the things which are likewise being everywhere unreasonably done by the governors."** He speaks to the Senators boldly, calling them **"men of like passions, and brethren, though ye know it**

[63] Marcus Aurelius, *Decree against New Religions*, quoted in Laux, *Church History*, p. 57.

not, and though ye be unwilling to acknowledge it on account of your glorying in what you esteem dignities."[64] He briefly recounts some of the outrages lately inflicted upon the Christian community and tries to appeal to their sense of justice and decency. Finally, making one last effort to distance himself from the slanderous old identification with the Gnostics, Justin writes:

> **And I [have] despised the wicked and deceitful teaching of Simon of my own nation. . . .**[65] **Our doctrines are not shameful, according to a sober judgment, but are indeed more lofty than all human philosophy. . . . And henceforth we shall be silent, having done as much as we could, and having added the prayer that all men everywhere may be counted worthy of the truth. And would that you also, in a manner becoming piety and philosophy, would for your own sakes judge justly!**[66]

The *Second Apology* also contains an ominous prophecy; proof that Justin foresees—at least in his own case—that all the careful, rational appeals in the world will come to nothing: **"I, too, therefore, expect to be plotted against"**, he writes, **"and fixed to the stake . . . perhaps by Crescens, that lover of bravado and boasting."**[67] Who was this Crescens? The answer to that question is a bitter pill indeed. Eusebius gives it in his chapter on the life of the great apologist: **"Justin, . . . after he had addressed a second work in behalf of our doctrines to the rulers already named,**

---

[64] Justin Martyr, *Second Apology*, chap. 1, in ANF 1:188.

[65] Justin, remember, was a Samaritan, as was Simon of Gitto.

[66] Justin Martyr, *Second Apology*, chap. 15, in ANF 1:193.

[67] Ibid., chap. 3, in ANF 1:189.

was crowned with divine martyrdom, in consequence of a plot laid against him by Crescens, a philosopher who emulated the life and manners of the Cynics, whose name he bore."[68] It was he who devised the plot against Justin, for **"Justin had repeatedly refuted him in public discussions."**[69] Justin's pupil Tatian, in his *Address to the Greeks*, sheds some additional light: **"Crescens, who made his nest in the great city, surpassed all men in unnatural love,**[70] **and was strongly addicted to the love of money. Yet this man, who professed to despise death, was so afraid of death, that he endeavoured to inflict on Justin, and indeed on me, the punishment of death, as being an evil, because by proclaiming the truth he convicted the philosophers of being gluttons and cheats."**[71]

Yes, like Jesus his Lord, Justin Martyr is betrayed into the hands of his enemies by one of his own friends—by one of the open-minded "lovers of truth" with whom he has been so trusting. But we must not be surprised, or too bitter. Some of our Savior's disciples, like gentle Nathanael, He commended for "guilelessness" and simplicity; surely Ignatius of Antioch was another of these. To others, however, Jesus committed a different role; that of being as **"wise as serpents, and innocent as doves"** (Mt 10:16). Justin of Neapolis was given this noble part to play; and he played it

---

[68] Cynicism was not just an attitude toward life in those days, but an actual school of philosophy whose most famous adherent was Diogenes.

[69] Eusebius, *Church History*, bk. 4, chap. 16, no. 1, trans. Arthur Cushman McGiffert, in NPNF2 1:193.

[70] The word used here is *paiderastia* (pederasty), a vice to which many of the Greek philosophers had been addicted ever since the days of Plato.

[71] Tatian of Syria, *Address to the Greeks*, chap. 19, trans. J. E. Ryland, in ANF 2:73.

to perfection for thirty years—a veritable Scarlet Pimpernel for Christ, skillfully outwitting the cleverest minds of the ancient world, for their own sakes and that of the kingdom. But surely Justin had known all along that it could not go on forever, that someday the time would come to pay the piper. The servant, after all, is not greater than his Master. It is enough for the servant to be like his Master.

The knock on the door (heard by so many successors to Justin since then, whether in Soviet Russia or China or in East Timor) came at night. Bible study was in session, at the home of Martinus. In a moment, Justin and six others were gone; their sacred scrolls carried away with them for the burning. And the house of Martinus stood quiet once more in the moonlight.

> **And when they had been brought before his judgment-seat, Rusticus the prefect said to Justin, "Obey the gods at once, and submit to the kings." Justin said, "To obey the commandments of our Saviour Jesus Christ is worthy neither of blame nor of condemnation." . . . Rusticus said, "Are you not, then, a Christian?" Justin said, "Yes, I am a Christian."** [The governor turned to Justin's pupils:] **Then said the prefect Rusticus to Chariton, "Tell me further, Chariton, are you also a Christian?" Chariton said, "I am a Christian by the command of God." Rusticus the prefect asked the woman Charito, "What say you, Charito?" Charito said, "I am a Christian by the grace of God." Rusticus said to Euelpistus, "And what are you?" Euelpistus, a servant of Caesar, answered, "I too am a Christian, having been freed by Christ; and by the grace of Christ I partake of the same hope." Rus-**

ticus the prefect said to Hierax, "And you, are you a Christian?" Hierax said, "Yes, I am a Christian, for I revere and worship the same God." Rusticus the prefect said, "Did Justin make you Christians?" Hierax said, "I was a Christian, and will be a Christian." And Paeon stood up and said, "I too am a Christian." Rusticus the prefect said, "Who taught you?" Paeon said, "From our parents we received this good confession." Euelpistus said, "I willingly heard the words of Justin. But from my parents also I learned to be a Christian." Rusticus the prefect said, "Where are your parents?" Euelpistus said, "In Cappadocia." Rusticus says to Hierax, "Where are your parents?" And he answered, and said, "Christ is our true father, and faith in Him is our mother; and my earthly parents died; and I, when I was driven from Iconium in Phrygia, came here." Rusticus the prefect said to Liberianus, "And what say you? Are you a Christian, and unwilling to worship [the gods]?" Liberianus said, "I too am a Christian, for I worship and reverence the only true God."[72]

What emotions must have surged through Justin during this interview! He knows that to confess Christianity is death, and therefore that he will probably see, in the next few minutes, all six of his precious companions beheaded before his eyes; for it was the custom of the Romans to make the shepherd of the flock watch the others go first. Yet how *proud* he was of them all! This was the very moment he had been training them for—and look! None of them

---

[72] *The Martyrdom of the Holy Martyrs*, chap. 1, trans. M. Dods, in ANF 1:305.

was a *bit* afraid! And though his eyes surely glistened with tears, Justin Martyr appears to have seen—not the guards with swords at the ready—but a vision of Paradise, and of the Lord Jesus Himself waiting there with arms open wide!

> **The prefect [turned] to Justin: "Hearken, you who are called learned, and think that you know true doctrines; if you are scourged and beheaded, do you believe you will ascend into heaven?" Justin said, "I [have] hope that, if I endure these things, I shall have His gifts. For I know that, to all who have thus lived, there abides the divine favour until the completion of the whole world." Rusticus the prefect said, "Do you suppose, then, that you will ascend into heaven to receive some recompense?" Justin said, "I do not suppose it, but I know and am fully persuaded of it."**[73]

Rusticus sighed. He had hoped that these poor, deluded people could be talked into abandoning their folly and thereby become useful members of society again. But now he could see that they were hopelessly fixed in their treason. The prefect sat back in the judgment-seat to address the group as a whole: "**'Let us, then, now come to the matter in hand, and which presses. Having come together, offer sacrifice with one accord to the gods.'**"[74]

Here was the moment of truth. And the great apologist paused not a moment:

> **Justin said, "No right-thinking person falls away from piety to impiety." Rusticus the prefect said, "Unless**

[73] Ibid., chap. 4, in ANF 1:306.

[74] Ibid.

ye obey, ye shall be mercilessly punished." Justin said, "Through prayer we can be saved on account of our Lord Jesus Christ, even when we have been punished, because this shall become to us salvation and confidence at the more fearful and universal judgment-seat of our Lord and Saviour." Thus also said the other martyrs: "Do what you will, for we are Christians, and do not sacrifice to idols." Rusticus the prefect [therefore] pronounced sentence, saying, "Let those who have refused to sacrifice to the gods and to yield to the command of the Emperor be scourged, and led away to suffer the punishment of decapitation, according to the laws." The holy martyrs having glorified God [by their confession], and having gone forth to the accustomed place, were beheaded, and perfected their testimony in the confession of the Saviour. And some of the faithful having secretly removed their bodies, laid them in a suitable place, the grace of our Lord Jesus Christ having wrought along with them, to whom be glory for ever and ever. Amen.[75]

There is one curious additional fact about this beautiful account of Justin's martyrdom. Though it is among the most authentic documents in all of Christian antiquity, several old copies of it would have Justin—not *beheaded*, as Marcus ordered—but dying in a different way: *by drinking a poisonous cup of hemlock*.

And though these odd variances are undoubtedly later interpolations on the original text, they do express symbolically a profound and vital reality, one that was noticed ear-

[75] Ibid., chaps. 4–5, in ANF 1:305–6.

lier by Justin himself in the pages of his last apology to the noble philosopher-kings:

> **And [even] those who by human birth were more ancient than Christ, when they attempted to consider and prove things by reason, were brought before the tribunals as impious persons and busybodies. And Socrates, who was more zealous in this direction than all of them, was accused of the very same crimes as ourselves. For they said that he was introducing new divinities, and did not consider those to be gods whom the state recognized. But he . . . taught men to reject the wicked demons and those who did the things which the poets related; and he exhorted them to become acquainted with the God who was to them unknown, by means of the investigation of reason, saying, "That it is neither easy to find the Father and Maker of all, nor, having found Him, is it safe to declare Him to all."[76] . . . In Christ, who was partially known even by Socrates (for He was and is the Word who is in every man . . .),[77] not only philosophers and scholars believed, but also artisans and people entirely uneducated, despising both glory, and fear, and death; since He is a power of the ineffable Father, and not the mere instrument of human reason.[78]**

---

[76] This is, indeed, a quote from Socrates himself, included in Plato's *Timaeus*.

[77] Compare with John 1:9: **"That was the true Light, which lighteth every man that cometh into the world"** (KJV).

[78] Justin Martyr, *Second Apology*, chap. 10, trans. Leslie William Barnard, in St. Justin Martyr, *First Apology*, in ANF 1:191.

To the Unknown God

Ever since the days of Abraham, who interceded for Sodom and Gomorrah, believers have sometimes felt that it is the presence or absence of a few holy people that makes the difference between life and death to a nation. While these saints are still at work—praying, striving, hoping—God Himself continues to strive, for their sakes and for those they care about. This strange feeling, rational or not, grows almost uncanny as we turn our thoughts to the tragic balance of Marcus Aurelius' life on earth.

After Justin's execution, war broke out almost immediately; a conflict known to history as the Parthian War. Marcus' brother Lucius, co-emperor and commander-in-chief, went to the front himself in 162 and took personal command of the troops. And it must be said that Antoninus' "other" son quitted himself gloriously, in an epic running battle across Syria, Cappadocia, Armenia, and Mesopotamia. Victory came in 166; but it was brief and all too ephemeral. Another conflict flared up almost immediately, then another. Soon the barbarians were truly at the gate—the Marcomanni, the Varistae, the Hermanduri, and the Vandals—all collected along the Danube, waiting to pour across the frontier into what had been the impregnable Rome. The situation became so frightening that even Marcus himself determined that his presence was needed on the battlefield, and in 169 he joined his brother there, at the remote, snowbound fortress of Sirmium in Pannonia.

Lucius Verus died that same year; and when he did, he left the prosecution of these vital wars entirely in the ineffectual hands of Marcus Aurelius. Marcus did his best to carry on alone, but it was little use. All of his chosen advisers were cast from the same hopeless mold as himself—schoolmasters and seers, teachers of philosophy and useless dilettantes. His generals were left to direct their own activities, with little coordination or central command. Every day the dispatches from home grew more desperate as well; Lucius' returning legions, it seems, had carried bubonic plague back with them from the East. Also, there had been a violent earthquake, and a famine caused when flood destroyed the royal granaries. Yet there were even worse reports. In the panic caused by these events, the people of the city were said to be reverting to the worst forms of heathen superstition. Sacrifices were being made by the thousands, of everything from bulls and goats to newborn babes, and the arenas of the Empire were being kept busy in shift work. Weird foreign gods had been imported, too, and the sacrifices *they* demanded were horrible even by the worst of Roman standards.

What did Marcus do? He sought the consolation of philosophy. Closing himself in a humble room at the bleak army camp, living on little more than bread and water, he retreated into self-examination and reverie. And while he did, the war raged on like a brush fire. No one knew it at the time, of course, but these events were the beginning of the end for Rome. Though it took over three hundred years for the tragedy to be complete, the "Fall of the Roman Empire", according to most historians, began—not with Caligula, or Claudius, or Trajan—but with Marcus Aurelius Antoninus. Reinhold Niebuhr called him "the noblest character of his time".[79] And the Catholic scholar Patrick Healy named him

[79] Quoted by Patrick J. Healy, in *The Catholic Encyclopedia*, Volume

"one of the best men of heathen antiquity"[80] But the same scholar was forced to say more: "It was a curse to mankind, finally, that 'he was a Stoic first and then a ruler.' . . . Philosophy became a disease in [Marcus'] mind and cut him off from the truths of practical life."[81]

It is true that his last reverie was a beautiful one. When Marcus, still living at his forbidding fortress along the Danube, finally collapsed and died on March 17, 180, the results of it were found nestled against his heart in the folds of his pallium: a diary, known to us today as his *Meditations*. Speaking of this book, M. Martha, the great historian of the Roman moralists, said, "The philosophy of Heathendom grows less proud, draws nearer to a Christianity which it ignored or which it despised, and is ready to fling itself into the arms of the Unknown God."[82]

We can only pray that Marcus Aurelius, having squandered such a fearful opportunity already, was given nevertheless a second chance so to fling himself before the end. Surely we may hope, by the grace of that same "unknown" God, that somehow a tender meeting, cruelly denied here on earth, has since occurred elsewhere—perhaps along some heavenly seashore; where the attention truly is not distracted, and converse uninterrupted for ages of ages, world without end.

Believe it or not, the philosopher's pallium—worn by Marcus, and Socrates, and Justin, and perhaps by Justin's mysterious Old Man—is still in use today. It survives, in a

---

II (Robert Appleton Co., 1907), www.newadvent.org/cathen/02109a.htm (Kevin Knight, 1999).

[80] Ibid.

[81] Ibid.

[82] Ibid.

slightly modified form, in many of the pulpits of Christendom; worn every Sunday by ministers of the liturgical tradition, in Catholic, Greek Orthodox, Anglican, and Lutheran churches. There, it serves a useful purpose; reminding us that all real truth is God's truth, that He answers every sincere knock on His door—but also, for those of us who know his story, reminding us of Justin Martyr of Neapolis, whom old Eusebius rightly called: **"truly, the most philosophical of men."**[83]

---

[83] Eusebius Pamphilus, *History of the Church*, bk. 4, chap. 16, in EHC 124.

Irenaeus of Lyons

The weary missionary prays as he walks, offering quiet thanks to God for the modest successes of the day. Little Blandina, the slave girl, has asked to be baptized, praise God, and Maturus, the village blacksmith, seems likely to do the same before much longer. True, the crowds were a little off today. Usually fifteen or twenty will listen, at least for a moment or two, as he preaches from that particular corner of the fish market. Still, by God's grace, he works relatively unhindered; speaking openly without much serious fear of persecution. So far organized opposition to the faith is practically unknown here on the barbarous outskirts of Empire, and the land of Gallia has yet to see its first Christian martyrdom. Irenaeus of Smyrna pauses briefly by the wayside and wonders if his home church back East has fared so well.

As his thoughts shift from the here and now to friends and family in Asia, our young evangelist notices that he has begun to think in his native Greek again, rather than in the strange local tongue he learned to speak for the sake of his mission here. The road Irenaeus travels today runs along the right bank of the broad river Rhone, and up ahead on a hilltop is the colonial capital of Lugdunum, standing on a narrow peninsula between that river and the Loire. The scene is beautiful no doubt—the fine spring weather has raised up a stunning crop of wildflowers along the roadside—but how very different this beauty, he reflects, from that of his dry, Anatolian birthplace! There, olive trees stand starkly against cloudless skies, and civilization is old, advanced, and sophisticated. The missionary catches himself short—was he feeling homesick again? A little, perhaps. But then he turns his thoughts back to Blandina once more, and to brave Maturus, and pushes ahead into the city with renewed vigor in his step.

Upon entering the city itself, Irenaeus suddenly notices his fellow presbyter Attalus rushing toward him in the street —another young Asian, this time out of Pergamum. Opening his mouth to greet him as he approaches, Irenaeus stops abruptly in mid-sentence. *The look on the man's face!* Dear God in heaven, what has happened? He catches Attalus by the shoulders as they meet. *What is it, friend? What's the matter?* The messenger is wide-eyed, and Irenaeus sees plainly that those eyes are red with weeping. But Attalus' expression is far from transparent; yes, there is fear, shock, anguish . . . but these darker emotions are mixed liberally with rapture and worship. Irenaeus shakes his fellow missionary roughly. *Open your mouth, man!* Finally, our weary evangelist is told simply *to run*, to run home and find the pastor at once, immediately. He does so without another instant of delay, leaving Attalus standing in the street alone.

A heavy beaded curtain is brushed roughly aside. Aged Pothinus, bishop of the fledgling church here at Lugdunum, is just where Irenaeus knew he would be; hard at prayer in the silken darkness of his prayer closet. Seeing his chamber flooded now with the afternoon light, the old man looks up at Irenaeus from his knees. He wears the same expression Attalus wore—though perhaps with less fear, more simple awe. And what is that spread out on the floor before him? A parchment? Irenaeus watches Pothinus rise slowly to his feet, sees him take the document carefully into his fingers, bringing it up with him as he rises. The bishop hands it to Irenaeus, then clutches the junior presbyter tightly to his breast, moistening his cheek with his tears. Then Pothinus turns away completely, lifting his face and hands toward the ceiling in wordless praise to heaven. The younger man carries the parchment out with him into the main room of their shared house.

Irenaeus sees at once that it is a letter from home—from **"the Church of God which resides as a stranger at Smyrna, to the Church of God residing at Philomelium,**[1] **and to all the communities of the holy and Catholic Church, residing in any place."** It begins simply:

> ***May mercy, and peace, and love* of God the Father and Our Lord Jesus Christ *be* yours *in abundance*!**
>
> **We are sending you, brethren, a written account of the martyrs and, in particular, of blessed Polycarp, whose witness to the faith as it were sealed the persecution and put an end to it. By almost every step that led up to it the Lord intended to exhibit to us anew the type of martyrdom narrated in the Gospel.**[2]

Polycarp martyred!

Polycarp had been Irenaeus' own father in the Lord—and was the initiator and patron of this very mission to the far West! And there was persecution of Polycarp's *church*

---

[1] Philomelium was another city in Asia Minor, and the church there probably had close ties with Smyrna.

[2] *The Martyrdom of St. Polycarp*, prologue and chap. 1, no. 1, in *The Didache, The Epistle of Barnabas, The Epistles and The Martyrdom of St. Polycarp, The Fragments of Papias, The Epistle to Diognetus*, trans. James A. Kleist, ACW, vol. 6 (Mahwah, N.J.: Paulist Press, 1948), p. 90.

as well—Irenaeus' own church home, with everything that meant for those he had left behind. The presbyter feels his face flush, feels the salt rushing into his eyes just as it had to those of his co-workers. And yet, he must not think first of the loss. Not the loss first, not for a Christian. He must turn his mind instead to the *obedience*—and to the glory. Irenaeus sinks to his knees in imitation of Pothinus.

When he can lift his head again he reads farther. It seems a small group of Smyrnaean believers had been rounded up in a spontaneous local outbreak. There were not many, but these few were so steadfast under torture that **"the whole mob, astonished at the heroism of the God-loving and God-fearing race of the Christians, shouted: 'Away with the atheists! Let Polycarp be searched for!'"**[3] Having pastored the church at Smyrna since apostolic times, and been himself a disciple of the Apostles, Polycarp was well known by Christian and pagan alike as the foremost bishop of the entire region. He became therefore the object of a massive manhunt; and finally, after a search of several days, was overtaken by the police in a farmhouse outside the city.

> **When he heard of their arrival** [the letter continued] **he came down and conversed with them. The onlookers were wondering at his age and his composure, and that there was so much ado about arresting a man so old. Then, late as it was, he at once ordered food and drink to be served them as much as they wished, and begged them to allow him an hour for undisturbed prayer. They granted his request; and there he stood, rapt in prayer, so overflowing with the grace of God that for two hours**

[3] Ibid., chap. 3, no. 2, ACW 6:92.

he was unable to stop speaking! Those that heard him were struck with admiration, and many were sorry they had come to fetch so old a man of God.

When he had at last ended his prayer, in which he remembered all that had met him at any time—both small and great, both known and unknown to fame, and the whole world-wide Catholic Church—the moment of departure arrived, and, seating him on an ass, they led him into the city.[4]

There was a trial, of course—the usual mockery of justice. And the defendant (also true to form) quickly found himself standing in the arena. Yet **"as Polycarp entered the arena,"** the letter recorded, **"a voice was heard from heaven: *'Be strong, Polycarp, and act manfully.'* Nobody saw the speaker, but those of our people who were present heard the voice."**[5]

Observing from his official box, the proconsul of the city gave Polycarp one last chance to apostatize:

When the proconsul insisted and said: "Take the oath and I will set you free; revile Christ," Polycarp replied: "For six and eighty years I have been serving Him, and He has done no wrong to me; how, then, dare I blaspheme my King who has saved me!"

But he again insisted and said: "Swear by the Fortune of Caesar."

He answered: "If you flatter yourself that I shall swear by the Fortune of Caesar, as you suggest, and if you

---

[4] Ibid., chap. 7, no. 2—chap. 8, no. 1, ACW 6:93.

[5] Ibid., chap. 9, no. 1, ACW 6:94.

pretend not to know me, let me frankly tell you: I am a Christian! If you wish to learn the teaching of Christianity, fix a day and let me explain." . . .

"Well," said the proconsul, "I have wild beasts, and shall have you thrown before them if you do not change your mind."

"Call for them," he replied, "to us a change from better to worse is impossible; but it is noble to change from what is evil to what is good."

Again he said to him: "If you make little of the beasts, I shall have you consumed by fire unless you change your mind."

"The fire which you threaten," replied Polycarp, "is one that burns for a little while, and after a short time goes out. You evidently do not know the fire of judgment to come and the eternal punishment, which awaits the wicked. But why do you delay? Go ahead; do what you want." . . .

Then the thing was done more quickly than can be told, the crowds being in so great a hurry to gather logs and firewood from the shops and baths! . . . Without delay the material prepared for the pyre was piled up round him; but when they intended to nail him as well, he said: "Leave me just as I am. He who enables me to endure the fire will also enable me to remain on the pyre unbudging, without the security afforded by your nails."

So they did not nail him, but just fastened him. And there he was, with his hands behind him, and fastened, like a ram towering above a large flock, ready for sacrifice, a holocaust prepared and acceptable to God! And he looked up to heaven and said:

"O Lord God, O Almighty, Father of Thy beloved and blessed Son Jesus Christ, through whom we have received the knowledge of you—God of angels and hosts and all creation—and of the whole race of saints who live under your eyes! I bless Thee, because Thou hast seen fit to bestow upon me this day and this hour, that I may share, among the number of the martyrs, the cup of Thy Anointed and rise to eternal life both in soul and in body, in virtue of the immortality of the Holy Spirit. May I be accepted among them in Thy sight today as a rich and pleasing sacrifice. . . ."

When he had wafted up the *Amen* and finished the prayer, the men attending to the fire lit it; and when a mighty flame shot up, we, who were privileged to see it, saw a wonderful thing; and we have been spared to tell the tale to the rest. The fire produced the likeness of a vaulted chamber, like a ship's sail bellying to the breeze, and surrounded the martyr's body as with a wall; and he was in the centre of it, not as burning flesh, but as bread that is baking, or as gold and silver refined in a furnace! In fact, we even caught an aroma such as the scent of incense or of some other precious spice.

At length, seeing that his body could not be consumed by fire, those impious people ordered an executioner to approach him and run a dagger into him. This done, there issued [a dove and] a great quantity of blood, with the result that the fire was quenched and the whole crowd was struck by the difference between unbelievers and elect.[6]

---

[6] Some manuscripts of the *Martyrdom of Polycarp* include an additional detail: that of a dove seen issuing from his pierced side along with the blood.

And of the elect the most wonderful Polycarp was certainly one—an apostolic and prophetic teacher in our times, and a bishop of the Catholic Church at Smyrna. . . .

We afterwards took up his bones, more precious than costly stones and more excellent than gold, and interred them in a decent place. There the Lord will permit us, as far as possible, to assemble in rapturous joy and celebrate his martyrdom—his birthday—both in order to commemorate the heroes that have gone before, and to train and prepare for heroes yet to come.[7]

Irenaeus pushes the letter aside, then falls weakly back from his knees into a sitting position on the floor. The

---

This was probably a later gloss on the original text—the early Christians often used a white dove as a symbol for the soul of a martyr just leaving his or her body.

[7] *Martyrdom of Polycarp*, chap. 9, no. 3—chap. 10, no. 1; chap. 11, nos. 1–2; chap. 13, no. 1a; chap. 13, no. 3—chap. 14, no. 2a; chap. 15, no. 1—chap. 16, no. 2; chap. 18, nos. 2–3, ACW 6:95–99. This passage, penned about A.D. 155, shows that the practice of keeping "saints' days" (in this case the anniversary of the martyrdom of Polycarp) dates from the earliest years of Christianity. Yet it should also be noticed that the Church was careful to maintain a sharp distinction between these honors and the worship paid to God alone. In a related verse, the author of Polycarp's *Martyrdom* writes: "**[Jesus] we *worship* as being the Son of God, the martyrs we *love* as being disciples and imitators of the Lord; and deservedly so, because of their unsurpassable devotion to their King and Teacher**" (*Martyrdom of Polycarp*, chap. 17, no. 3 [emphasis added], ACW 6:99). It would likewise appear from the passage being discussed that the remains (or "relics") of these martyrs were also kept in the churches early on and played some part in these anniversary celebrations. This was another dramatic way to contrast Gnosticism (which despised the body and denied its redemption) with Catholic Christianity (which insisted so strongly on the salvation of the flesh that a martyr's very bones were considered holy).

tears are flowing freely now, and, unconscious of manners, he wipes at them with the sleeve of his robe. He must give thanks, of course. That was the first thing to do. No greater tale of courage had been told in the Church since Polycarp's old friend Ignatius Theophorus had gone to his own reward. And yet—though he knows it is wrong—Irenaeus feels a nasty tug of *fear* in his heart. Not for his own life, of course, not even for his loved ones at home anymore, but for *the future of Christianity.*

How can we do it? How can we go on—*alone?*

So long as Polycarp lived, it was still possible to learn the message of the Apostles directly from one of their own personal disciples. Whenever lawless innovators like the Docetists had come forward to expound their novel theories, the Church had been able to say, quite simply, "*Ask Polycarp . . .* Polycarp will know. He can tell you what the Apostles would have said." But with Polycarp gone, the last of his kind . . . well, with that tremendous milestone passed the apostolic age had truly come to an end. From this point on, all gospel preaching would have to come *second-hand:* either from a third-generation messenger like himself, or (for those who were able to read Greek) out of scrolls copied from the memoirs of the Apostles. Irenaeus has not, of course, been so foolish as to think that this day was not inevitable. But perhaps he would admit to hoping, along with the rest of the Church, that the Lord would have returned by now, before any of this became an issue.

He had thought of the apostolic writings—would these be sufficient, by themselves, to stand in for the living voices that were now silenced? Well, undoubtedly, all such *authentic* memoirs were to be regarded as the very Word of

God itself; and the most reliable of them had for years been referred to as Scripture in the churches, on an equal par with Moses and the prophets. But alas, the still coalescing New Testament had not come with an inspired "contents page". Irenaeus must have known that other "gospels" had begun making the rounds as well: already there was a *Gospel of Thomas*, a *Gospel of Nicodemus*, and other such books attributed to Andrew, Philip, Bartholomew, and Matthias. That these falsified chronicles had not, in truth, been composed by apostolic men was, of course, a fact—but it was a fact for which anyone other than a history scholar would simply have to take the Church's word. Even more vexing, orthodox Christians themselves were still debating which books should and should not be admitted. Quite apart from the myriad Gnostic fabrications, there were many *legitimate* candidates for inclusion about which the Church remained unsure. There was a solid core collection in use, certainly: the four genuine Gospels, the Acts of the Apostles, the letters of Paul. But many felt that questions still remained, for example, about the authorship of Hebrews, about the canonicity of the book of Revelation, or about whether Peter had really written a second general epistle. Other teachers—also entirely orthodox—wished to include later writings on the approved list as well; books like *The Shepherd of Hermas* and even Clement's own *Epistle to the Corinthians*.[8] Irenaeus

[8] To get a clear picture of this process, it might be helpful to note some of the many variations of opinion within the Church in those days. One of the earliest attempts at a New Testament canon—that contained in the famous *Muratorian Fragment* (ca. A.D. 140)—explicitly rejected the book of Hebrews. Origen, on the other hand, accepted it . . . along with the *Didache*, the *Epistle of Barnabas*, and the *Shepherd of Hermas*. In fact, Irenaeus

himself had no doubt whatever that the Holy Spirit would eventually guide the Church to the correct and final list, but that, once again, would be something for which the world would be forced to take her word.

No, Irenaeus saw immediately that it would not do. It would be impossible to rely upon documents alone, however holy, because *documents have to be vouched for by somebody*. And if potential converts were led to distrust the very messengers doing the vouching (as had been Simon Magus' *modus operandi* from the beginning), well, then, how long could such people be expected to reverence the books these discredited messengers happened to have brought along with them? Obviously, if their whole mission was a fake to begin with (as the Gnostics slanderously maintained), then they might have faked their scriptures as well. And, of course, the old issue of interpretation had not gone away either. A living man like Polycarp could correct you as he spoke, could let you know when you were misunderstanding him or when you had misrepresented his meaning to others. The brief

---

himself speaks of the *Shepherd* as "scripture". Clement of Alexandria excluded these later books, but wished, on the other hand, to include the far more dubious *Apocalypse of Peter*. Cyprian of Carthage, whose words carried great weight in the early Church, rejected Hebrews, James, and Jude. Eusebius, along with many others, doubted the inspiration of the book of Revelation, and almost everyone had questions about the authenticity of Second Peter. Should these facts lead us to doubt the final canon or to blur the lines between inspired and merely human books? No, but they should help us to understand that the Church came to recognize the true canon by a gradual process, rather than by receiving it ready-made from Christ Himself or the Apostles. To accept her word, however, that she recognized the *correct* list of books does require faith in her continued guidance by the Holy Spirit as well as faith that her rivals, with their various alternative canons, did not have this guidance.

collection of books and letters that had managed to survive from the Apostles—precious as they were and inspired by God—had not this power. In fact, Irenaeus could see nothing at all to replace it: the living voice in **"the household of God, which is the church of the living God, the pillar and bulwark of the truth"** (1 Tim 3:15). Without that voice—the living voice of Christ's disciples elucidating their own writings to their own people—the Scriptures, in day-to-day practice, would never be much more than an ink-blot test.

Our young missionary wanders absently back out into the street. The sun is setting now, turning the western sky over Gallia a deep, darkening wine-red; and everywhere lamps are being lighted in windows and the smell of supper pours out into the street. Always with the heart of an evangelist, Irenaeus' thoughts turn once more to the people, to the souls he came here to save. He struggles, for their sake, to regain his composure, his confidence, but he feels as if a chair has been kicked out from under him. Yes, there were still many, many holy men in the churches. Polycarp and the others like him had been careful to leave hundreds of their own fully trained children and grandchildren in Christ. But now Irenaeus sees with frightening clarity that each new degree of separation will mean new opportunities for Satan . . . and for Simon. With no one left to contradict them directly, the Gnostics (and other alternative Christians) will begin to claim anything and be believed. In fact, he had already heard that some of them were starting to imitate even the Church's own claim to apostolic origins. Gnostic missions were now purporting to have been blessed at some point by one of the minor names on the list of Apostles (Apostles whose true movements had been lost to history), or to have been based on "later, fuller" revelations passed down by Peter or Paul in secret, to their more "advanced" pupils. What had been impossible for the Magus himself to maintain—the idea that Jesus had approved of and established his devilish mission—had now become possible to his successors with nothing else but the mere passage of time.

Blood red now, the sun can be seen dipping below the horizon; Irenaeus watches it as best he can through tear-dimmed eyes. Darkness will follow in a moment or two—and our missionary feels the coming chill. Now the flood-gates will spring wide, he reflects bitterly. New "churches" will open for business every day, and all of them preaching a different brand of "truth" from the one next door. And what could the poor pagans hope to do with this pathetic welter of competing Christianities? Simon's work would be complete. In fact, Irenaeus is suddenly able to foresee a time when even the very idea of one holy, catholic, and apostolic Church might be lost and forgotten by many. That, God help us, would be a sign of the end, surely. Then, the poor sad world would have come full circle. The false prophets would have returned victorious, and to the little lost sheep it would be as if the Good Shepherd had never come at all. And every man would be forced to do once more what seems right in his own eyes . . . and call it *freedom*.

And yet, there in the gathering gloom, Irenaeus pauses. Suddenly, with what feels like an interior rush of wind, he remembers a voice out of the Lord's own dark night of the soul. Had not Jesus, in His great high-priestly prayer, spoken to these very fears directly? Speaking of His Apostles, had not the Savior said: **"I do not pray for these only, but also for those who believe in me through their word, that**

they may all be one; even as thou, Father, art in me, and I in thee, that they also may be in us, so that the world may believe that thou hast sent me. . . . I in them and thou in me, that they may become perfectly one, so that the world may know that thou hast sent me and hast loved them even as thou hast loved me" (Jn 17:20–21, 23).

So that *the world* may know! For the sake of the lost world, Christ has prayed that His true Church would become ever more perfectly one. And *visibly* one—with a unity even unbelievers would be able to see! Irenaeus' heart leaps. Praise God, the Lord had *foreseen* this nightmare of his! Jesus had *known* what the Gnostics would attempt and had struggled against it in spiritual warfare! He prayed (as had Ignatius of Antioch) for "one prayer, one supplication, one mind, one hope, one temple and one altar". . . *so that the world may know!*

And could the prayer of Christ go unanswered? Irenaeus catches his breath again. If the Father has promised to hear even miserable sinners like himself, how much more must He be willing to give His only Son anything and everything He asks?

Night falls—perhaps as dark as Irenaeus feared. But now the young presbyter has joined Pothinus within; he and the bishop together, hearts uplifted in an ecstasy of thanksgiving.

Mission of Mercy

The remote mission we have just visited in semi-barbaric Gallia was the first Christian church in a country we now refer to as *France*—and Irenaeus of Smyrna has become known to history as Irenaeus of Lyons (Lyons being the modern name for the ancient military colony of Lugdunum). The people living there at that time did not speak French—a language that did not exist in the second century A.D. and would be, when it did come, an altered form of the Latin spoken by their Roman conquerors. No, these people were the *Celts*, and their language (the speech Irenaeus learned in order to minister to them) was Gaulic—or *Gaelic*, as it is known today where it still lingers, among the Irish and in the isolated Hebrides of Scotland. Historians tell us that the Church there among the Celts was definitely founded by missionaries from Asia Minor. A brisk trade flourished at that time between Smyrna and Marseilles, and Christian emissaries from the east probably hitched a ride on one of these commercial vessels, sailing the whole length of the Mediterranean before progressing up the Rhone to settle at Lugdunum. The future city of Lyons was situated at the very crossroads of ancient France, on the main highway junction of the nation and at a great inland port on the river route north to Colonia Agrippina. It was, therefore, the perfect hub from which to begin the centuries-long process of evangelizing pagan Gaul.

The year of our brief visit to Lyons was A.D. 155 or 156, the year of the martyrdom of Polycarp. Antoninus Pius was still on the throne of the Caesars, and Justin of Neapolis had recently sent the *First Apology* for his consideration. And it seems to have been Polycarp himself who conceived this mission to Gallia and who selected one of his own presbyters from Smyrna, Pothinus, as its first bishop. Among the younger men who likely accompanied Pothinus on this trek into the "wild west" was Irenaeus, who would have been at this time about twenty-five years of age. Of

Irenaeus' background in Asia very little is known. His name is a Latinization of a Greek word meaning "peacemaker" —from which we might guess that though he was born in Greek-speaking Asia, Irenaeus' parents were Latin émigrés, possibly Christians who gave him a name with a Christian meaning. At any rate, Irenaeus himself tells us that he sat under the preaching of Polycarp from an early age. Among the peers who sat with him were Attalus of Pergamum (whom we met briefly in the streets of Lyons) and a dashing young scholar named Florinus, from whom many expected great things in the Church.

With the death of Antoninus in 161 began the persecution that was to claim, along with so many others, the life of Justin Martyr. But in distant Celtica (as Gaul was also known at that time) there was little impact at first. In fact, the years following the martyrdom of Polycarp (leading up to about A.D. 177) seem to have been something of a golden age in Irenaeus' church. The harvest of converts was plentiful, and Pothinus began sending church planters from Lyons into every part of the country. Yet most striking of all to modern readers is the abundance of *miraculous gifts* that still flourished in the Church in those days—especially in missionary lands. We have not focused on this phenomenon thus far, but the early Church apparently retained for many decades the signs and wonders that had so characterized the Pentecostal outpouring of apostolic times.

Jesus Himself, of course, had prophesied these gifts: **"And these signs shall follow them that believe; In my name shall they cast out devils; they shall speak with new tongues; They shall take up serpents; and if they drink any deadly thing, it shall not hurt them; they shall lay hands on the**

sick, and they shall recover" (Mk 16:17–18 KJV). The Apostle Paul recorded even more varieties of gifts in his day: **"To one is given through the Spirit the utterance of wisdom, and to another the utterance of knowledge according to the same Spirit, to another faith by the same Spirit, to another gifts of healing by the one Spirit, to another the working of miracles, to another prophecy, to another the ability to distinguish between spirits, to another various kinds of tongues, to another the interpretation of tongues"** (1 Cor 12:8–10). And while their occurrence does seem to have gradually lessened with time (without ever disappearing completely) there is ample evidence in the writings of our four witnesses that they knew these *charisms* well and had seen them in operation in their churches. Clement, in his letter to Corinth, speaks admiringly about gifts of discernment and the word of knowledge, and Justin states plainly that **"the prophetical gifts remain with us, even to the present time."**[9] When debating with Trypho the Jew, Justin had used the existence of these gifts as a proof of the power of the gospel: **"Daily, some [of you] are becoming disciples in the name of Christ, and quitting the path of error; who are also receiving gifts, each as he is worthy, illumined through the name of this Christ. For one receives the spirit of understanding, another of counsel, another of strength, another of healing, another of foreknowledge, another of teaching, another of the fear of God."**[10]

---

[9] Justin Martyr, *Dialogue with Trypho, a Jew*, chap. 82, trans. Alexander Roberts and James Donaldson, in ANF 1:240.

[10] Ibid.

Irenaeus himself seems to have witnessed the most striking of these signs:

> **Those who are in truth His disciples, receiving grace from Him, do in His name perform [miracles], so as to promote the welfare of other men, according to the gift which each one has received from Him. For some do certainly and truly drive out devils, so that those who have thus been cleansed from evil spirits frequently both believe [in Christ], and join themselves to the Church. Others have foreknowledge of things to come: they see visions, and utter prophetic expressions. Others still, heal the sick by laying their hands upon them, and they are made whole. Yea, moreover, . . . the dead even have been raised up, and remained among us for many years.**[11]

This last astounding gift Irenaeus uses as another illustration of the mighty contrast between the true Church and the disciples of Simon Magus:

> **So far are they from being able to raise the dead, as the Lord raised them, and the apostles did by means of prayer, and as has been frequently done in the brotherhood on account of some necessity—the entire Church in that particular locality entreating . . . with much fasting and prayer, the spirit of the dead man has returned, and he has been bestowed in answer to the prayers of the saints—that they do not even believe this can possibly be done, [and hold] that the resurrection of the**

[11] Irenaeus of Lyons, *Against Heresies*, bk. 2, chap. 32, no. 4, trans. Alexander Roberts and James Donaldson, in ANF 1:409.

dead is simply an acquaintance with that truth which they proclaim.[12]

The fact that Irenaeus was so firmly convinced of these miracles, and so open to their continued place in the Church, made him an ideal candidate for a certain *mission of mercy;* and it was this mission (which took place in the latter half of A.D. 177) that first wrote his name upon the page of history.

Earlier that same year, Marcus Aurelius' persecution finally reached Gallia. It began slowly, but already some of Irenaeus' fellow Christians had been imprisoned and the Church was forced to begin meeting in secret. But worse by far than this external assault was another internal division among the brethren. As in the days of Clement, storms without became the prelude to trouble within—though this time (quite unlike the trouble at Corinth) it was not so easy to determine who was at fault. Eusebius records it this way: **"It was at that very time, in Phrygia, that Montanus, Alcibiades, Theodotus, and their followers began to acquire a widespread reputation for prophecy; for numerous other manifestations of the miraculous gift of God, still occurring in various churches, led many to believe that these men too were prophets."**[13] Who were these Phrygians and what were they up to? Eusebius includes the testimony of a churchman named Apolinarius; an eyewitness (but not, as will be seen, a very unbiased one):

There is, it appears, a village near the Phrygian border of Mysia called Ardabau. There it is said that a recent

[12] Ibid., chap. 31, no. 2, in ANF 1:407.

[13] Eusebius Pamphilus, *History of the Church*, bk. 5, chap. 3, in EHC 150.

convert named Montanus, while Gratus was proconsul of Syria, in his unbridled ambition to reach the top laid himself open to the adversary, was filled with spiritual excitement and suddenly fell into a kind of trance and unnatural ecstasy. He raved, and began to chatter and talk nonsense, prophesying in a way that conflicted with the practice of the Church handed down generation by generation from the beginning. Of those who listened at that time to his sham utterances some were annoyed, regarding him as possessed, a demoniac in the grip of a spirit of error, a disturber of the masses. They rebuked him and tried to stop his chatter, remembering the distinction drawn by the Lord, and His warning to guard vigilantly against the coming of false prophets. Others were elated as if by the Holy Spirit or a prophetic gift, were filled with conceit, and forgot the Lord's distinction. They welcomed a spirit that injured and deluded the mind and led the people astray: they were beguiled and deceived by it, so that it could not now be reduced to silence.[14]

How familiar this account sounds to those of us—on either side of the question—who lived through the upheavals that accompanied the advent of the charismatic movement in the 1970s! Then, as in the days of Irenaeus, even Christians who may have been open to the idea of miracles in the Church remained suspicious of abuses and spiritual counterfeits. And since, of course, the Apostles warned us that there really are such counterfeits, finding exactly the right

[14] Ibid., chap. 16, in EHC 161. (Here Eusebius is quoting one of the writers associated with Apolinarius.)

response to these new phenomena was as great a problem in the twentieth century as it had been, apparently, in the second. Clearly, then, with half the faithful embracing these manifestations as the work of the Spirit and the other half attributing them to demonic forces, the danger of division in the Church of Gaul was immediate—and the situation seemed to call for decisive action.

Continuing to speak about these "Montanists" (as they came to be called) Eusebius has these words:

> **When there was a difference of opinion about them, the Gallic Christians again submitted their own careful and most orthodox conclusions on the question, attaching various letters from the martyrs fulfilled in their midst —letters penned while they were still in prison to their brothers in Asia and Phrygia, and also to Eleutherus [Eleutherius], then Bishop of Rome, in an effort to ensure peace in the churches. The same martyrs commended Irenaeus, already a presbyter in the Lyons diocese, to the Bishop of Rome just mentioned, paying warm tribute to his character, as is clear from their words: "Greeting once more, Father Eleutherus:[15] may**

[15] The title "Father" used here is the Greek word *papas*, from which we derive both our familiar family term "papa" and the ecclesiastical designation of "pope". And though Eleutherius was indeed the bishop of Rome, the word had not yet, at this early date, been restricted to that use only; it was often applied (up until about the fifth century) to any bishop of the Catholic Church. As for the use of "father" itself, in apparent contradiction of Matthew 23:9 (**"call no man your father on earth"**), we can only say that the early Church, as evidenced in her writings, did not interpret this command literally. The use of "father", as a title of respect to elders in the Lord, appears early on and often in the writings of the Church; in-

God bless you always. We are entrusting this letter to our brother and companion Irenaeus to convey to you. We are anxious that you should hold him in high regard, as a man devoted to the covenant of Christ. For if we had thought that position conferred righteousness on anyone, we should have recommended him first as a presbyter of the Church, which indeed he is."[16]

Irenaeus' mission, then, was to travel five hundred miles across Europe, taking to the bishop of Rome a letter (probably from Pothinus and the other senior pastors in Gaul) describing the situation and asking for his input. Clement, after all, who had occupied this same prestigious office eighty years earlier, had been able to use that prestige to intervene successfully for peace at Corinth under similar circumstances. Eleutherius, his successor, might do the same in the current crisis. What were these "careful and most orthodox conclusions" Irenaeus carried? Eusebius himself does not tell us, but a close study of the life of Eleutherius and of other key figures in the controversy seems to give the answer. It appears that though the elders of Gaul were highly concerned about the strange Montanist manifestations (which included a practice of prophesying in the first

---

deed, there is evidence that the word was used in this way even in apostolic times. Paul, for example (in 1 Cor 4:15), speaks of himself as the "father" of the Corinthian church, and also (in 1 Tim 1:2, 18) as being Timothy's father in Christ. Likewise, the martyr Stephen (under, we are told, the direct inspiration of the Holy Ghost) calls even the corrupt elders of the Pharisees his "fathers" (Acts 7:2). It appears, then, that the early Christians understood Matthew 23:9 to be another instance in which our Lord employed powerful Hebrew hyperbole—akin to His similar directive in Luke 14:26, that a Christian must **"hate his own father and mother"**.

[16] Eusebius, *Church History*, bk. 5, chaps. 3–4, in EHC 150.

person, saying "I am the Father, the Word, and the Paraclete" as if possessed by God), they were not inclined to take harsh action against them. Irenaeus' letter seems to have counseled a "wait and see" approach; for that, we believe, was Eleutherius' own initial recommendation.[17] The truth would out, surely, and the true character of the new movement would doubtless be revealed in time by the quality of its fruit. So far, the Montanists had espoused no false doctrines, and the recommendation from Lyons was apparently to maintain them in the unity of the Church up until such time as they did. Irenaeus' own cautious attitude is perhaps revealed in later comments he made about some extreme anti-Montanists he had seen in the churches: **"Wishing to have no false prophets . . . , they drive away the grace of prophecy from the Church; resembling persons who, in order to avoid those who come in hypocrisy, withdraw from communion even with brethren."**[18]

Irenaeus did undertake this mission of peace and unity, and he completed it successfully. And this was no small accomplishment, involving, as it did, a passage through enemy lines—for the fierce wars that so plagued the last days of Marcus Aurelius were then in full tilt. Irenaeus appears to have wintered with the brethren at Rome, enjoying their world-famous faith and hospitality, before setting out for home in the spring of 178, bringing with him the word

---

[17] Tertullian says that the bishop of Rome was inclined at first to approve of the new prophecies but was eventually dissuaded by his advisors.

[18] Irenaeus of Lyons, *Against Heresies*, bk. 3, chap. 11, no. 9, quoted by John Chapman, in *The Catholic Encyclopedia*, Volume X (Robert Appleton Company, 1911), www.newadvent.org/cathen/10521a.htm (Kevin Knight, 1999).

of reconciliation from Eleutherius. With the matter of the Montanists thus settled for the moment, our Gallican presbyter (now in his mid-forties) felt that he might at last be able to return to his true calling: that of evangelism and the conversion of the West.

We have no record of what adventures Irenaeus may have encountered on the long road back to ancient France, but he undertook them all with good cheer, little dreaming what he would find when he got there.

Bishop Irenaeus

Beginning on August 8, 177, while Irenaeus was absent in Italy, the church of Lyons had been decimated by what was probably the worst wave of persecution to hit any church since Nero's great tribulation at Rome.

Irenaeus received the terrible news upon his return: he was perhaps the only member of the Lugdunum clergy left alive. Bishop Pothinus, at ninety years of age, had followed in the footsteps of Polycarp. He had been taken by a mob, beaten half to death by soldiers, and flung at last into a rancid cell, where—cheating the lions—he died of his injuries. Likewise, Irenaeus' dear co-worker from Pergamum had been led around the amphitheater with a sign pinned to his chest, saying, "This is Attalus the Christian"—before being tortured to death. In all, forty-eight such martyrs had gone to God in one two-week period. Being, then, the most senior man remaining in the entire mission, Irenaeus of Smyrna was immediately ordained as Pothinus' successor and became the second bishop of Lyons.

As such, it is thought that Irenaeus himself composed the

famous letter—included in Eusebius—that has preserved the details of this great trial for the ages. His first official act as bishop, after compiling all the various eyewitness reports, was to send out this heartbreaking history; addressed, as it is, from

The servants of Christ at Vienne and Lyons, in Gaul to our brothers in Asia and Phrygia who have the same faith and hope of redemption as we: peace, grace, and glory from God the Father and Christ Jesus our Lord. . . .

The severity of our trials here, the unbridled fury of the heathen against God's people, the untold sufferings of the blessed martyrs, we are incapable of describing in detail: indeed, no pen could do them justice. The adversary swooped on us with all his might, giving us now a foretaste of his advent, which undoubtedly is imminent. . . . But against [him] the grace of God put itself at our head, rescuing the weak and deploying against our enemies unshakable pillars, able by their endurance to draw upon themselves the whole onslaught of the evil one. These charged into the fight, standing up to every kind of abuse and punishment, and made light of their heavy load as they hastened to Christ, proving beyond a doubt that the sufferings of this present time are not to be compared with the glory that is in store for us.

To begin with, they heroically endured whatever the surging crowd heaped on them, noisy abuse, blows, dragging along the ground, plundering, stoning, imprisonment, and everything that an infuriated mob normally does to hated enemies. . . . [At the trial] it was clear that some were ready to be the first Gallic martyrs: they made

a full confession of their testimony with the greatest eagerness. It was equally clear that others were not ready, that they had not trained and were still flabby, in no fit condition to face the strain of a struggle to the death. Of these, some ten proved stillborn, causing us great distress and inexpressible grief, and damping the enthusiasm of those not yet arrested. . . . But the arrests went on and on, and day after day those who were worthy filled up the number of the martyrs, so that from the two dioceses were collected all the active members who had done the most to build up our church life. . . .

The whole fury of the crowd, governor, and soldiers fell with crushing force on Sanctus, the deacon from Vienne; on Maturus, very recently baptized but heroic in facing his ordeal; on Attalus, who had always been a pillar and support of the church in his native Pergamum; and on Blandina, through whom Christ proved that things which men regard as mean, unlovely, and contemptible are by God deemed worthy of great glory, because of her love for Him shown in power and not vaunted in appearance. When we were all afraid, and her earthly mistress (who was herself facing the ordeal of martyrdom) was in agony lest she should be unable to make a bold confession of Christ because of bodily weakness, Blandina was filled with such power that those who took it in turns to subject her to every kind of torture from morning to night were exhausted by their efforts and confessed themselves beaten — they could think of nothing else to do to her. They were amazed that she was still breathing, for her whole body was mangled and her wounds gaped; they declared that torment of any one kind was enough to part soul and body, let alone a succession of torments of such extreme severity. But the blessed woman, wrestling magnificently, grew in strength as she proclaimed her faith, and found refreshment, rest, and insensibility to her sufferings in uttering the words: "I am a Christian: we do nothing to be ashamed of."

Sanctus was another who with magnificent, superhuman courage nobly withstood the entire range of human cruelty. Wicked people hoped that the persistence and severity of his tortures would force him to utter something improper, but with such determination did he stand up to their onslaughts that he would not tell them his own name, race, and birthplace, or whether he was slave or free; to every question he replied in Latin: "I am a Christian." This he proclaimed over and over again, instead of name, birthplace, nationality, and everything else, and not another word did the heathen hear from him. . . .

Then occurred a great dispensation of God, and the infinite mercy of Jesus was revealed to a degree rarely known in the brotherhood of Christians, but not beyond the skill of Christ. Those who when the first arrests took place had denied Him were gaoled with the others and shared their sufferings: on this occasion they gained nothing by their denial, for whereas those who declared that they were gaoled as Christians, no other charge being brought against them, the others were further detained as foul murderers and punished twice as much as the rest. For the faithful were relieved of half their burden by the joy of martyrdom and hope of the promises, and by love towards Christ and the Spirit of the Father, but the unfaithful were tormented by their conscience, so that as they passed they could easily be picked out from the rest by the look on their faces. The faithful stepped out with a happy smile, wondrous glory and grace blended on their faces, so that even their fetters hung like beautiful ornaments around them and they resembled a bride adorned with golden lace elaborately wrought, they were perfumed also with the sweet savour of Christ, so that some people thought they had smeared themselves with worldly cosmetics. The unfaithful were dejected, downcast, ill-favoured, and devoid of charm; in addition they were jibed at by the heathen as contemptible cowards; they were accused of homicide, and had lost the honourable, glorious, life-giving name. The sight of this stiffened the resistance of the rest: those who were arrested unhesitatingly declared their faith without one thought for the devil's promptings.

From that time on, their martyrdoms embraced death in all its forms. . . . Maturus and Sanctus were again taken through the whole series of punishments, as if they had suffered nothing at all before, or rather as if they had defeated their opponents in bout after bout and were now battling for the victor's crown. Again they ran the gauntlet of whips, in accordance with local custom; they were mauled by the beasts, and endured every torment that the frenzied mob on one side or the other demanded and howled for, culminating in the iron chair which roasted their flesh and suffocated them with the reek. Not even then were their tormentors satisfied: they grew more and more frenzied in their desire to overwhelm the resistance of the martyrs, but do what they might they heard nothing from Sanctus beyond the words he had repeated from the beginning—the declaration of his faith.

In these two, despite their prolonged and terrible ordeal, life still lingered; but in the end they were sacrificed, after being made all day long a spectacle to the world. . . .

To crown all this, on the last day of the sports Blandina was again brought in, and with her Ponticus, a lad of about fifteen. Day after day they had been taken in to watch the rest being punished, and attempts were made to make them swear by the heathen idols. When they stood firm and treated these efforts with contempt, the mob was infuriated with them, so that the boy's tender age called forth no pity and the woman no respect. They subjected them to every horror and inflicted every punishment in turn, attempting again and again to make them swear, but to no purpose. Ponticus was encouraged by his sister in Christ, so that the heathen saw that she was urging him on and stiffening his resistance, and he bravely endured every punishment till he gave back his spirit to God. Last of all, like a noble mother who had encouraged her children and sent them before her in triumph to the King, blessed Blandina herself passed through all the ordeals of her children and hastened to rejoin them, rejoicing and exulting at her departure as if invited to a wedding supper, not thrown to the beasts.[19]

[19] Eusebius, *History of the Church*, bk. 5, chap. 1, in EHC 139–41, 143–47.

Bishop Irenaeus carefully recorded all these things—and it must have been a terrible ordeal for him; the document has a horrible clarity of detail and was drawn up with the fastidiousness of a court reporter. There must have been interviews with the survivors and with the family and friends of those who had not survived. Perhaps our bishop put it all down so carefully as a sort of self-imposed penance, to punish himself (though it certainly was not his own fault) for having been, once again, safely elsewhere when the axe fell. Proud as he was, like Justin, of his brave, holy little flock, Irenaeus must also, like Theophorus, have felt something wanting in his own discipleship for him to have been denied once more the privilege of bearing witness unto death.

Nevertheless, Irenaeus of Lyons had been reborn in the ordeal. Though he would certainly have denied it, his own tortures had been as genuine as those of his departed companions—just as Mary of Nazareth, in watching her Son die on the Cross, found, in fulfillment of prophecy, that a sword had pierced her own soul, too (cf. Lk 2:35). And Irenaeus found himself shepherding a church now purged and purified as well, washed white as snow in the blood of her martyrs. The new bishop grimly vowed, with the Lord's help, to keep her that way—alive, unified, vigorous, holy—for the sake of that future day when, in God's good time, the pagans would come back to the church at Lyons, and come back to bless rather than to curse.

Until then he would cherish the blessed thought (so memorably phrased by Tertullian) that strengthened all suffering believers during those dark days: **"Crucify us, torture us, condemn us, destroy us! . . . The more we are hewn down**

by you, the more numerous do we become. The blood of martyrs is the seed of Christians!"[20]

A Means of Defense

Satan failed spectacularly at Gaul, failed in one of his greatest attempts to overthrow the Church by terror and intimidation. And this, according to Eusebius, brought about a new era in Church history:

> **Like dazzling lights the churches were now shining all over the world, and to the limits of the human race faith in our Saviour and Lord Jesus Christ was at its peak, when the demon who hates the good, sworn enemy of truth and inveterate foe of man's salvation, turned all his weapons against the Church. In earlier days he had attacked her with persecutions from without; but now that he was debarred from this, he resorted to unscrupulous impostors as instruments of spiritual corruption and ministers of destruction, and employed new tactics, contriving by every possible means that impostors and cheats, by cloaking themselves with the same name as our religion, should at one and the same time bring to the abyss of destruction every believer they could entrap, and by their own actions and endeavours turn those ignorant of the Faith away from the path that leads to the message of salvation. . . .**
>
> **Consequently, while a great number of churchmen were busy at the time fighting for the truth and elo-**

---

[20] Tertullian, *Apology*, chap. 50, nos. 12–13, in FEF 1:117, no. 285.

quently championing the beliefs of the apostles and the Church, some also set down on paper for the benefit of later generations the means of defence against these very heresies. . . .

Hegesippus we have met already. There was also Bishop Dionysius of Corinth and Bishop Pinytus of Crete, as well as Philip, Apolinarius, Melito, Musanus, Modestus, and above all Irenaeus.[21] In every case writings which show their orthodoxy and unshakable devotion to the apostolic tradition have come into my hands.[22]

Beginning shortly after his ordination as bishop, Irenaeus of Lyons began to compose the monumental work for which he is most remembered. Its formal title is *The Refutation and Overthrow of the Gnosis Falsely So-called*, but it is generally known today by the less formidable title *Against Heresies*. It consists of five books, written in Greek, the composition of which occupied most of the remainder of his life. The original object of this undertaking was to refute one heresy only—that of Valentinianism, another Gnostic

---

[21] Hegesippus was the traveler who gave us the welcome report about Clement's effect at Corinth; he is sometimes known as "the father of Church history" even though his priceless works have perished. Dionysius of Corinth seems to have been a great Scripture scholar in the latter half of the second century, and Philip of Gortyna composed a treatise against Marcionism. Apolinarius was the writer already quoted by Eusebius in opposition to Montanism. Melito of Sardis was a philosophical writer who, like Justin, sent an apology to Marcus Aurelius. Pinytus of Crete, Musanus, and Modestus are known chiefly from their names on this list.

[22] Eusebius, *History of the Church*, bk. 4, chaps. 7 and 21, in EHC 108, 128.

offshoot (founded by Valentine of Egypt) that had much in common with Docetism. Irenaeus tells us that though errors such as this had troubled the Christian East since the days of Ignatius, it was during his own bishopric in Gaul that they began to penetrate the newly evangelized West as well. Yet as the writing of this original book continued, Satan's work continued also. A second book soon became necessary, then a third, and finally Irenaeus found himself exposing and disproving practically the entire range of multiform Gnostic heresy.

Some modern writers have attempted to portray Gnosticism as a religion almost completely distinct from Christianity, running separately from it on a parallel course and drawing most of its converts directly from paganism. This hypothesis does not fit the facts or the tone of the times. Irenaeus and all those working with him write as *shepherds protecting their flocks*, and it is quite clear that the danger to the flocks had to be real and immediate. Probably Irenaeus himself had witnessed many distressing losses to the various Gnostic sects. It was his compassion, then, that moved him to this new task—a task that was not perhaps entirely congenial to him by nature. One contemporary writer tells us that Irenaeus' first love was always evangelism, and his chief characteristic a zeal for the conversion of the lost. But his love for the little lambs remained after their conversion as well, and it was this kind of love—rather than any natural appetite for debate—that led Irenaeus to immerse himself, for their sakes, in a detailed analysis of the enemy and his strategies.

In the preface to books 1 and 3, he gives in his own words his reasons for taking up the pen:

Lest, therefore, through my neglect, some should be carried off, even as sheep are by wolves, while they perceive not the true character of these men, —because they outwardly are covered with sheep's clothing (against whom the Lord has enjoined us to be on our guard), and because their language resembles ours, while their sentiments are very different, —I have deemed it my duty (after reading some of the *Commentaries*, as they call them, of the disciples of Valentinus, and after making myself acquainted with their tenets through personal intercourse with some of them) to unfold to thee, my friend, these portentous and profound mysteries. . . . Showing that they spring from Simon, the father of all heretics . . . [I intend] to exhibit both their doctrines and successions, and to set forth arguments against them all . . . [so that you may] receive from me the means of combating and vanquishing those who, in whatever manner, are propagating falsehood . . . and faithfully and strenuously . . . resist them in defence of the only true and life-giving faith, which the Church has received from the apostles and imparted to her sons. For the Lord of all gave to His apostles the power of the Gospel, through whom also we have known the truth, that is, the doctrine of the Son of God; to whom also did the Lord declare: "He that heareth you, heareth Me; and he that despiseth you, despiseth Me, and Him that sent Me" [Lk 10:16].[23]

---

[23] Irenaeus, *Against Heresies*, bk. 1, prologue, no. 2; bk. 3, prologue, in ANF 1:315, 414.

Even the most cursory examination of Irenaeus' first two volumes makes it clear that, in one sense, his dark forebodings after the loss of Polycarp had come true in spades. Already, not 150 years from the day of Pentecost, there were dozens of tiny independent denominations at work, all operating on a free-lance basis, all differing (on one point or another) both from the *Katholikē Ekklēsia* and from the other schismatic groups as well. Some of them were strange and extravagant, with theologies that sound more like Greek mythology than any kind of Christianity. Others were less so, having quarreled with the apostolic Church mainly on disciplinary rather than doctrinal grounds. But they all had at least two things in common. First, they all shared the old antipathy to physical reality: their Christ was always a ghost, their Church a voluntary association of cognoscenti, their salvation a familiarity with the "true" theology. And secondly, they were all quite content to go about their business (despite Ignatius' famous warnings) entirely without the bishop, presbyters, and deacons—and let God sort it out.

To what then did they appeal when offering their various "insights"? *To Scripture always* . . . though always to Scripture "properly understood", of course. Yet **"since they differ so widely among themselves both as respects doctrine and tradition,"** complains Irenaeus, **"and since those of them who are recognised as being most modern make it their effort daily to invent some new opinion, and to bring out what no one ever before thought of, it is a difficult matter to describe all their opinions. . . ."**[24] As he said earlier,

[24] Ibid., bk. 1, chap. 21, no. 5, in ANF 1:347.

"There are as many schemes of 'redemption' as there are teachers. . . ."[25] He attributes this to **"the fact that numbers of them—indeed, we may say all—desire themselves to be teachers, and to break off from the particular heresy in which they have been involved. Forming one set of doctrines out of a totally different system of opinions, and then again others from others, they insist upon teaching something new, declaring themselves the inventors of any sort of opinion which they may have been able to call into existence."**[26]

Had Irenaeus' worst fears come to pass, then, in spite of everything? Had Christ's prayer for unity come to nothing after all?

Irenaeus would demonstrate otherwise. First, he takes the remainder of books 1 and 2 to catalogue carefully all these multitudinous opinions, along with their alleged "scriptural" footings. Then, beginning in earnest with book 3, he starts to refute them—using Scripture himself, it is true—but with something *more* also. Were he to add merely one more private interpretation into the mix, Irenaeus knows that he would accomplish nothing. He would be playing the same pointless word game with which the Gnostics had been entertaining themselves. Our bishop understands all too well that even the most sincere Scripture student needs some way, at the end of the day, to know that his interpretation—careful, prayerful as it may be—is, in fact, *God's interpretation*. Without that, it is back to square one, and the wolf goes back on the prowl.

---

[25] Ibid., no. 1, in ANF 1:345.

[26] Ibid., chap. 28, in ANF 1:353.

What is this "something more" that Irenaeus brings?

It is a simple gift; a gift handed down to the Church Catholic—and to her *alone*—by the Lord Jesus Himself. It is, in fact, the self-same *something more* that distinguished His own teaching from that of the self-proclaimed "Scripture experts" He encountered: **"And when Jesus finished these sayings, the crowds were astonished at his teaching, for he taught them as one who had authority, and not as their scribes"** (Mt 7:29).

The Certain Gift of Truth

"We have judged it well to point out, first of all, in what respects the very fathers of this fable differ among themselves, as if they were inspired by different spirits of error. For this very fact forms an *a priori* proof that the truth proclaimed by the Church is immoveable, and that the theories of these men are but a tissue of falsehoods."[27] Right at the outset Irenaeus offers a stunning and well-nigh unanswerable argument. The Gnostics can agree on only one thing: that the apostolic Church had gotten it wrong. Irenaeus' people, on the other hand, having agreed that the Church is apostolic, now *agree on everything else*.

> **As many as they are, [the Gnostics] all depart [from each other], holding so many opinions as to one thing, and bearing about their clever notions in secret within themselves. . . . In the meanwhile, however, [they] convict themselves, since they are not of one mind with regard to the same words. But as we follow for our teacher**

[27] Ibid., chap. 9, no. 5, in ANF 1:330.

> **the one and only true God, and possess His words as the rule of truth, we do all speak alike with regard to the same things.**[28]

Here, Irenaeus is echoing the command of the Apostle Paul, who said to the Corinthians, **"I beseech you, brethren, by the name of our Lord Jesus Christ, that ye all speak the same thing, and that there be no divisions among you; but that ye be perfectly joined together in the same mind and in the same judgment"** (1 Cor 1:10, KJV). And was not Paul himself echoing Christ's great prayer here, "that they all may become perfectly one"? But is such a thing really possible? Can any society made up of fallen men ever even dream to attain so perfect a unanimity?

Irenaeus not only affirms that it can, but asserts, as a historical fact, that one in particular has actually done so:

> **The Church, having received this preaching and this faith, although scattered throughout the whole world, yet, as if occupying but one house, carefully preserves it. She also believes these points [of doctrine] just as if she had but one soul, and one and the same heart, and she proclaims them, and teaches them, and hands them down, with perfect harmony, as if she possessed only one mouth. For, although the languages of the world are dissimilar, yet the import of the tradition is one and the same. For the Churches which have been planted in Germany do not believe or hand down anything different, nor do those in Spain, nor those in Gaul, nor those in the East, nor those in Egypt, nor those in Libya, nor**

[28] Ibid., bk. 4, chap. 35, no. 4, in ANF 1:514.

those which have been established in the central regions of the world. But as the sun, that creature of God, is one and the same throughout the whole world, so also the preaching of the truth shineth everywhere, and enlightens all men that are willing to come to a knowledge of the truth.[29]

How has this incredible unity been achieved? *By clinging rigidly to the principle of discipleship*—Christ's own pattern for the Church. As Jesus passed down His authority to speak for God to the disciples he made, so had they, in turn, passed this authority down to their own successors.

Polycarp [for example] was not only instructed by apostles, and conversed with many who had seen Christ, but was also, by apostles in Asia, appointed bishop of the Church in Smyrna, whom I also saw in my early youth, for he tarried [on earth] a very long time, and, when a very old man, gloriously and most nobly suffering martyrdom, departed this life, having always taught the things which he had learned from the apostles, and which the Church has handed down, and which alone are true. To these things all the Asiatic Churches testify, as do also those men who have succeeded Polycarp down to the present time,—a man who was of much greater weight, and a more stedfast witness of truth, than Valentinus, and Marcion, and the rest of the heretics. He it was who, coming to Rome in the time of Anicetus caused many to turn away from the aforesaid heretics to the Church of God, proclaiming that he had

[29] Ibid., bk. 1, chap. 10, no. 2, in ANF 1:331; [brackets in original].

> received this one and sole truth from the apostles,—that, namely, which is handed down by the Church. . . . Since therefore we have such proofs, it is not necessary to seek the truth among others which it is easy to obtain from the Church; since the apostles, like a rich man [depositing his money] in a bank, lodged in her hands most copiously all things pertaining to the truth: so that every man, whosoever will, can draw from her the water of life. For she is the entrance to life; all others are thieves and robbers.[30]

Yet each individual Gnostic proposed to correct the Catholic Church, as he saw fit, by means of the Scriptures, setting the apostolic books against the apostolic disciples. Irenaeus saw the absurdity of this plainly:

> In this way no one will possess the rule of truth; but in accordance with the number of persons who explain the parables will be found the various systems of truth, in mutual opposition to each other, and setting forth antagonistic doctrines, like the questions current among the Gentile philosophers. According to this course of procedure, therefore, man would always be inquiring but never finding, because he has rejected the very method of discovery. . . . For how stands the case? Suppose there arise a dispute relative to some important question among us, should we not have recourse to the most ancient Churches with which the apostles held constant intercourse, and learn from them what is cer-

[30] Ibid., bk. 4, chap. 3, no. 4; chap. 4, no. 1, in ANF 1:416; [final brackets in original].

tain and clear in regard to the present question? For how should it be if the apostles themselves had not left us writings? Would it not be necessary, [in that case,] to follow the course of the tradition which they handed down to those to whom they did commit the Churches?[31]

Speaking from his missionary experience, Irenaeus *knew* this principle was sound, for he had seen it in action:

Those barbarians who believe in Christ do assent [to the faith], having salvation written in their hearts by the Spirit, without paper or ink, and carefully preserve the ancient tradition. . . . Those who, in the absence of written documents, have believed this faith, are barbarians, so far as regards our language; but as regards doctrine, manner, and tenor of life, they are, because of faith, very wise indeed; and they do please God, ordering their conversation in all righteousness, chastity, and wisdom. If any one were to preach to these men the inventions of the heretics, speaking to them in their own language, they would at once stop their ears, and flee as far off as possible, not enduring even to listen to the blasphemous address. Thus, by means of that ancient tradition of the apostles, they do not suffer their mind to conceive anything of the [doctrines suggested by the] portentous language of these teachers, among whom neither Church nor doctrine has ever been established.[32]

---

[31] Ibid., bk. 2, chap. 27, nos. 1–2; bk. 3, chap. 4, no. 1, in ANF 1:398, 417.

[32] Ibid., bk. 3, chap. 4, no. 2, in ANF 1:417; [final brackets in original].

Since, therefore, the tradition from the apostles does thus exist in the Church, and is permanent among us, let us revert to the Scriptural proof furnished by those apostles who did also write the Gospel, in which they recorded the doctrine regarding God, pointing out that our Lord Jesus Christ is the truth, and that no lie is in Him. As also David says, prophesying His birth from a virgin, and the resurrection from the dead, "Truth has sprung out of the earth" [Ps 85:11]. The apostles, likewise, being disciples of the truth, are above all falsehood; for a lie has no fellowship with the truth, just as darkness has none with light, but the presence of the one shuts out that of the other. . . . These men [on the other hand] are proved to be not disciples of the apostles, but of their own wicked notions. To this cause also are due the various opinions which exist among them, inasmuch as each one adopted error just as he was capable. But the Church throughout all the world, having its origin firm from the apostles, perseveres in one and the same opinion with regard to God and His Son.[33]

What then of the Gnostic claim that the Church, being mere flesh, is not really necessary—and that a man needs only the Holy Spirit to guide him through the Scriptures? Irenaeus answers thus:

This gift of God has been entrusted to the Church, as breath was to the first created man, for this purpose, that all the members receiving it may be vivified; and the [means of] communion with Christ has been distributed

[33] Ibid., chap. 5, no. 1; bk. 3, chap. 12, no. 7, in ANF 1:417, 433.

throughout it, that is, the Holy Spirit, the earnest of incorruption, the means of confirming our faith, and the ladder of ascent to God. "For in the Church," it is said, "God hath set apostles, prophets, teachers" [1 Cor 12:28], and all the other means through which the Spirit works; of which all those are not partakers who do not join themselves to the Church, but defraud themselves of life through their perverse opinions and infamous behaviour. For where the Church is, there is the Spirit of God; and where the Spirit of God is, there is the Church, and every kind of grace; but the Spirit is truth. Those, therefore, who do not partake of Him, are neither nourished into life from the mother's breasts, nor do they enjoy that most limpid fountain which issues from the body of Christ; but they dig for themselves broken cisterns out of earthly trenches. . . . Alienated thus from the truth, they do deservedly wallow in all error, tossed to and fro by it, thinking differently in regard to the same things at different times, and never attaining to a well-grounded knowledge, being more anxious to be sophists of words than disciples of the truth. For they have not been founded upon the one rock, but upon the sand, which has in itself a multitude of stones.[34]

Wherefore it is incumbent to obey the presbyters who are in the Church,—those who, as I have shown, possess the succession from the apostles; those who, together with the succession of the episcopate, have received the certain gift of truth, according to the good pleasure of the Father. But [it is also incumbent] to hold in suspi-

[34] Ibid., bk. 3, chap. 24, nos. 1–2, in ANF 1:458.

cion others who depart from the primitive succession, and assemble themselves together in any place whatsoever, [looking upon them] either as heretics of perverse minds, or as schismatics puffed up and self-pleasing, or again as hypocrites, acting thus for the sake of lucre and vainglory. For all these have fallen from the truth. . . . From all such persons, therefore, it behoves us to keep aloof, but to adhere to those who, as I have already observed, do hold the doctrine of the apostles, and who, together with the order of the priesthood . . . display sound speech and blameless conduct for the confirmation and correction of others. . . . Paul then, teaching us where one may find such, says, "God hath placed in the Church, first, apostles; secondly, prophets; thirdly, teachers." Where, therefore, the gifts of the Lord have been placed, there it behoves us to learn the truth, [namely,] from those who possess that succession of the Church which is from the apostles, and among whom exists that which is sound and blameless in conduct, as well as that which is unadulterated and incorrupt in speech. . . . They expound the Scriptures to us without danger, neither blaspheming God, nor dishonouring the patriarchs, nor despising the prophets. . . . Then shall every word also seem consistent to him, if he for his part diligently read the Scriptures in company with those who are presbyters in the Church, among whom is the apostolic doctrine, as I have pointed out. . . .[35]

---

[35] Ibid., bk. 4, chap. 26, nos. 2, 4, 5; chap. 32, no. 1, in ANF 1:497–98, 506.

Now all these [heretics] are of much later date than the bishops to whom the apostles committed the Churches. . . . It follows, then, as a matter of course, that these heretics aforementioned, since they are blind to the truth, and deviate from the [right] way, will walk in various roads; and therefore the footsteps of their doctrine are scattered here and there without agreement or connection. But the path of those belonging to the Church circumscribes the whole world, as possessing the sure tradition from the apostles, and gives unto us to see that the faith of all is one and the same, since all receive one and the same God the Father, and believe in the same dispensation regarding the incarnation of the Son of God, and are cognizant of the same gift of the Spirit, and are conversant with the same commandments, and preserve the same form of ecclesiastical constitution, and expect the same advent of the Lord, and await the same salvation of the complete man, that is, of the soul and body. And undoubtedly the preaching of the Church is true and stedfast, in which one and the same way of salvation is shown throughout the whole world. For to her is entrusted the light of God. . . . For the Church preaches the truth everywhere, and she is the seven-branched candlestick which bears the light of Christ.[36]

Irenaeus culminates his powerful argument against the abuse of Scripture by drawing an analogy from the book of *Genesis*:

---

[36] Ibid., bk. 5, chap. 20, no. 1, in ANF 1:547–48.

It behoves us, therefore . . . to flee to the Church, and be brought up in her bosom, and be nourished with the Lord's Scriptures. For the Church has been planted as a garden [*paradisus*] in this world; therefore says the Spirit of God, "Thou mayest freely eat from every tree of the garden" [Gen 2:16], **that is, Eat ye from every Scripture of the Lord; but ye shall not eat with an uplifted mind, nor touch any heretical discord. For these men do profess that they have themselves the knowledge of good and evil; and they set their own impious minds above the God who made them. . . . For this cause also the apostle says, "Be not wise beyond what it is fitting to be wise, but be wise prudently"** [Rom 12:3], **that we be not cast forth by eating of the "knowledge" [*gnosis*] of these men (that knowledge which knows more than it should do) from the paradise of life.**[37]

Writing just fifteen or so years later, Tertullian of Carthage memorably recapitulated this argument against private interpretation—showing both his debt to Irenaeus and also the permanent validity of his case. With these strong words, the early Church reveals her mind on this topic in the plainest possible fashion:

In order that we may be judged to have the truth—we who walk in the rule which the Churches have handed down from the Apostles, the Apostles from Christ, and Christ from God,—admit that the reasonableness of our position is clear, defining as it does that heretics ought not to be allowed to challenge [us by] an appeal to the

[37] Ibid., no. 2, in ANF 1:548.

Scriptures, since we, without using Scripture, prove that they have nothing to do with the Scriptures. If they are heretics, they cannot be Christians, because it is not from Christ that they have gotten what they pursue of their own choosing, and from which they incur the name heretic.[38]

Not being Christians, they have acquired no right to Christian literature; and it might be justly said to them, "Who are you? When and from where did you come? Since you are not of mine, what are you doing with what is mine? Indeed, Marcion, by what right do you chop in my forest? By whose permission, Valentine, do you divert my streams? By what authority, Apelles,[39] do you move my boundary markers? And the rest of you, why do you sow and graze here at your own pleasure? This is my property, which I have long possessed, which I possessed before you came, and for which I have a sure title from the very authors whose property it was. I am the heir of the Apostles. As they carefully prepared their will, as they committed it to a trust, and as they sealed it with an oath, so do I hold the inheritance. You, certainly, they always held as disinherited, and rejected you as strangers and enemies."[40]

"God's word read by God's people—but read in God's Church, God's way." This was the rule of life followed by the earliest

[38] The English word "heresy" comes to us from a Greek root that means "to pick and choose".

[39] Apelles was another Gnostic heretic of the late second century, the pupil of Marcion.

[40] Tertullian, *Demurrer against the Heretics*, chap. 37, nos. 1–6, in FEF 1:122–23, no. 298.

Christians—and it kept their faith sound through the centuries, in a world where the Bible was still being born and printed books were a dream for the distant future.

The Mischief of Schism

One more section of Irenaeus' masterpiece requires comment—but in order to understand it fully we will need to spend a moment catching up with the Montanists.

Montanus of Phrygia himself seems to have died—probably in full communion with the Catholic Church—about the time that Irenaeus began writing *Against Heresies*. And his followers up to this point had also maintained their place in the Church, thanks to the moderate policies promoted by Eleutherius. Yet as time went on, this precious bond of unity became more and more strained. To put it shortly, the Montanists grew impatient with their old-fashioned brethren; they were not embracing the new "move of God" quickly enough; they were holding back the revival. And, to be fair, we need not doubt that there might have been some truth in this. Even the holiest of churches will have areas that could stand improvement or even blind spots calling for reform, and it may well be that some members of the Church at this time really were excessively cautious about the new prophecies. Be that as it may, we do know that the disciples of Montanus responded to this resistance badly. They began to speak of "dead Christians" clogging up the Churches, by which they meant the ordinary "Sunday-go-to-meeting" sort of Christians who contented themselves with prayer and worship and works of charity. Soon, the Montanists started distancing themselves from these donkey-like traditionalists, began referring to them as mere *psychic* (or "animal") Christians—while they themselves made up a hidden or *pneumatic* church within the Church.

Then the Montanists became rigorists. They advocated the harshest possible moral standards for the Church in an effort to weed out anyone not truly "with it" or "tuned in to what the Spirit is saying". Any second marriage, for instance—even by a widow trying to provide for herself and her children—was considered rank adultery and cause for excommunication. Likewise, even the simplest attempt to avoid getting into trouble with the authorities began to be considered cowardice by the Montanists. True Christians, they held, should *seek out* opportunities to suffer—and not to do so was obviously the sign of a lesser class of believer. Paradoxically however, the Montanists simultaneously began to tolerate within their own ranks behavior that ordinary Christians considered fleshly. Eusebius' eyewitness, for example, had these penetrating questions:

> **Don't you agree that all scripture debars a prophet from accepting gifts and money? When I see that a prophetess has accepted gold and silver and expensive clothing, am I not justified in keeping her at arm's length? . . .**
>
> **The Lord said: "Do not provide yourselves with gold or silver or two coats", [Mt 10:9–10] but these people have done the exact opposite—they have transgressed by providing themselves with these forbidden things. I can prove that their so-called prophets and martyrs rake in the shekels not only from the rich but from poor people, orphans, and widows. . . .**
>
> **Tell me, does a prophet dye his hair? Does a prophet**

> **paint his eyelids? Does a prophet love ornaments? Does a prophet visit the gaming tables and play dice? Does a prophet do business as a moneylender? Let them say plainly whether these things are permissible or not, and I will prove that they have been going on in their circles.**[41]

Perhaps inevitably, then, the Montanists began to separate themselves from the *psychici*. Soon they were assembling together into their own "pure" congregations, congregations that—while technically in communion with the apostolic Church—began nevertheless to be called *Montanist churches*. Freed now, as a practical matter, from the restraints of association with the conservative majority, their prophecies became wilder, less defensible. Before long, they were speaking of Montanus as a virtual incarnation of the Paraclete and treating his recorded sayings as Scripture. Because God had largely failed, they now said, to accomplish the salvation of the world by means of the Apostles, the Holy Ghost had been forced to descend upon Montanus in a greater fullness, with more plenitude of power. Finally, says Eusebius, the Montanists were led

> **by this arrogant spirit to denigrate the entire Catholic Church throughout the world, because the spirit of pseudo-prophecy received neither honour nor admission into it; for the Asian believers repeatedly and in many parts of Asia had met for this purpose, and after investigating the recent utterances pronounced them profane and rejected the heresy. Then at last its devo-**

---

[41] Eusebius, *History of the Church*, bk. 5, chap. 18, in EHC 165–66.

> **tees were turned out of the Church and excommunicated.**[42]

Among these Asian believers was, undoubtedly, Irenaeus of Lyons—probably called back for a time to his home church to assist in evaluating the new errors. And his witness was an important one, for it vividly established the Church's impartiality in her assessment of these new developments. It was, after all, Irenaeus himself who had originally intervened with Eleutherius, at the outset of the movement, on behalf of the Montanists. Yet in the interval our subject had been forced to alter his stance toward the innovators; the movement had had time to reveal its true character. Writing in book 4, composed about A.D. 186, Irenaeus says this:

> **[The spiritual man] shall judge false prophets, who, without having received the gift of prophecy from God . . . pretend to utter prophecies, while all the time they lie against God. He shall also judge those who give rise to schisms, who are destitute of the love of God, and who look to their own special advantage rather than to the unity of the Church; and who for trifling reasons, or any kind of reason which occurs to them, cut in pieces and divide the great and glorious body of Christ, and so far as in them lies, destroy it,—men who prate of peace while they give rise to war, and do in truth strain out a gnat, but swallow a camel. For no reformation of so great importance can be effected by them, as will compensate for the mischief arising from their schism.**[43]

---

[42] Ibid., chap. 16, in EHC 161.

[43] Irenaeus, *Against Heresies*, bk. 4, chap. 33, nos. 6–7, in ANF 1:508.

In another sad bit of irony, one of the ringleaders of this new schism seems to have been Florinus of Smyrna—Irenaeus' old friend from his days as the student of Polycarp.[44] Florinus fancied himself a teacher of doctrine by this time and had many disciples; but now, with the link to the Catholic Church completely severed, Montanist doctrine had become as grotesque as any Gnosticism. One contemporary writer tells us that the Montanists of this period practiced baptism for the dead; another, that they taught eight heavens and eight degrees of damnation. In short, their "pure, pneumatic" church, once cut off from the true vine, quickly degenerated into just another cult.

In response to one of Florinus' books of theology, Irenaeus wrote this to his estranged friend in a letter:

> **These doctrines, Florinus, to put it mildly, are not of sound judgment. These doctrines are not in accord with the Church, and they involve those who accept them in the greatest of impiety. . . . These doctrines were not handed down to you by the presbyters who came before us and who were companions of the Apostles. When I was still a boy I saw you in Asia Minor with Polycarp, doing splendidly in the royal court and striving to gain his approbation. I remember the events of those days better than the ones of recent years. What a boy learns grows with the mind and becomes a part of him, so**

[44] The exact nature of Florinus' heresy is difficult to pin down—though Eusebius does mention him first in a section dealing with "the Phrygian heresy". Later, we are told, Florinus became "inveigled in the error of Valentinus", but he may have passed into this from an earlier Montanism; once the break with the Church was complete there seems to have been a rather free cross-fertilization of Gnostic and Montanist ideas.

that I am able to describe the very place in which the blessed Polycarp sat as he discoursed, his goings and his comings, the manner of his life, his physical appearance, as well as the discourses he delivered to the people, and how he spoke of his familiar conversation with John and with the rest of those who had seen the Lord, and how he would recall their words to mind. All that he had heard from them concerning the Lord or about His miracles and about His teaching, having received it from eyewitnesses of the Word of Life, Polycarp related in harmony with the Scriptures. These things were told me at that time through the mercy of God; and I listened to them attentively and noted them down, not on paper but in my heart. Continually, by the grace of God, I recall them exactly to mind. I am able to bear witness in the presence of God that if that blessed and apostolic old man had heard any such thing, he would have cried out and stopped his ears; and, as was his custom, he would have said, "O good God, to what times you have spared me, that I should endure these things!" He would have fled away from the place where, sitting or standing, he had heard such words.[45]

Feed My Sheep

Yet the presence of Florinus among the schismatics raises a troubling question. Could not Florinus—as much a student of Polycarp as Irenaeus—also have claimed for that reason

[45] Irenaeus, *Fragment* 2, quoted in Eusebius, bk. 5, chap. 20, nos. 4–7, in FEF 1:106, no. 264.

to be included in the apostolic succession? If having been the disciple of apostolic men is enough to ensure trustworthiness, then what happened in Florinus' case? Does his fate not prove that discipleship alone *is not* infallible—that an apostolic presbyter can go astray just like anyone else, just as Judas Iscariot betrayed the Lord in person?

Responding to this problem in A.D. 200, Tertullian[46] lays out the bigger picture:

> **The Apostles—a title which means "those who have been sent forth"[47]—immediately chose by lot Matthias as the twelfth, in the place of Judas. . . . They obtained the promised power of the Holy Spirit for miracles and**

---

[46] It is true, but bitterly ironic, that Tertullian later abandoned these principles and joined the Montanist schism himself—one of the greatest and saddest shocks in early Church history. Even so, he never bothered to pretend that his new ideas were in any way apostolic or that his earlier statements had not, in fact, accurately expressed the mind of the early Church. Instead, he took the more radical approach: Montanus had brought new revelation. Like Muhammad or Joseph Smith, Montanus came to overthrow the original Christianity altogether with "another testament of Jesus Christ". Thus, while the famous Carthaginian did not live up to his own principles, the quotes offered here are still valid. Having failed to do so, however, Tertullian finished his life in a fashion sadder still. Not content with Montanism finally, he eventually founded a sect of his own called the Tertullianists; a tiny remnant of this group survived into the fifth century. The best happy ending we can salvage out of this gloomy tale is that another great African, Augustine of Hippo, was eventually able to undo some of this damage—by preaching to this unhappy little faction and receiving its members back into the unity of the Catholic Church.

[47] Interestingly enough, Justin Martyr speaks of Christ Himself as an "apostle" in this sense—as "one who has been sent out on a mission". And in John 20:21 the Greek word in its verb form is used by Jesus to make clear the connection between His own ministry and that of His chosen spokesmen: As the Father has *apostled* me, even so I *apostle* you.

eloquence, and after first bearing witness to faith in Jesus Christ in Judea, and having established Churches there, they next went forth into the world and preached the same doctrine of the same faith to the gentiles. They then founded Churches in cities one after another, from which other churches borrow the sprout of faith and seeds of doctrine, and are daily borrowing them, so that they may become Churches. And it is in this way that they may regard themselves as apostolic; for they are the offspring of apostolic Churches.

Any group of things must be classified according to its origin. Therefore although the Churches are so many and so great, there is but one primitive Church of the Apostles, from which all others are derived. . . .[48]

From this then, we draw up our demurrer: if the Lord Jesus Christ sent the Apostles to preach, no others ought to be received except those appointed by Christ: For no one knows the Father except the Son, and him to whom the Son gives a revelation [Mt 11:27]. Nor does it seem that the Son has given revelation to any others than the Apostles, whom He sent forth to preach what He had revealed to them. But what they preached, that is, what Christ revealed to them—and here again I must enter a demurrer—can be proved in no other way except through the same Churches which the Apostles founded, preaching in them themselves *viva voce* as they say, and afterwards by their Epistles. If these things are so, then it follows that all doctrine which agrees with the apostolic Churches, those nurseries and origi-

[48] Tertullian, *Demurrer*, chap. 20, nos. 4–7, in FEF 1:120, no. 292.

> **nal depositories of the faith, must be regarded as truth, and as undoubtedly constituting what the Churches received from the Apostles, what the Apostles received from Christ, and what Christ received from God. And indeed, every doctrine must be prejudged as false, if it smells of anything contrary to the truth of the Churches and of the Apostles of Christ and God.**[49]

Yet could not Florinus' "church" claim to be connected to the Apostles through him, by way of Polycarp, to John the Beloved? Could they not, in this way, crib together their own sort of ersatz apostolic succession? Tertullian continues:

> **Let the heretics invent something like it. After their blasphemies, what could be unlawful for them? But even if they should contrive it, they will accomplish nothing; for their doctrine itself, when compared with that of the Apostles, will show by its own diversity and contrariety that it has for its author neither an Apostle nor an apostolic man. The Apostles would not have differed among themselves in teaching, nor would an apostolic man have taught contrary to the Apostles. . . . Those [Churches] which agree in the same faith are reckoned as apostolic on account of the blood ties in their doctrine. . . .**[50]

> **Come now, if you would indulge a better curiosity in the business of your salvation, run through the apostolic Churches in which the very thrones of the Apostles remain still in place; in which their own authentic**

---

[49] Ibid., chap. 21, nos. 1–4, in FEF 1:120–21, no. 293.

[50] Ibid., chap. 32, nos. 4–6, in FEF 1:122, no. 296.

writings are read, giving sound to the voice and recalling the faces of each. Achaia is near you, so you have Corinth. If you are not far from Macedonia, you have Philippi. If you can cross into Asia, you have Ephesus. But if you are near to Italy, you have Rome, whence also our authority derives.[51]

Crowning this line of argumentation is our final section from Irenaeus himself. In his most powerful words on the subject, Irenaeus gives his own prescription against the virus of heresy—a prescription useful for all churches everywhere:

It is possible, then, for everyone in every Church, who may wish to know the truth, to contemplate the tradition of the Apostles which has been made known throughout the whole world. And we are in a position to enumerate those who were instituted bishops by the Apostles, and their successors to our own times: men who neither knew nor taught anything like these heretics rave about. For if the Apostles had known hidden mysteries which they taught to the elite secretly and apart from the rest, they would have handed them down especially to those very ones to whom they were committing the self-same Churches. For surely they wished all those and their successors to be perfect and without reproach, to whom they handed on their authority. . . .

But since it would be too long to enumerate in such a volume as this the successions of all the Churches, we shall confound all those who, in whatever manner, whether through self-satisfaction or vainglory, or

---

[51] Ibid., chap. 36, nos. 1–2, in FEF 1:122, no. 297.

> through blindness and wicked opinion, assemble other than where it is proper, by pointing out here the successions of the bishops of the greatest and most ancient Church known to all, founded and organized at Rome by the two most glorious Apostles, Peter and Paul, that Church which has the tradition and the faith which comes down to us after having been announced to men by the Apostles. For with this Church, because of its superior origin, all Churches must agree, that is, all the faithful in the whole world; and it is in her that the faithful everywhere have maintained the Apostolic tradition.
>
> The blessed Apostles [Peter and Paul], having founded and built up the Church [of Rome], they handed over the office of the episcopate to Linus. . . . To him succeeded Anencletus; and after him, in the third place from the Apostles, Clement was chosen for the episcopate. . . . To this Clement, Evaristus succeeded; and Alexander succeeded Evaristus. Then, sixth after the Apostles, Sixtus was appointed; after him, Telesphorus, who also was gloriously martyred. Then Hyginus; after him, Pius; and after him, Anicetus. Soter succeeded Anicetus, and now, in the twelfth place after the Apostles, the lot of the episcopate has fallen to Eleutherus. In this order, and by the teaching of the Apostles handed down in the Church, the preaching of the truth has come down to us.[52]

"Because of its superior origin. . . ." In this phrase we see that Irenaeus' mind has been turned back to the very

[52] Irenaeus, *Against Heresies*, bk. 3, chap. 3, nos. 1–3, in FEF 1:89–90, nos. 209–11.

beginning—back to the start of our story, where the risen Lord once breakfasted with His disciples along the shore of Tiberias. Had not the Good Shepherd committed some kind of special role to Peter, when He took him apart from the others, when He solemnly commanded him three times to "feed my sheep"? And in more recent days, had not Peter's successors at Rome always acted with an awareness of this special destiny? Had not Clement written from Rome to intervene in the affairs of the church at Corinth—saying, **"should any disobey what has been said by Him through us, let them understand that they will entangle themselves in transgression and no small danger"**?[53] Had not Ignatius, when writing to the Roman Church, spoken of her as **"presiding in love"**?[54] And had not our subject himself, while working for peace with the Montanists, carried his letters to Eleutherius, bishop of the church at Rome? Why? Irenaeus saw it clearly now—the fires of opposition have revealed the fullness contained in that long-ago commission.

If Jesus really has established *one true Church on earth* with authority to speak in His name, then that one Church must be *preserved* by Him somehow—preserved in such a way that it can never open the Good Shepherd Himself to the charge of leading the lambs astray. Such a Church would have to speak as He did—clearly, plainly, in the power of the Holy Spirit. It would have to speak with no uncertainty in its voice, would have to teach with authority—not as the

---

[53] Clement of Rome, *First Epistle of Clement to the Corinthians*, chap. 59, no. 1, in *The Epistles of St. Clement of Rome and St. Ignatius of Antioch*, trans. James A. Kleist, ACW, vol. 1 (Mahwah, N.J.: Paulist Press, 1948), p. 45.

[54] Ignatius of Antioch, *Epistle to the Romans*, prologue, in *Epistles*, ACW 1:80.

scribes and Pharisees. In short, it must be a Church *sanctified in the truth*. And therefore, as a matter of necessity, there has to be a way, even when orthodox Christians disagree, to find —not more theology, however steeped in Bible verses—but simply *the truth*. The buck, in other words, must stop somewhere, and the little lambs must have some way to know with certainty when it has. In fact, if there is ever going to be any *certainty* anywhere in matters of faith then there must be a final answer—even within the Church herself—to our haunting old riddle: "Who's to say?" Is there any evidence that such an answer was given?

The early Christians believed there was. Writing just a few decades after Irenaeus (in A.D. 251), Cyprian of Carthage —a bishop and martyr in Africa—completes Irenaeus' argument and summarizes the ancient understanding of the Church in a few elegant words:

> **The Lord says to Peter: "I say to you," He says, "that you are Peter, and upon this rock I will build my Church, and the gates of hell will not overcome it. And to you I will give the keys of the kingdom of heaven: and whatever things you bind on earth shall be bound also in heaven, and whatever you loose on earth, they shall be loosed also in heaven"** [Mt 16:18–19]. **And again He says to him after His resurrection: "Feed my sheep"** [Jn 21:17]. **On him He builds the Church, and to him He gives the command to feed the sheep; and although He assigns a like power to all the Apostles, yet He founded a single chair, and He established by His own authority a source and an intrinsic reason for that unity. Indeed, the others were that also which Peter was; but a primacy is given**

> **to Peter, whereby it is made clear that there is but one Church and one chair.[55] So too, all are shepherds, and the flock is shown to be one, fed by all the Apostles in single-minded accord. If someone does not hold fast to this unity of Peter, can he imagine that he still holds the faith? If he desert the chair of Peter upon whom the Church was built, can he still be confident that he is in the Church?[56]**

Irenaeus of Lyons, the great "peacemaker" of Gaul, completed *Against Heresies* about A.D. 188, having fully succeeded in his ambition to refute all the errors of his day and to put their adherents to flight. Yet Irenaeus, for all his intellectual victories, retained the heart of a soul-winner to the end. Included in the pages of his great opus is this touching prayer for the heretics he has just vanquished:

> **[I] pray that these men may not remain in the pit which they themselves have dug, but [that they may] . . . stand away from the void, and relinquish the shadow; and that they, being converted to the Church of God, may be lawfully begotten, and that Christ may be formed in them,**

---

[55] It is useful in this context to compare two important verses from the Gospels. Speaking to Peter alone in Matthew 16:19, Jesus said: **"I will give you the keys of the kingdom of heaven, and whatever you bind on earth shall be bound in heaven, and whatever you loose on earth shall be loosed in heaven."** Later, in John 20:23, Jesus bestows a similar commission on all of the Apostles assembled together: **"If you forgive the sins of any, they are forgiven; if you retain the sins of any, they are retained."** Yet here there is no reference to the ability to "bind in heaven" and no mention of the keys.

[56] Cyprian of Carthage, *On the Unity of the Catholic Church*, no. 4, in FEF 1:220–21, nos. 555–56.

> **and that they may know the Framer and Maker of this universe, the only true God and Lord of all. We pray for these things on their behalf, loving them better than they seem to love themselves. For our love, inasmuch as it is true, is salutary to them, if they will but receive it. It may be compared to a severe remedy, extirpating the proud and sloughing flesh [off] a wound; for it puts an end to their pride and haughtiness. Wherefore it shall not weary us, to endeavour with all our might to stretch out the hand unto them.**[57]

Sadly, the story of Irenaeus' remaining years has been lost. We do know that he wrote, about A.D. 195, a catechism for the church in Celtica called *The Proof of the Apostolic Preaching*. This work, though misplaced for many centuries, was rediscovered in the twentieth and makes excellent, orthodox reading for those who would know our subject's mind more fully. Then he was briefly involved—also in the early 190s—in another peace mission to Rome, during what is known today as the "Quartodeciman Controversy".[58] But by the end of the second century A.D. Irenaeus of Lyons had passed quietly and completely from the pages of the historic record.

[57] Irenaeus, *Against Heresies*, bk. 3, chap. 25, no. 7, in ANF 1:460.

[58] At this time Easter was not celebrated on the same day in all Christian communities; the Eastern churches kept it always on the fourteenth day of Nisan, no matter what day of the week, since they held this day to be the actual anniversary of the Resurrection; the Western churches, including Rome, maintained that the celebration must always take place on a Sunday. About 190, Victor, the immediate successor of Eleutherius as bishop of Rome, wished to universalize the Roman usage and prescribed it for the whole Church. When they refused, he excommunicated the churches of Asia. Irenaeus, an Asian himself, acted as go-between once more and intervened to restore peace.

In stark contrast to our knowledge about Ignatius and Justin, we know next to nothing about his death. Some writers assert that about the year 202 he finally followed his friends Pothinus, Attalus, and Blandina in martyrdom—caught up in the next great wave of persecution under Emperor Septimus Severus. Unfortunately, the evidence for this is very inconclusive; while Jerome claims it for a fact, Eusebius and Tertullian are silent.

This much we do know, however: Roman Gaul—and the Celtic people Irenaeus loved—became fully Christian within 150 years. In fact, it is among Irenaeus' own flock that we find the earliest known use of the *ichthus*—that symbolic figure of a fish that now adorns the bumpers of so many Christian-owned automobiles. Mighty Rome herself, on the other hand, was fated to fall . . . , and fall she did, for all practical purposes, not long afterward. Yet we can happily say that before the end much of Irenaeus' great hope came to pass: the pagans returned, in vast numbers, to bless rather than to curse. They had heard the voice of God—just as Paul heard it on the road to Damascus: **"Saul, Saul, why do you persecute me?"** (Acts 9:4). The Church is, after all, nothing less than the Body of Christ, and every arrow they had hurled against her was another wound in His side. Yet this same Lord who told us to pray for our persecutors was victorious at last; and His persecutors—in Gaul and then all across the Empire—found ultimately that they had wounded Him by their own transgressions, and by His stripes they had been healed.

The Gnostics, conversely, denied that Christ had a Body. And if His own Incarnation among us had been a trumped-up fraud, how much more so this crude physical organism claiming to be His Body now, this so-called *Katholikē Ekklēsia?* Spiritual things must remain spiritual; that is, they must remain bodiless, phantasmagoric, symbolic. In this way the Church of Christ will be kept safe in the heavenly places and free from all human contamination, by never becoming real at all. This is the legacy of Simon Magus. And while the Magician himself did not survive the first century, his obstinate disciples pursued this fatal vision of Christianity for the next five hundred years; whether the latest and greatest version called itself Arianism or Albigensianism, whether its devotees were known as Manichees or Monophysites. Finally, by the end of the first millennium, most true Gnosticism had vanished, and few today remember it by name. But do not its hollow, lifeless echoes still sound? Are not its broken cisterns still breaking thirsty hearts slowly—wherever the Apostles are said to have failed, wherever the little lambs are taught that the gates of hell did prevail, anyplace where the Household of God is a theory, and not a *thing?*

Yet nothing, praise God, can hide a city set on a hill. Ezekiel had promised one flock, with one Good Shepherd ruling over it forever—and that prophecy was fulfilled when our Lord Jesus sat upon the throne of his father David. Yet when the Good Shepherd commissioned the Apostles—with Peter as their head—to shepherd His flock until the day of His return in glory, it was the prophecy of Jeremiah that came to pass: **"And I will give you shepherds after my own heart, who will feed you with knowledge and understanding"** (Jer 3:15).

Eusebius, the first great Church historian, who has been our guide through so much of this journey, seems the proper man to draw this story of four witnesses to a close. His short epilogue to Irenaeus is really the prologue to our own Church Age, and a message of hope for the twenty-first century and beyond:

> **Truth asserted herself, and with the march of time shone with increasing light. For by her activity the machinations of her foes were promptly shown up and extinguished, though one after another new heresies were invented, the earlier ones constantly passing away and disappearing, in different ways at different times, into forms of every shape and character. But the splendor of the Catholic and only true Church, always remaining the same and unchanged, grew steadily in greatness and strength, shedding on every race of Greeks and non-Greeks alike the majestic, spotless, free, sober, pure light of her inspired citizenship and philosophy.**[59]

[59] Eusebius, *History of the Church*, bk. 4, chap. 7, in EHC 110.

I can do nothing on My own initiative. As I hear, I judge; and My judgment is just, because I do not seek My own will, but the will of Him who sent Me. If I alone testify about Myself, My testimony is not true. . . . For I did not speak on My own initiative, but the Father Himself who sent Me has given Me a commandment as to what to say and what to speak. I know that His commandment is eternal life; therefore the things I speak, I speak just as the Father has told Me.

John 5:30–31, 12:49–50

Afterword

The early Church is no mystery, but I must say that, for me personally, it *was* a terrible challenge. I studied the writings of the four witnesses. I studied everything else I could find from the early Church. I looked and looked for something resembling my own faith, for something at least similar to the distinctives and practices of my own local church . . . and found only Catholicism.

It was like something out of a dream, a nightmare. I had always believed, on the best authority I knew, that Roman Catholicism as it exists today is a rigid, clotted relic of the Middle Ages, the faded and fading memory of a Christianity distorted beyond all recognition by centuries of syncretism and superstition. Its organization and its officers were nothing but the christianized fossils of Emperor Constantine and his lieutenants; its transubstantiating Mass and its regenerating baptism, the ghosts of pagan mystery religion lingering over Vatican Hill. Catholicism represented to me the very opposite of primitive Christianity. The idea that anything remotely like it should be found in the first and second centuries was laughable, preposterous. I knew, like everyone else, that the early Church was a loose fraternity of simple, autonomous, spontaneous believers, with no rituals, no organization, who got their beliefs from the Bible only and who always, therefore, got it right . . . like me. I also knew that the object of the Christian game, here in the modern world, is to "put things back to the way they were in the early Church". That, after all, was what our glorious Reformation had been all about. That, for crying out loud, was the whole meaning of Protestantism. So, as you might guess, finding apostolic succession in A.D. 96, or the Sacrifice of the Altar in 150, did my settled Evangelical way of life no good at all.

Since that time I have learned that many other Evangelical Christians have experienced this same painful discovery. One of the greatest and holiest, and a role model of mine on this challenging journey, was the Englishman John Henry Newman—to whom I have dedicated this book. Newman began his Christian walk, early in the nineteenth century, as a staunch Evangelical whose beliefs were quite consistent in most respects with those of today's American Evangelicals. Though he was a member (like practically everyone else in England at that time) of the episcopal Anglican Church, Newman's faith was of the "Bible only" variety, and he felt, as I did for most of my life, that the beliefs to be mined out of that Bible were anything but Catholic. But Newman became a scholar; became, in fact, one of the most important faculty members at Oxford University. And as time went on, he used this scholarship to investigate his own presuppositions. He began to learn about the Church Fathers, and then to develop a ravenous hunger—based, ironically enough, on his Evangelical drive to "put things back to the early Church"—to know everything that could be known about them. It did not take him long to discover (as perhaps some of you have discovered) that this mysterious thing called the *Katholikē Ekklēsia* was there from the very beginning.

Newman summarized the results of his agonizing quest

in a paper called *The Church of the Fathers*. In it he wrote this:

> History is not a creed or a catechism, it gives lessons rather than rules; still no one can mistake its general teaching in this matter, whether he accept it or stumble at it. Bold outlines and broad masses of colour rise out of the records of the past. They may be dim, they may be incomplete; but they are definite. And this one thing at least is certain; whatever history teaches, whatever it omits, whatever it exaggerates or extenuates, whatever it says and unsays, at least the Christianity of history is not Protestantism. If ever there were a safe truth, it is this. . . .
>
> And this utter incongruity between Protestantism and historical Christianity is a plain fact, whether the latter be regarded in its earlier or in its later centuries. . . . So much must the Protestant grant that, if such a system of doctrine as he would now introduce ever existed in early times, it has been clean swept away as if by a deluge, suddenly, silently, and without memorial; by a deluge coming in a night, and utterly soaking, rotting, heaving up, and hurrying off every vestige of what it found in the Church, before cock-crowing: so that "when they rose in the morning" her true seed "were all dead corpses"—Nay dead and buried—and without gravestone. "The waters went over them; there was not one of them left; they sunk like lead in the mighty waters." . . . Let him take which of his doctrines he will, his peculiar view of self-righteousness, of formality, of superstition; his notion of faith, or of spirituality in religious worship; his denial of the virtue of the sacraments, or of the ministerial commission, or of the visible Church; or his doctrine of the divine efficacy of the Scriptures as the one appointed instrument of religious teaching; and let him consider how far Antiquity, as it has come down to us, will countenance him in it. No; he must allow that the alleged

> deluge has done its work; yes, and has in turn disappeared itself; it has been swallowed up by the earth, mercilessly as itself was merciless.[1]

In our own times, Steve Ray, a former Baptist Bible teacher, has followed Newman on this same path and made the same startling discovery. He records the experience in his book *Crossing the Tiber:*

> It is important to consider the *silence* of the early Church as well as what she proclaimed. If the idea of sacrifice and Real Presence [in the Eucharist] were an early invention and diversion from the apostle's proclamation, why do we hear nothing from those great writers and preachers of the truth who spoke out so quickly against other heresies and false teaching? When the deity of Christ was challenged, when the Trinity was attacked, when the visible, organic unity of the Church was questioned, what did the early Fathers do? They fought vociferously with tongue and pen. They left no stone unturned, no argument unused. Where is their diatribe against the Real Presence? Where are their invectives against the sacrificial nature of the Mass? . . . As an Evangelical anxious to disprove the Catholic Church's dogmas, I searched in vain for the Fathers who would come to my rescue, but I found none. The more I read, the more I realized that the early Church was Catholic and did not support my Evangelical conclusions.[2]

In spite of these things, neither Steve Ray nor John Newman was willing to jump into the deep end immediately,

---

[1] John Henry Newman, *An Essay on the Development of Christian Doctrine*, nos. 5–6 (1878; reprint, Westminster, Md.: Christian Classics, 1968), pp. 7–9.

[2] Stephen Ray, *Crossing the Tiber* (San Francisco: Ignatius Press, 1997), pp. 271–72.

and neither was I. Whatever else this "Catholic Church" may have been in the early centuries, she surely was not the same grotesque body that today postures about bearing that name. What about devotions to Mary? What about purgatory? What about prayers to the saints and indulgences? Were not all these things conclusive proof that the modern Roman Church is just as man-made and fallible as any other human institution?

John Henry Newman thought so at first, and continued to speak out against "the errors of the Papists" for some time. Nevertheless, how could he simply walk away and forget the new facts he had learned about the early Church? He felt compelled to incorporate them into his outlook somehow. As a result, Newman became one of the key figures in a new movement within the English church: the "Oxford Movement", as it was known. The thesis was fairly simple: what was needed was some kind of *via media*—or "middle way"—between Catholicism and Protestantism; between the Church of Rome (encrusted as she was with the mere traditions of men) and the new churches of Luther and company (which had perhaps gone too far in their efforts to strip these off). Might it not be possible that Anglicanism itself—which, for historical reasons, is a less radical branch of the Reformation (retaining as it does, bishops, priests, and sacraments)—might this not be a providentially provided *via media* in its own right?

Newman spent years trying to prove that it was; and I myself have spent time in several such "middle way" churches. This being the case, I can attest from experience that many of the Christians in these groups—whether they are called Evangelical Orthodox, "High Church" Episcopalians, or

Oxford Movement Anglicans—are sincere, godly people who have found that they can content themselves with such a *via media*. Impressive theories really can be built up showing that this *Katholikē Ekklēsia* of the primitive age—apparently centered at Rome—is today represented someplace else: in Moscow, at Canterbury, in Constantinople, or in a hidden remnant of bishops scattered through them all and known only to God. Yes, "High Church" Episcopalians do claim to be able to find their religion in the writings of our four witnesses. And yes, the Eastern churches do venerate these very writings, almost on an equal level with Scripture, insisting that theirs is the faith revealed in those pages. But to a downright Evangelical like myself—who saw practically nothing there that was not a rebuff—such stopgap solutions began to ring hollow. Like Newman himself, I gradually realized that I now had a "problem about the early Church"—a problem that no human compromise, however well meaning, would ever fix for long.

Newman describes his own moment of truth vividly:

> About the middle of June [1839] I began to study and master the history of the Monophysites. . . . It was during this course of reading that for the first time a doubt came upon me of the tenableness of Anglicanism. . . . Here, in the middle of the fifth century, I found . . . Christendom of the sixteenth and the nineteenth centuries reflected. I saw my face in that mirror, and I was a Monophysite. The Church of the *Via Media* was in the position of the [Monophysites], Rome was where she now is; and the Protestants were the Eutychians [plain schismatics who departed from Catholic tradition without apology]. . . . It was difficult to make out how the Eutychians or Monophysites were heretics, unless Protestants and Anglicans were heretics also . . . difficult to

> condemn the Popes of the sixteenth century, without condemning the Popes of the fifth. The drama of religion, and the combat of truth and error, were ever one and the same. The principles and proceedings of the Church now, were those of the Church then; the principles and proceedings of heretics then, were those of Protestants now.[3]

I mentioned in my introduction that I was raised in a Christian home, raised to love God and love the Bible, and to try and do right by them both. It was quite a shock, therefore, suddenly to start entertaining the thought that I might, in reality, belong to a mere schismatic sect, with a faulty man-made theology. I was unaware at the time that the Catholic Church herself actually had much subtler ideas about my position. In reality, she *does not* teach that everyone outside the Roman communion is simply lost and wandering in the dark. The Catholic Church has always acknowledged (in her doctrine if not always in practice) the existence of a genuine spiritual bond linking all baptized Christians—and she would not have faulted me personally for winding up on the wrong side in this five-hundred-year-old "custody battle" in the Body of Christ. Had I but known it, the Church would have *honored* my love of the Bible and would have seconded my testimony to the saving work of Jesus in my life up to that point—while continuing to maintain, of course, her claim to be the one true apostolic *Ekklēsia* founded by Him. But I had not heard these things. I was left only with Cyprian's haunting question ringing in my ears: "If [a man] desert the chair of Peter upon whom the Church was built,

---

[3] John Henry Newman, *Apologia Pro Vita Sua* (New York: Image Books, 1989), p. 217.

can he still be confident that he is in the Church?" Looking back, I think the Lord did this on purpose. The Good Shepherd, I believe, wanted to test my willingness to follow Him—and follow no matter where He led, even if the path were through the valley of the shadow of death.

For me, the fatal blow came in 1992, when Pope John Paul II promulgated the *Catechism of the Catholic Church*. In its pages I read these words:

> "The one mediator, Christ, established and ever sustains here on earth his holy Church, the community of faith, hope, and charity, as a visible organization through which he communicates truth and grace to all men."[4]

> The Lord Jesus endowed his community with a structure that will remain until the Kingdom is fully achieved. Before all else there is the choice of the Twelve with Peter as their head [cf. Mk 3:14–15]. Representing the twelve tribes of Israel, they are the foundation stones of the new Jerusalem [cf. Mt 19:28; Lk 22:30; Rev 21:12–14]. The Twelve and the other disciples share in Christ's mission and his power, but also in his lot [cf. Mk 6:7; Lk 10:1–2; Mt 10:25; Jn 15:20].[5]

> "In order that the mission entrusted to them might be continued after their death, [the apostles] consigned, by will and testament, as it were, to their immediate collaborators the duty of completing and consolidating the work they had begun, urging them to tend to the whole flock, in which the Holy Spirit had appointed them to shepherd the Church of God. They accordingly designated such men and then

[4] CCC 771, quoting *Lumen Gentium* 8 § 1.

[5] CCC 765.

> made the ruling that likewise on their death other proven men should take over their ministry."[6]
>
> Hence the Church teaches that "the bishops have by divine institution taken the place of the apostles as pastors of the Church, in such wise that whoever listens to them is listening to Christ and whoever despises them despises Christ and him who sent Christ."[7]
>
> They are "heralds of faith, who draw new disciples to Christ; they are authentic teachers" of the apostolic faith "endowed with the authority of Christ."[8]
>
> In order to preserve this Church in the purity of the faith handed on by the apostles, Christ who is the Truth willed to confer on her a share in his own infallibility. By a "supernatural sense of faith" the People of God, under the guidance of the Church's living Magisterium [or "teaching office"], "unfailingly adheres to this faith."[9]
>
> The mission of the Magisterium is linked to the definitive nature of the covenant established by God with his people in Christ. It is this Magisterium's task to preserve God's people from deviations and defections and to guarantee them the objective possibility of professing the true faith without error.[10]

I recognized it immediately: *this* was the faith I had found with Clement and Ignatius, with Justin and Irenaeus. And if the Catholic Church in the late twentieth century was

[6] CCC 861, quoting *Lumen Gentium* 20, cf. Acts 20:28; St. Clement of Rome, *Ad Cor.* 42, 44; PG 1, 291–300.

[7] CCC 862, quoting *Lumen Gentium* 20 § 2.

[8] CCC 888, quoting *Lumen Gentium* 25.

[9] CCC 889, quoting *Lumen Gentium* 12, cf. *Dei Verbum* 10; [bracketed explanation added].

[10] CCC 890.

saying the same things my four witnesses had said in the first and second, I knew I was in big, big trouble. Especially since I also recognized something else—that my Evangelical brothers and sisters were not saying these things. And so, incredibly, my own cherished principles seemed to demand it: I needed (in my own life, at any rate) to "put things back to the way they were in the early Church".

But, once again, *what about the Bible?* What about Mary and purgatory and the Immaculate Conception? Yes, I could already see that having some kind of "pope"—someplace for the buck to stop—would make a lot of good, useful sense. Even as a convinced Protestant I had been growing more and more appalled by the constant fissuring in Evangelical circles, the endless church splits, and the hundreds upon hundreds of competing denominations. In other words, the problem of "who's to say?" had already become very real in my mind. And also, by this time, I had learned enough additional information from my Catechism to see that many of my objections to the papacy were just red herrings to begin with. I discovered, for instance, that the pope has never been held by the Church to be *impeccable* (incapable of sin) but only *infallible* (incapable of error)—preserved, as the chief teacher of the Church, from teaching falsehood in Christ's name, but not preserved, as a mere human being, from personal folly or guilt. Likewise, I learned that the pope is not said to be a source of *new revelation*; God's final revelation, as much in Catholicism as in my own Evangelicalism, was complete in Christ. All the pope is held to be is an infallible *interpreter* of that original revelation, someone who, by the gift of the Holy Ghost, will never say that something is part of the original revelation if it was not, or subtract something from that original revelation that truly belongs there. All these things I had learned and was perhaps willing, at this point, to entertain.

Yet there was still that terrible stumbling block. Had not the popes and the other Catholic bishops *contradicted* the Bible on many points? Could not these "apostolic ministers"—whatever else might be said for their position—be demonstrably proven to have *departed* from Bible doctrine in numerous places? I thought they could and recoiled. True, I had learned from my reading that the papacy (in the persons of Peter, Linus, Cletus, and Clement, at least) actually *predates* much of the Bible, and certainly predates the final canon of the Bible. I also learned that the Christian Church had never been "based on" the Bible in the first place, but that the Bible had been based on the Church—in the sense that it was bishops of the Catholic Church who preserved it, who compiled it, who passed it down through the ages, and who vouched for it to the world. But *still*—outright contradiction would shatter everything. The Holy Spirit of God, assuredly, does not "speak with forked tongue".

It only remained, then, actually to turn to the Church and see what she had to say about these "contradictions". How did the Catholic Church herself account for my alleged departures? At first, I was quite prepared to believe—as I had been taught in the traditions of my Protestant fathers—that she simply did not bother. She ignored the Bible, supposedly, and this is why she had often forbidden her children to read it. Or worse still, she had fabricated her own "Catholic" Bible—a faulty partisan translation based on Latin corruptions rather than the true texts, full of spurious "extra" books which do not truly belong. All these things, I have since discovered, were simply untruths. The Church has never forbidden the Scriptures to anyone, and the so-called "apocryphal" books she includes in her Old Testament were present in the Bible used by Jesus and the Apostles. It was all anti-Catholic rhetoric from start to finish. The actual fact, I finally realized, is that I had never in my life up to that point been willing to hear one single word from the Catholics themselves in their own defense; everything I "knew" about the Catholic Church I had learned from her enemies. I could not have given a decent explanation of Catholic doctrine if my life had depended upon it, and to compare, therefore, my reckless distorted version of it with Scripture was stacking the deck from the get-go.

A few genuine biblical problems did remain, however—of two distinct types. The first kind, I found, had become fairly easy to resolve now that I had the history of the four witnesses under my belt. These were the traditional charges that such and such a doctrine was "not found in Scripture"—something like the Assumption of Mary, for example. This teaching, held by the Catholic Church since the earliest times, records that Jesus' mother, at the time of her falling asleep in Christ, was received bodily into heaven without first suffering corruption—much like Enoch and Elijah under the old Covenant. This event, obviously, is not included in the Gospels; it is quite possible that Mary, at the time the Synoptics were first published, was still alive and active at the Church of Ephesus. Be that as it may, the bare assertion that this dogma—which is undeniably *extra-biblical*—is for that reason alone *unbiblical* would have struck our four witnesses as odd indeed. Whoever *said* that the Bible contains everything God wants to say to the world? After all, it was not even finished yet in their time—and yet they were preaching and living out its truths every day. No, in the minds of Clement and the others, the Bible itself was something the world was receiving *from the Church*. And if the very same people who told you there was any Bible in the first place also tell you that Mary was assumed into heaven, well, who are we to pick and choose? Another Catholic convert, the journalist G. K. Chesterton, once expressed this truth in a memorable analogy:

> The ordinary sensible sceptic or pagan is standing in the street . . . and he sees a procession go by of the priests of some strange cult, carrying their object of worship under a canopy, some of them wearing high head-dresses and carrying symbolical staffs, others carrying scrolls and sacred records, others carrying sacred images and lighted candles before them, others sacred relics in caskets or cases, and so on. I can understand the spectator saying, "This is all hocus-pocus"; . . . I can understand his saying, "Your croziers are bosh, your candles are bosh, your statues and scrolls and relics and all the rest of it are bosh." But in what conceivable frame of mind does he rush in to select one particular scroll of the scriptures of this one particular group (a scroll which had always belonged to them and been a part of their hocus-pocus, if it was hocus-pocus); why in the world should the man in the street say that one particular scroll was *not* bosh, but was the one and only truth by which all the other things were to be condemned? Why should it not be as superstitious to worship the scrolls as the statues, of that one particular procession? Why should it not be as reasonable to preserve the statues as the scrolls, by the tenets of that particular creed? To say to the priests, "Your statues and scrolls are condemned by our common sense," is sensible. To say, "Your statues are condemned by

> your scrolls, and we are going to worship one part of your procession and wreck the rest," is not sensible from any standpoint, least of all that of the man in the street.[11]

Here at last I saw the logical lapse in my old watchword of *Sola Scriptura*—"the Bible and the Bible alone". Get in a time machine, go back to A.D. 180, and use it in a dispute with Irenaeus, and he simply would not know what you were talking about.

These "where's that in the Bible?" difficulties, then, were not really *contradictions* of the Scriptures at all; but there *was* a second class of problem verses. These were the passages where I saw what looked like actual *conflict* between Catholic teaching and Scripture; things like the perpetual virginity of Mary, for example, or the concept of a New Testament priesthood. Yet here once again, I quickly found that the mere fact of having experienced the story of the four witnesses had worked a peculiar kind of magic in my life. With my anti-Catholic suspicions quieted a bit, with my distinctively American anti-authoritarianism softened somewhat, I realized that I could now *listen* to the Catholic Church for the first time—really listen and give her a fair hearing. And when I did, believe it or not, I found that the Catholic Church had a rational, logical, and *biblical* explanation for every one of my objections. Not just some kind of "after the fact" apology for them, mind you, but real *explanations* that actually fit the facts better than what I had been offering and that illumined, in turn, *other* passages elsewhere in the Bible that had always been dark to me before. This

[11] G. K. Chesterton, *The Catholic Church and Conversion*, in *The Collected Works of G. K. Chesterton*, vol. 3 (San Francisco: Ignatius Press, 1990), p. 73.

was the most startling fact of all. Later, I found that my experiences in this had paralleled those of the young St. Augustine of Hippo. After years wandering in the wilderness as a member of a strange Gnostic-influenced sect called the Manichees, he was forced by his unhappiness and despair (and by the prayers of his saintly mother Monica) to re-examine the claims of the apostolic Church. Augustine had been given by his Manichean preachers nothing but the most slanted and distorted picture of her teachings and had been taught, in place of her true doctrines, ugly cartoonish caricatures of them. But when he finally looked for himself, when he finally took the trouble to hear both sides of the story and to read their books on his own—the result was a spiritual earthquake, a revolution: "A great hope has dawned!" he wrote in his autobiography. "The Catholic Faith does not teach the things I thought it did and vainly accused it of teaching. . . ."[12] Soon afterward, Augustine asked to be received into the Catholic Church and was welcomed with open arms by his mother's pastor, Bishop Ambrose of Milan.

Was I now willing to do the same? No, I hate to admit, I was not—not quite. One by one, my doubts about the Church's claims were vanishing, but not my fears. I wrote a moment ago that the Good Shepherd seemed to be leading me through the valley of the shadow of death; and at this point in my life the very notion that I might have to join the *Roman Catholic Church*—which I had heard called everything from a pathetic ruin of medievalism to the Great Whore of Babylon—sounded very much like a death sentence. John

---

[12] St. Augustine of Hippo, *Confessions*, trans. Rex Warner (London: Penguin Books, 1963), p. 128.

Henry Newman's conversion process, as a matter of fact, was quite a lot like dying: another slow-motion martyrdom, you might say. In Newman's day, an Englishman who converted to Catholicism was considered a traitor to his country. He stood to lose his job, his friends, his family, and many of his civil rights. I certainly had nothing like *that* to go through, praise God, and have been treated more kindly than I deserved as I made my various religious adjustments. But I do think that God sent us both on a journey somewhat akin to Paul's—like that zealous teacher of Israel struck down on the road to Damascus. Paul was still Saul at that time, still the "Hebrew of the Hebrews" and was following the best faith he knew—indeed, the best faith that anyone had known until recently. Yet God had a greater plan for his life: it was time to learn more. This greater call would not be easy. It involved learning somehow that his treasured childhood faith (holy as it was on its own terms) had been incomplete, imperfect, and in danger of becoming a rival to God's work now rather than an embodiment of it. It involved admitting that he had been wrong and bowing the knee to people he had formerly despised. He might easily have rejected the call, might have found another explanation for his "paranormal" experience on that Syrian roadside. But no . . . no, Paul had seen too much. And while the vision I received from my four witnesses was a bit less dramatic, so had I.

Newman simply lost his faith for a while. Not his faith in Jesus—never that. But he lost his faith in Christianity, or in what his Protestant critics insisted was Christianity. "We uphold the pure unmutilated Scripture", they told him; "the Bible, and the Bible only, is the religion of Protestants; the

Bible and our own sense of the Bible. We claim a sort of parliamentary privilege to interpret its laws in our own way, and not to suffer an appeal to any court beyond ourselves. We know, and we view it with consternation, that all Antiquity runs counter to our interpretation; and therefore, alas, the Church was corrupt from very early times indeed . . . We confess facts are against us; we do but claim the liberty of theorizing in spite of them. Far be it from us to say that we are certainly right; we only say that the whole early Church was certainly wrong."[13] Steve Ray, though it was the end of his life as a Protestant Evangelical, could not continue to believe this scheme of religion either—not after having spent time with the four witnesses. He reached an inescapable—but dismaying—conclusion:

> The Reformation was not a recovery of what had been lost; rather, it was a radical departure from that which had always been. . . .
>
> We must be connected to our roots, or we must be honest and forsake our claim to be the progeny of the first believers. We cannot claim to be followers of Jesus and his apostles if we condemn their students, the bishops, presbyters, and deacons, who carried out their commands and practices with detailed precision in the first centuries of the Church. Can we really think we are the true followers of Christ if we ignore his Church and follow our own private judgment based on the Bible alone? Is it logical to insist on our own interpretation of the New Testament and yet ignore, or even condemn as "paganized", those who formed

[13] John Henry Newman, *Historical Sketches* 1:420, quoted in *John Henry Newman: A Biography*, by Ian Kerr (Oxford: Oxford University Press, 1988), p. 140.

> the very canon of books Evangelicals and Catholics alike call the New Testament?[14]

Both these men, finally, admitted that it was not logical—then broke down and made their choice. If the only way to save their faith in Christ was to follow him into someplace dark, frightening, and unfamiliar—to walk down to Nineveh with Jonah—then their response, ultimately, would have to be that of faith alone: "Behold, I am the handmaid of the Lord; let it be done to me according to your word" (Lk 1:38).

I am a far less important, far less faithful man than either Newman or Ray; but by the grace of God, I was able to follow in their footsteps on April 6, 1996, when, at the great vigil of Easter, I was confirmed as a Catholic. I chose St. Augustine of Hippo as my patron saint. And I mean literally that I made my decision by God's grace alone. No intellectual process, no course of reading, can ever, in and of itself, bring a man to faith—either in Christ or in His kingdom, the Church. Faith is a miracle. And what the four witnesses had offered to me was the story of another miracle—*another incarnation*. I knew, and already believed with all my heart, that the Son of God had become Man at Bethlehem for my salvation; "the Word became flesh and dwelt among us" (Jn 1:14). But now I could see that the early Fathers believed more: *They believed that His Bride had become flesh too.*

The Church of Christ is present in the world but, like the Apostles who are her foundation, she is "not of the world, even as I am not of this world" (Jn 17:16). Yes, the invasion

---

[14] Ray, *Crossing the Tiber*, pp. 274–75.

of history that began at Bethlehem *continues*—and is permanent among us. The Body of Christ did not dematerialize at the Ascension; Jesus dwells in it today in heaven—glorified yet still fully human. Likewise, His larger Body is real, as well. This Man gives us His flesh to eat, and thus, "Because there is one bread, we who are many are one body, for we all partake of the one bread" (1 Cor 10:17). The Bride of Christ did not become a ghost on the day she was born, nor did she vanish like a hare into a thicket of bickering denominations. No, she is as real as her divine Spouse and one with Him; "the two will become one flesh," writes Paul, "and I am applying it to Christ and the Church" (Eph 5:31–32, NAS). Yes, both wheat and tares will grow within her gates until the end, and the human element in her constitution sometimes clouds the brightness of her glory. Nevertheless, the Savior's promise stands firm forever: this is the Church to whose founders Jesus declared: "He who hears you hears me, and he who rejects you rejects me, and he who rejects me rejects him who sent me" (Lk 10:16). No "Great Apostasy" can ever prevail against *her*; no free-lance prophet can ever find her again, hidden under a bushel in Wittenberg, Germany, or Palmyra, New York. She is the Household of God. She is the kingdom of God within us—*among us*—down at Sacred Heart Parish on Mulberry Street. And this incarnational principle—shocking as it may be—extends to everything she is and does; her sacraments are symbols that actually *embody* the things they symbolize; her saints move through history as the prophets and Apostles move through Scripture—literally raising the dead and making the blind to see. This is the Bible story that, God bless them, my

Sunday School teachers never taught me. This is the "Full Gospel" I never heard at any Full Gospel Businessmen's Meeting.

And does not the *Gnostic* impulse rise in us at these words! I know it did in me. *Spiritual things must remain spiritual.* God is in His heaven. God is in a Book. But I stumbled at a God who entangles Himself in filthy flesh—in candles and relics, in holy water and holy places. Yet soon I noticed something else about these feelings. These terrors and falterings were familiar. They were the same ones that had gripped me just before "walking the aisle" to become a Christian in the first place. When Jesus came, they told me "Here is a Man who is more than a man." When the Church came, they told me "Here is a human society which is more than human." Both claims were enormous—and equally enormous—but Christianity is the religion of enormous claims. Faith is a miracle, and miracles require faith.

Chesterton compared the final moment in his own conversion (when he lay completely paralyzed with indecision) to "the last instant before an iron springs to the magnet". As for me, I can say only that God Himself provided the strength that I could never have mustered. But when that faith finally came, it came with the power of a resurrection—I felt *young* again. When I finally let go of my thoughtless suspicions, when I finally looked at the Catholic Church with the eyes of a child rather than with those of prejudice, I cried out with King David: "I was glad when they said unto me, let us go into the House of the LORD!" (Ps 122:1, KJV). Since that time, my experiences have paralleled, once more, those of John Henry Newman—better known today, of course, as the venerable Cardinal Newman. Though he faced loneliness from time to time in his new surroundings, and misunderstanding from both his old friends and his new, he never ceased to give thanks for everything God had brought him through: "From the time that I became a Catholic," he wrote, ". . . I . . . have had no anxiety of heart whatever. I have been in perfect peace and contentment; I never have had one doubt. . . . It was like coming into port after a rough sea; and my happiness on that score remains to this day without interruption."[15]

To any of my Evangelical brothers and sisters who may be faced at this time with a similar decision, let me say that you have my fervent prayers. But if you do come home, the dropping of your uncertainties will be the sweetest part; like a heavy winter overcoat—worn so long that it has nearly been forgotten—slipping from your shoulders on a fine spring day.

The One, Holy, Catholic and Apostolic Church—of which I do not deserve to be a member—teaches that Clement of Rome, Ignatius of Antioch, Irenaeus of Lyons, and Justin Martyr are *still alive today*, more alive now than when they lived the stories you have read. Moreover, she teaches that they are still *awake*, as well—enfolded into Christ now, no longer seeing through a glass darkly but knowing fully, even as they are known (1 Cor 13:12). They have perhaps been watching me as I write, and you as you read. In my firm confidence, then, that the true Church established by Jesus can never deceive or be deceived, I now offer this request—for myself and for all who have honored me by reading this book:

---

[15] Newman, *Apologia*, p. 317.

You holy men of God—disciples of the Apostles, now glorified and reigning with them in heaven—pray, I entreat you, for us poor sinners still on earth. In the name of the Father, and of the Son, and of the Holy Ghost. Amen.

Appendix

CATHOLIC TEACHING IN THE EARLY CHURCH

"If Christianity is historical, Catholicism is Christianity."

—Cardinal Henry Manning,
convert from Protestantism

This appendix presents a collection of additional quotations from the Church Fathers and a comparison of their teachings with those of the present-day Roman Catholic Church. The patristic selections are taken (unless otherwise noted) from W. A. Jurgens' indispensable compendium *The Faith of the Early Fathers,* published by the Liturgical Press of Collegeville, Minnesota. The current Catholic teachings are taken from authoritative modern sources. For the purposes of this appendix, "the early Church" has been defined as the first six hundred years after Pentecost—a period during which she remained, even according to John Calvin, "pure and undefiled".

The Nature of the Church

TODAY'S CATHOLIC TEACHING

Christ, the one Mediator, established and continually sustains here on earth His holy Church, the community of faith, hope and charity, as an entity with visible delineation through which He communicated truth and grace to all. . . . That divine mission, entrusted by Christ to the apostles, will last until the end of the world (Mt 28:20), since the Gospel they are to teach is for all time the source of all life for the Church. And for this reason the apostles, appointed as rulers in this society, took care to appoint successors.

For they not only had helpers in their ministry, but also, in order that the mission assigned to them might continue after their death, they passed on to their immediate cooperators, as it were, in the form of a testament, the duty of confirming and finishing the work begun by themselves, recommending to them that they attend to the whole flock in which the Holy Spirit placed them to shepherd the Church of God. They therefore appointed such men, and gave them the order that, when they should have died, other approved men would take up their ministry. . . . Therefore, the Sacred Council teaches that bishops by divine institution have succeeded to the place of the apostles, as shepherds of the Church, and he who hears them, hears Christ, and he who rejects them, rejects Christ and Him who sent Christ.

—Vatican II, *Lumen Gentium*, nos. 8, 20.

CATHOLIC TEACHING IN THE EARLY CHURCH

The true gnosis [knowledge] is the doctrine of the Apostles, and the ancient organization of the Church throughout the whole world, and the manifestations of the body of Christ according to the successions of bishops, by which successions the bishops have handed down the Church which is found everywhere; and the very complete tradition of the

Scriptures, which have come down to us by being guarded against falsification, and which are received without addition or deletion; and reading without falsification, and a legitimate and diligent exposition according to the Scriptures, without danger and without blasphemy; and the preeminent gift of love, which is more precious than knowledge, more glorious than prophecy, and more honored than all the other charismatic gifts.

— Ca. A.D. 180: Irenaeus of Lyons, *Against Heresies*, bk. 4, chap. 33, no. 8, in FEF 1:97, no. 242.

Grant, then, that all have erred; that the Apostle was mistaken in bearing witness; that the Holy Spirit had no such consideration for any one Church as to lead it into truth, although He was sent for that purpose by Christ [Jn 14:26], who had asked the Father to make Him the Teacher of truth [Jn 15:26]; that the Steward of God and Vicar of Christ [the Holy Spirit] neglected His office, and permitted the Churches for a time to understand otherwise and to believe otherwise than He Himself had preached through the Apostles: now, is it likely that so many and such great Churches should have gone astray into a unity of faith?

— Ca. A.D. 200: Tertullian of Carthage, *The Demurrer against the Heretics*, chap. 28, no. 1, in FEF 1:121, no. 295.

Christ breathed upon the Apostles alone, saying to them: "Receive the Holy Spirit: if you forgive any man his sins, they shall be forgiven; and if you retain any man's sins, they shall be retained" [Jn 20:22–23]. Therefore, the power of forgiving sins was given to the Apostles and to the Churches which these men, sent by Christ, established; and to the bishops who succeeded them by being ordained in their place.

— Ca. A.D. 255: Firmilian of Caesarea, *Letter to Cyprian*, chap. 75, no. 16, in FEF 1:245, no. 602.

In addition to this pious belief in regard to the Father and the Son, we confess, as the divine writings teach us, one Holy Spirit, who moved both the holy men of the Old Testament and the divine teachers of that styled the New. And in one only Catholic Church, that which is Apostolic.

— A.D. 324: Alexander of Alexandria, *Encyclical Letter to Another Bishop Alexander and All Non-Egyptian Bishops*, no. 12, in FEF 1:301, no. 680.

[The Church] is called Catholic, then, because it extends over the whole world, from end to end of the earth; and because it teaches universally and infallibly each and every doctrine which must come to the knowledge of men, concerning things visible and invisible, heavenly and earthly; and because it brings every race of men into subjection to godliness, governors and governed, learned and unlearned; and because it universally treats and heals every class of sins, those committed with the soul and those with the body; and it possesses within itself every conceivable form of virtue, in deeds and in words and in spiritual gifts of every description.

— Ca. A.D. 350: Cyril of Jerusalem, *Catechetical Lectures*, lec. 18, no. 23, in FEF 1:359, no. 838.

We believe . . . in one holy, catholic, and apostolic Church.

— A.D. 363/374: The Nicene Creed, in FEF 1:399, no. 910a.

In the Catholic Church, there are many other things which, most properly, can keep me in her bosom. The unanimity of peoples and nations keeps me here. Her authority, inaugurated in miracles, nourished by hope, augmented by love, and confirmed by her age, keeps me here. The succession of priests, from the very see of the Apostle Peter, to whom our Lord, after His resurrection, gave the charge of feeding His sheep, up to the present episcopate, keeps me here. And at last, the very name of Catholic, which, not without reason, belongs to this Church alone, in the face of so many heretics, so much that, although all heretics want to be called Catholic, when a stranger inquires where the Catholic Church meets, none of the heretics would dare to point out his own basilica or house.

— A.D. 397: Augustine of Hippo, *Against the Letter of Mani Called "The Foundation"*, chap. 4, no. 5, in FEF 3:51, no. 1580.

Let us love our Lord God, let us love His Church; Him as a Father, her as a Mother; Him as a Master, her as His Handmaid; for we are the children of the Handmaid herself. But this marriage is held together by a great love; no one offends the one and gains favor with the other. No one can say: "Certainly I go to idols, I consult demoniacs and fortune-tellers; but I do not abandon the Church of God. I am a Catholic." While clinging to your Mother, you have offended your Father. Another says likewise: "Far be it from me. I consult no fortune-teller, I seek out no demoniac, I look to no sacrilegious divinations, I do not go to the worship of idols, nor do I bow down to stones; but I am in the party of Donatus." What does it profit you not to have offended your Father, when He will vindicate your offended Mother? What does it profit you to confess the Lord, to honor God, to preach Him, to acknowledge His Son, to confess the Son seated at the right hand of the Father, if you blaspheme His Church? . . . Cling, then, beloved, cling all with one mind to God our Father and to the Church our Mother.

— Ca. A.D. 400: Augustine of Hippo, *Explanations of the Psalms* 88, 2, 14, in FEF 3:19, no. 1478.

The disciples receive as their lot the preeminence of celestial judgment, so that, in God's stead, they retain sins for some and for some they forgive them [Jn 20:22–23]. It was fitting that they be so raised up by God, when they had consented to be so grossly humiliated for God's sake. See, they who feared the strict judgment of God have become judges of souls, and they who feared that they would themselves be condemned now either condemn others or release them. Certainly it is now the bishops who hold their place in the Church. They receive the authority of binding and of loosing, who have as their lot a degree of governing. It is a magnificent honor, but that honor carries with it a heavy burden.

— A.D. 590: Pope Gregory I, *Homilies on the Gospels* 12, 26, 4, in FEF 3:323–24, no. 2332.

The Papacy

TODAY'S CATHOLIC TEACHING

That which our Lord Jesus Christ, the prince of shepherds and great shepherd of the sheep, established in the blessed apostle Peter, for the continual salvation and permanent benefit of the Church, must of necessity remain for ever, by Christ's authority, in the church which, founded as it is upon a rock, will stand firm until the end of time. For no one can be in doubt, indeed it was known in every age that the holy and most blessed Peter, prince and head of the apostles, the pillar of faith and the foundation of the Catholic Church, received the keys of the kingdom from our Lord Jesus Christ, the saviour and redeemer of the human race, and that to this day and for ever he lives and presides and exercises judgment in his successors the bishops of the holy Roman see, which he founded and consecrated with his blood. *Therefore* whoever succeeds to the chair of Peter obtains by the institution of Christ himself, the primacy of Peter over the whole Church. So what the truth has ordained stands firm, and blessed Peter perseveres in the rock-like strength he was granted, and does not abandon that guidance of the Church which he once received. For this reason it has always been necessary for every church —that to say the faithful throughout the world—to be in agreement with the Roman Church because of its more effective leadership.

— Vatican I, *First Dogmatic Constitution on the Church of Christ.*

Nor does the kingdom of heaven belong to the sleeping and the lazy; rather, the violent take it by force [Mt 11:12]. . . . On hearing these words, the blessed Peter, the chosen, the pre-eminent, the first among the disciples, for whom alone with Himself the Savior paid the tribute [Mt 17:27], quickly grasped and understood their meaning. And what does he say? "Behold, we have left all and have followed you!" [Mt 19:27; Mk 10:28].

— Ca. A.D. 200: Clement of Alexandria, *Who Is the Rich Man that Is Saved?* chap. 21, no. 1, in FEF 1:187, no. 436.

Peter, upon whom is built the Church of Christ, against which the gates of hell shall not prevail, left only one Epistle of acknowledged genuinity. Let us concede also a second, which, however, is doubtful.

— Ca. A.D. 230: Origen, *Commentaries on John* 5, 3, according to Eusebius, *History of the Church*, bk. 6, chap. 25, in FEF 1:202, no. 479a.

Our Lord, whose commands we ought to fear and observe, says in the Gospel, by way of assigning the episcopal dignity settling the plan of his Church: "I say to you that you are Peter, and upon this rock I will build my Church, and the gates of hell will not overcome it. And to you I will give the keys of the kingdom of heaven: and whatever things you bind on earth will be bound also in heaven, and whatever you loose on earth, they will be loosed also in heaven" [Mt 16:18–19]. From that time the ordination of bishops and the plan of the Church flows on through the changes of time and successions; for the Church is founded upon the bishops, and every act of the Church is controlled by these same rulers. Since this has indeed been established by divine law, I marvel at the rash boldness of certain persons who have desired to write to me as if they were writing letters in the name of the Church, "since the Church is established upon the bishop and upon the clergy and upon all who stand firm in the faith."

— A.D. 250: Cyprian of Carthage, *Letter . . . to the Lapsed* 33 (27), no. 1, in FEF 1:229, no. 571.

There is one God and one Christ, and one Church, and one Chair founded on Peter by the word of the Lord. It is not possible to set up another altar or for there to be another priesthood besides that one altar and that one priesthood. Whoever has gathered elsewhere is scattering.

— A.D. 251: Cyprian of Carthage, *Letter to All His People* 43 (40), no. 5, in FEF 1:229, no. 573.

We are not ignorant of the fact that there is one God, and one Christ the Lord whom we confess, and one Holy Spirit; and that there must be one bishop in the Catholic Church.

— A.D. 252: Pope Cornelius I, *Letter to Cyprian*, in *Cyp. Epist.* 49 (*al.* 46), no. 2, in FEF 1:216, no. 546.

Simon, My follower, I have made you the foundation of the holy Church. I betimes called you Peter, because you will support all its buildings. You are the inspector of those who will build on earth a Church for Me. If they should wish to build what is false, you, the foundation, will condemn them. You are the head of the fountain from which My teaching flows, you are the chief of My disciples. Through you I will give drink to all peoples. Yours is that life-giving sweetness which I dispense. I have chosen you to be, as it were, the first-born in My institution, and so that, as the heir, you may be executor of My treasures. I have given you the keys of My kingdom. Behold, I have given you authority over all My treasures!

— Ca. A.D. 350: Ephraim of Nisibis, *Homily* 4, no. 1, FEF 1:311, no. 706.

You cannot deny that you are aware that in the city of Rome the episcopal chair was given first to Peter; the chair in which Peter sat, the same who was head—that is why he is also called Cephas—of all the Apostles; the one chair in which unity is maintained by all. Neither do other Apostles proceed individually on their own; and anyone who would set up another chair in opposition to that single chair would, by that very fact, be a schismatic and a sinner.

— Ca. A.D. 367: Optatus of Milevis, *The Schism of the Donatists* 2, 2, in FEF 2:140, no. 1242.

I follow no leader but Christ and join in communion with none but Your Blessedness, that is, with the chair of Peter. I know that this is the rock on which the Church has been built. Whoever eats the Lamb outside this house is profane.

Anyone who is not in the ark of Noah will perish when the flood prevails.

— Ca. A.D. 375: Jerome, *Letter to Pope Damasus* 15, no. 2, in FEF 2:183–84, no. 1346.

Although all the Catholic Churches spread abroad through the world comprise but one bridal chamber of Christ, nevertheless, the holy Roman Church has been placed at the forefront not by the conciliar decisions of other Churches, but has received the primacy by the evangelic voice of our Lord and Savior, who says: "You are Peter, and upon this rock I will build My Church, and the gates of hell will not prevail against it; and I will give you the keys of the kingdom of heaven, and whatever you shall have bound on earth will be bound in heaven, and whatever you shall have loosed on earth shall be loosed in heaven" [Mt 16:18–19]. . . . The first see, therefore, is that of Peter the Apostle, that of the Roman Church, which has neither stain nor blemish nor anything like it.

— A.D. 382: Pope Damasus I, *Decree of Damasus*, no. 3, in FEF 1:406, no. 910u.

Before His suffering the Lord Jesus Christ, as you know, chose His disciples, whom He called Apostles. Among these Apostles almost everywhere Peter alone merited to represent the whole Church. For the sake of his representing the whole Church, which he alone could do, he merited to hear: "I will give you the keys of the kingdom of Heaven" [Mt 16:19]. For it was not one man, but the unity of the

Church, which received those keys. In that way, therefore, Peter's own excellence is foretold, because he acted the part of the unity and totality of the Church herself, when to him it was said, "I hand over to you," what was in fact handed over to all.

— Ca. A.D. 410: Augustine of Hippo, *Sermon* 295, no. 2, in FEF 3:32, no. 1526.

We exhort you in every respect, honorable brother, to heed obediently what has been written by the Most Blessed Pope of the City of Rome; for Blessed Peter, who lives and presides in his own see, provides the truth of faith to those who seek it.

— A.D. 449: Peter Chrysologus, *Letter to Eutyches* 25, no. 2, in FEF 3:268, no. 2178.

From the whole world only one, Peter, is chosen to preside over the calling of all nations, and over all the other Apostles, and over the Fathers of the Church. Thus, although among the people of God there are many priests and many pastors, it is really Peter who rules them all, of whom, too, it is Christ who is their chief ruler.

— Ca. A.D. 460: Pope Leo I, *Sermon* 4, no. 2, in FEF 3:275, no. 2191.

Baptism

TODAY'S CATHOLIC TEACHING

The sacrament of Baptism confers first sanctifying grace by which original sin is washed away, as well as all actual sin if any such exists; it remits all punishment due on account of such sins; it imprints the character of a Christian; it makes us children of God, members of the Church, and heirs to Paradise, and enables us to receive the other sacraments.

— Catechism of St. Pius X

CATHOLIC TEACHING IN THE EARLY CHURCH

Baptize as follows: after first explaining all these points, baptize in the name of the Father and of the Son and of the Holy Spirit, in running water. But if you have no running water, baptize in other water; and if you cannot in cold, then in warm. But if you have neither, pour water on the head three times in the name of the Father and of the Son and of the Holy Spirit. . . .

Let no one eat or drink of your Eucharist but those baptized in the name of the Lord; for concerning this also did the Lord say: "Do not give to dogs what is sacred."

— Ca. A.D. 70: *The Didache*, in *The Didache, The Epistle of Barnabas, The Epistles and The Martyrdom of St. Polycarp, The Fragments of Papias, The Epistle to Diognetus*, trans. James A. Kleist, ACW vol. 6 (Mahwah, N.J.: Paulist Press, 1948), pp. 19, 20.

What else does [God] say? "And there was a river flowing on the right, and beautiful trees grew beside it, and whoever shall eat of them shall live forever" [cf. Ezek 47:1–12]. In this way He says that we descend into the water full of sins and foulness, and we come up bearing fruit in our heart, having fear and hope in Jesus in the spirit.

— Ca. A.D. 79: *The Epistle of Barnabas*, chap. 11, no. 10, in FEF 1:15, no. 34.

Let your baptism be your armour; for your faith, your helmet, your love, your spear; your patient endurance, your panoply. Your deposits should be your works, that you may receive your savings to the exact amount.

— Ca. A.D. 107: Ignatius of Antioch, *Epistle to Polycarp*, in *The Epistles of St. Clement of Rome and St. Ignatius of Antioch*, trans. James A. Kleist, ACW, vol. 1 (Mahwah, N.J.: Paulist Press, 1948), p. 98.

"They had need," [the shepherd] said, "to come up through the water, so that they might be made alive; for they could not otherwise enter into the kingdom of God, except by putting away the mortality of their former life. These also, then, who had fallen asleep, received the seal of the Son of God, and entered into the kingdom of God. For," he said, "before a man bears the name of the Son of God, he is dead. But when he receives the seal, he puts mortality aside and again receives life. The seal, therefore, is the water. They go down into the water dead, and come out of it alive."

— Ca. A.D. 140: Hermas, *The Shepherd*, par. 9, 16, 2, in FEF 1:36, no. 92.

Moreover, those things which were created from the waters were blessed by God, so that this might also be a sign that men would at a future time receive repentance and remission of sins through water and the bath of regeneration—all who proceed to the truth and are born again and receive a blessing from God.

— Ca. A.D. 180: Theophilus of Antioch, *To Autolycus*, bk. 2, no. 16, in FEF 1:75, no. 181.

And again, giving the disciples the power of regenerating in God, He said to them: "Go and teach all nations, and baptize them in the name of the Father, and of the Son, and of the Holy Spirit" [Mt 28:19]. . . . The Lord promised to send us the Paraclete, who would make us ready for God. Just as dry wheat without moisture cannot become one dough or one loaf, so also, we who are many cannot be made one in Christ Jesus, without the water from heaven. Just as dry earth cannot bring forth fruit unless it receive moisture, so also we, being at first a dry tree, can never bring forth fruit unto life, without the voluntary rain from above. Our bodies achieve unity through the washing which leads to incorruption; our souls, however, through the Spirit. Both, then, are necessary, for both lead us on to the life of God.

— Ca. A.D. 180: Irenaeus of Lyons, *Against Heresies*, bk. 3, chap. 17, nos. 1–2, in FEF 1:92, nos. 219–20.

Happy is our sacrament of water, in that, by washing away the sins of our early blindness, we are set free *and admitted* into eternal life!

— Ca. A.D. 200: Tertullian of Carthage, *On Baptism*, chap. 1, trans. Alexander Roberts and James Donaldson, in ANF 2:669.

Formerly there was Baptism, in an obscure way, in the cloud and in the sea; now however, in full view, there is regeneration in water and in the Holy Spirit.

—A.D. 244: Origen, *Homily on Numbers*, hom. 7, no. 2, in FEF 1:206, no. 491.

And I myself was bound fast, held by so many errors of my past life, from which I did not believe that I could extricate myself. I was disposed, therefore, to yield to my clinging vices; and, despairing of better ways, I indulged my sins as if they were actually part and parcel of myself. But afterwards, when the stain of my past life had been washed away by means of the water of re-birth, a light from above poured itself upon my chastened and now pure heart; afterwards through the Spirit which is breathed from heaven, a second birth made of me a new man. And then in a marvelous manner, doubts immediately clarified themselves, the closed opened, the darkness became illuminated, what before had seemed difficult offered a way of accomplishment, and what had been thought impossible was able to be done. Thus it had to be acknowledged that what was of the earth and was born of the flesh and had lived submissive to sins, had now begun to be of God, as the Holy Spirit was animating it.

—A.D. 246/247: Cyprian of Carthage, *To Donatus* 4, in FEF 1:217, no. 548.

Since man is of a twofold nature, composed of body and soul, the purification also is twofold: the corporeal for the corporeal and the incorporeal for the incorporeal. The water cleanses the body, and the Spirit seals the soul. Thus, having our heart sprinkled by the Spirit and our body washed with pure water, we may draw near to God. When you go down into the water, then, regard not simply the water, but look for salvation through the power of the Holy Spirit. For without both you cannot attain to salvation. It is not I who say this, but the Lord Jesus Christ, who has the power in this matter. And He says, "Unless a man be born again" —and He adds the words "of water and of the Spirit—he cannot enter into the kingdom of God" [Jn 3:5].

— Ca. A.D. 350: Cyril of Jerusalem, *Catechetical Lectures*, lec. 3, no. 4, in FEF 1:348–49, no. 810a.

The Church was redeemed at the price of Christ's blood. Jew or Greek, it makes no difference; but if he has believed, he must circumcise himself from his sins so that he can be saved . . . for no one ascends into the kingdom of heaven except through the Sacrament of Baptism.

— A.D. 387: Ambrose of Milan, *Abraham*, bk. 2, chap. 11, no. 79, in FEF 2:169, no. 1323.

Let no one say: "I did that; perhaps I will not be forgiven." Because you did it? How great is the sin you committed? Tell me what you have done, something serious, something horrible, something terrifying even to think about. Whatever you might have done, did you kill Christ? There is nothing worse than having done that, because there is nothing better than Christ. How great a wrong is it to kill Christ? But the Jews killed Him; and afterwards many of them believed in Him and drank His Blood; and the sin which they had committed was forgiven them. When you shall have been baptized, keep to a good life in the commandments of God, so that you may preserve your Baptism to the very end. I do not tell you that you will live here without sin, but they are venial sins which this life is never without. Baptism was instituted for all sins; for light sins, without which we cannot live, prayer was instituted. What does the prayer say? "Forgive us our debts as we too forgive our debtors." We are cleansed once by Baptism; by prayer we are cleansed daily. But do not commit those sins on account of which you would have to be separated from the Body of Christ; perish the thought! For those whom you see doing penance have committed crimes, either adultery or some other enormities: that is why they are doing penance. If their sins were light, daily prayer would suffice to blot them out. In the Church, therefore, there are three ways in which sins are forgiven: in Baptism, in prayer, and in the greater humility of penance; yet, God does not forgive sins except to the baptized.

— Ca. A.D. 395: Augustine of Hippo, *Sermon to Catechumens* 7, no. 15, in FEF 3:35, no. 1536.

The Lord's Supper

TODAY'S CATHOLIC TEACHING

At the Last Supper, on the night he was betrayed, our Savior instituted the eucharistic sacrifice of his Body and Blood. This he did in order to perpetuate the sacrifice of the Cross throughout the ages until he should come again, and so to entrust to his beloved Spouse, the Church, a memorial of his death and resurrection: a sacrament of love, a sign of unity, a bond of charity, a paschal banquet in which Christ is consumed, the mind is filled with grace, and a pledge of future glory is given to us.

— Vatican II, *Sacrosanctum Concilium*, no. 47.

CATHOLIC TEACHING IN THE EARLY CHURCH

On the Lord's own day, assemble in common to break bread and offer thanks; but first confess your sins, so that your sacrifice may be pure. However, no one quarrelling with his brother may join your meeting until they are reconciled; your sacrifice must not be defiled. For here we have the saying of the Lord: "In every place and time offer me a pure sacrifice; for I am a mighty King, says the Lord; and my name spreads terror among the nations [cf. Mal 1:11]."

— Ca. A.D. 70: *The Didache*, in ACW, vol. 6, p. 23.

Accordingly, as wine is blended with water, so is the Spirit with man. And the one, the mixture of wine and water, nourishes to faith; while the other, the Spirit, conducts to immortality. And the mixture of both—of the water and of the Word—is called *Eucharist*, renowned and glorious grace; and they who by faith partake of it are sanctified both in body and soul.

— Ca. A.D. 200: Clement of Alexandria, *The Instructor*, chap. 2, trans. Alexander Roberts and James Donaldson, in ANF 2:242.

We take also, in congregations before daybreak, and from the hand of none but the presidents, the sacrament of the Eucharist, which the Lord both commanded to be eaten at meal-times, and enjoined to be taken by all alike. . . . We feel pained should any wine or bread, even though our own, be cast upon the ground.

— Ca. A.D. 204: Tertullian of Carthage, *The Chaplet*, chap. 3, trans. Alexander Roberts and James Donaldson, in ANF 3:94.

If Christ Jesus, our Lord and God, is Himself the High Priest of God the Father; and if He offered Himself as a sacrifice to the Father; and if He commanded that this be done in commemoration of Himself—then certainly the priest, who imitates that which Christ did, truly functions in the place of Christ.

— Ca. A.D. 250: Cyprian of Carthage, *Letter to a Certain Cecil* 63, no. 14, in FEF 1:232–33, no. 584.

As the prayer continues, we ask and say, "Give us this day our daily bread" [Mt 6:11]. . . . And we ask that this bread be given us daily, so that we who are in Christ and daily receive the Eucharist as the food of salvation, may not, by falling into some more grievous sin and then in abstaining from communicating, be withheld from the heavenly Bread, and be separated from Christ's Body. . . . He Himself warns us, saying, "Unless you eat the flesh of the Son of Man and drink His blood, you shall not have life in you" [Jn 6:54]. Therefore do we ask that our Bread, which is Christ, be given to us daily, so that we who abide and live in Christ may not withdraw from His sanctification and from His Body.

— Ca. A.D. 251: Cyprian of Carthage, *The Lord's Prayer*, no. 18, in FEF 1:223, no. 559.

This one teaching of the blessed Paul is enough to give you complete certainty about the Divine Mysteries, by your having been deemed worthy of which, you have become united in body and soul with Christ. For Paul proclaimed clearly that: "On the night in which He was betrayed, our Lord Jesus Christ, taking bread and giving thanks, broke it and gave it to His disciples, saying, 'Take, eat, This is My Body.' And taking the cup and giving thanks, He said, 'Take, drink, This is My Blood' [cf. 1 Cor 11:23–25]." He Himself, therefore, having declared and said of the Bread, "This is My Body," who will dare any longer to doubt? And when He Himself has affirmed and said, "This is My Blood," who can ever hesitate and say it is not His Blood? . . . Do not, therefore, regard the Bread and the Wine as simply that;

for they are, according to the Master's declaration, the Body and Blood of Christ. Even though the senses suggest to you the other, let faith make you firm. Do not judge in this matter by taste, but—be fully assured by the faith, not doubting that you have been deemed worthy of the Body and Blood of Christ.

— Ca. A.D. 350: Cyril of Jerusalem, *Catechetical Lectures*, lec. 22 (*Mystagogic* 4), nos. 1, 6, in FEF 1:360, 361, nos. 843, 846.

Our Lord Jesus took in His hands what in the beginning was only bread; and He blessed it, and signed it, and made it holy in the name of the Father and in the name of the Spirit; and He broke it and in His gracious kindness He distributed it to all His disciples one by one. He called the bread His living Body, and did Himself fill it with Himself and the Spirit. And extending His hand, He gave them the Bread which His right hand had made holy: "Take, all of you eat of this, which My word has made holy. Do not now regard as bread that which I have given you; but take, eat this Bread, and do not scatter the crumbs; for what I have called My Body, that it is indeed. One particle from its crumbs is able to sanctify thousands and thousands, and is sufficient to afford life to those who eat of it. Take, eat, entertaining no doubt of faith, because this is My Body, and whoever eats it in belief eats it in Fire and Spirit. . . ." But if anyone despise or reject it or treat it with ignominy, it may be taken as a certainty that he treats with ignominy the Son, who called it and actually made it to be His Body.

— Ca. A.D. 350: Ephraim of Nisibis, *Homily*, 4, no. 4, in FEF 1:311, no. 707.

Cease not to pray and plead for me when you draw down the Word by your word, when in an unbloody cutting you cut the Body and Blood of the Lord, using your voice for a sword.

— Ca. A.D. 383: Gregory Nazianzen, *Letter to Amphilochius, Bishop of Iconium* 171, in FEF 2:41, no. 1019.

We saw the Prince of Peace coming to us, we saw and heard Him offering His blood for us. We follow, inasmuch as we are able, being priests; and we offer the sacrifice on behalf of the people. And even if we are of but little merit, still, in the sacrifice, we are honorable. For even if Christ is not now seen as the one who offers the sacrifice, nevertheless it is He Himself that is offered in sacrifice here on earth when the Body of Christ is offered. Indeed, to offer Himself He is made visible in us, He whose word makes holy the sacrifice that is offered.

— Ca. A.D. 390: Ambrose of Milan, *Commentaries on Twelve of David's Psalms* 38, 25, in FEF 2:150, no. 1260.

When you see the [Body of Christ] lying on the altar, say to yourself, "Because of this Body I am no longer earth and ash, no longer a prisoner, but free. Because of this Body I hope for heaven, and I hope to receive the good things that are in heaven, immortal life, the lot of angels, familiar conversation with Christ. This Body, scourged and crucified, has not been fetched by death. . . . This is that Body which was blood-stained, which was pierced by a lance, and from which gushed forth those saving fountains, one of blood and the other of water, for all the world." . . . This is the Body which He gave us, both to hold in reserve and to eat, which was appropriate to intense love; for those whom we kiss with abandon we often even bite with our teeth.

— Ca. A.D. 392: John Chrysostom, *Homilies on the First Epistle to the Corinthians*, hom. 24, no. 4 (7), in FEF 2:117–18, no. 1195.

It is proper, therefore, that when [Christ] gave the Bread He did not say, "This is the symbol of My Body," but, "This is My Body." In the same way when He gave the Cup He did not say, "This is the symbol of My Blood," but, "This is My Blood"; for He wanted us to look upon the [Eucharistic elements] after their reception of grace and the coming of the Holy Spirit not according to their nature, but [that we should] receive them as they are, the Body and Blood of our Lord. We ought . . . not regard the [Eucharistic elements] merely as bread and cup, but as the Body and Blood of Christ, into which they were transformed by the descent of the Holy Spirit.

— Ca. A.D. 410: Theodore of Mopsuestia, *Catechetical Homilies* 5, in FEF 2:82, no. 1113f.

" 'From the rising of the sun even to its setting My name is great among the Gentiles, and in every place sacrifice is offered to My name, a clean oblation; for My name is great among the Gentiles,' says the Lord Almighty" [Mal 1:11]. What do you answer to that? Open your eyes at last, then, any time, and see, from the rising of the sun to its setting, the Sacrifice of Christians is offered, not in one place only, as was established with you Jews, but everywhere; and not to just any god at all, but to Him who foretold it, the God of Israel. . . . Not in one place, as was prescribed for you in the earthly Jerusalem, but in every place, even in Jerusalem herself. Not according to the order of Aaron, but according to the order of Melchisedech.

— Ca. A.D. 425: Augustine of Hippo, *Sermon against the Jews* 9, no. 13, in FEF 3:168, no. 1977.

This Victim alone saves the soul from eternal ruin, the sacrificing of which presents to us in a mystical way the death of the Only-begotten, who,—though He is now risen from the dead and dies no more, and death will no longer have dominion over Him, for He lives immortally and incorruptibly in Himself,—is immolated for us again in this mystery of the sacred oblation. For His body is eaten there, His flesh is distributed among the people unto salvation, His blood is poured out, no longer in the hands of the faithless but in the mouth of the faithful. Let us take thought, therefore, of what this sacrifice means for us, which is in constant representation of the suffering of the Only-begotten Son, for the sake of our forgiveness.

— Ca. A.D. 593: Pope Gregory I, *Dialogues*, bk. 4, chap. 60, in FEF 3:320–21, no. 2323.

TODAY'S CATHOLIC TEACHING

What the Catholic faith believes about Mary is based on what it believes about Christ, and what it teaches about Mary illumines in turn its faith in Christ.

—CCC 487.

Called in the Gospels "the mother of Jesus," Mary is acclaimed by Elizabeth, at the prompting of the Spirit and even before the birth of her son, as "the mother of my Lord" [Lk 1:43; Jn 2:1; 19:25; cf. Mt 13:55; et al.]. In fact, the One whom she conceived as man by the Holy Spirit, who truly became her Son according to the flesh, was none other than the Father's eternal Son, the second person of the Holy Trinity. Hence the Church confesses that Mary is truly "Mother of God" (*Theotokos*).

—CCC 495, quoting the Council of Ephesus (431): DS 251.

Mary "remained a virgin in conceiving her Son, a virgin in giving birth to him, a virgin in carrying him, a virgin in nursing him at her breast, always a virgin" (St. Augustine, *Serm.* 186, 1: PL 38, 999): with her whole being she is "the handmaid of the Lord" (Lk 1:38).

—CCC 510.

"Finally the Immaculate Virgin, preserved free from all stain of original sin, when the course of her earthly life was finished, was taken up body and soul into heavenly glory . . ." [*Lumen Gentium* 59; cf. Pius XII, *Munificentissimus Deus* (1950): DS 3903; cf. Rev 19:16]. The Assumption of the Blessed Virgin is a singular participation in her Son's Resurrection and an anticipation of the resurrection of other Christians.

—CCC 966.

CATHOLIC TEACHING IN THE EARLY CHURCH

For our God, Jesus Christ, was conceived by Mary in accord with God's plan: of the seed of David, it is true, but also of the Holy Spirit.

—Ca. A.D. 107: Ignatius of Antioch, *Letter to the Ephesians*, chap. 18, no. 2, in FEF 1:18, no. 42.

"Since it is written of Him in the Memoirs of the Apostles that He is the Son of God, and since we call Him Son, we have understood that before all creatures He proceeded from the Father by His will and power . . . and that He became Man by the Virgin so that the course which was taken by disobedience in the beginning through the agency of the serpent, might be also the very course by which it would be put down. For Eve, a virgin and undefiled, conceived the word of the serpent, and bore disobedience and death. But the Virgin Mary received faith and joy when the angel Gabriel announced to her the glad tidings that the Spirit of the Lord would come upon her and the power of the Most High would overshadow her, for which reason the Holy One being born of her is the Son of God. And she replied, 'Be it done unto me according to thy word' [Lk 1:38]."

— Ca. A.D. 160: Justin Martyr, *Dialogue with Trypho the Jew*, chap. 100, in FEF 1:62, no. 141.

The Virgin Mary, . . . being obedient to His word, received from an angel the glad tidings that she would bear God.

— Ca. A.D. 180: Irenaeus of Lyons, *Against Heresies*, bk. 5, chap. 19, no. 1, in FEF 1:101, no. 256a.

Through a Virgin, the Word of God was introduced to set up a structure of life. Thus, what had been laid waste in ruin by this sex, was by the same sex re-established in salvation. Eve had believed the serpent; Mary believed Gabriel. That which the one destroyed by believing, the other, by believing, set straight.

— Ca. A.D. 210: Tertullian of Carthage, *The Flesh of Christ*, chap. 17, no. 5, in FEF 1:147, no. 358.

In the womb of Mary the Infant was formed,
who from eternity is equal to the Father.
He imparted to us His greatness,
and took on our infirmity.
He became mortal like us and joined His life to ours, so
that we might die no more.

This Virgin became a Mother
while preserving her virginity;
And though still a Virgin
she carried a Child in her womb;
And the handmaid of His Wisdom
became the Mother of God.

—Ca. A.D. 350: Ephraim of Nisibis, *Songs of Praise*, 1, nos. 12 and 20, in FEF 1:312, no. 711.

You alone and your Mother
are more beautiful than any others;
For there is no blemish in you,
nor any stains upon your Mother.
Who of my children
can compare in beauty to these?

—Ca. A.D. 350: Ephraim of Nisibis, *Nisibene Hymns* 27, no. 8, in FEF 1:313, no. 719.

Let those, therefore, who deny that the Son is by nature from the Father and proper to His essence, deny also that He took true human flesh from the Ever-Virgin Mary.

—Ca. A.D. 360: Athanasius, *Discourses against the Arians* 2, no. 70, in FEF 1:330, no. 767a.

Come, then, and search out Your sheep, not through Your servants or hired men, but do it Yourself. Lift me up bodily and in the flesh, which is fallen in Adam. Lift me up not from Sara but from Mary, a Virgin not only undefiled but a Virgin whom grace has made inviolate, free of every stain of sin.

— Ca. A.D. 388: Ambrose of Milan, *Commentary on Psalm 118*, 22, 30, in FEF 2:166, no. 1314.

Tell me how Jesus entered through closed doors [Jn 20:19] . . . and I will explain how Saint Mary can be both Mother and Virgin. A Mother before she married, she remained a Virgin after bearing her Son.

— Ca. A.D. 393: Jerome, *Letter to Pammachius* 48, no. 21, in FEF 2:185, no. 1350.

Our Lord Jesus Christ . . . , who came to liberate mankind, in which both males and females are destined to salvation, was not averse to males, for He took the form of a male, nor to females, for of a female He was born. Besides, there is a great mystery here: that just as death comes to us through a woman, Life is born to us through a woman; that the devil, defeated, would be tormented by each nature, feminine and masculine, since he had taken delight in the defection of both.

— Ca. A.D. 397: Augustine of Hippo, *Christian Combat* 22, 24, in FEF 3:50, no. 1578.

Having excepted the Holy Virgin Mary, concerning whom, on account of the honor of the Lord, I wish to have absolutely no question when treating of sins,—for how do we know what abundance of grace for the total overcoming of sin was conferred upon her, who merited to conceive and bear Him in whom there was no sin?—so, I say, with the exception of the Virgin, if we could have gathered together all those holy men and women [of past ages] . . . and had asked them whether they were without sin, what do we suppose would have been their answer? . . . Would they not have declared in a single voice: "If we say we have no sin, we deceive ourselves, and the truth is not in us!" [1 Jn 1:8]?

—A.D. 415: Augustine of Hippo, *Nature and Grace*, chaps. 36 and 42, in FEF 3:111, no. 1794.

Heretics called Antidicomarites are those who contradict the perpetual virginity of Mary, and affirm that after Christ was born she was joined as one with her husband.

—A.D. 428: Augustine of Hippo, *Heresies* 56, in FEF 3:166, no. 1974d.

I have been amazed that some are utterly in doubt as to whether or not the Holy Virgin is able to be called Mother of God. For if our Lord Jesus Christ is God, how should the Holy Virgin who bore Him not be the Mother of God?

—Ca. A.D. 430: Cyril of Alexandria, *Letter to the Monks of Egypt* 1, in FEF 3:206, no. 2058.

Now, heretic, you say, whoever you are who deny that God was born of the Virgin, that Mary, the Mother of our Lord Jesus Christ, cannot be called Theotokos, that is, the Mother of God, but Christokos, that is, the Mother only of Christ, and not of God. For no one, you say, gives birth to one older than herself. And of this utterly stupid argument, wherein you suppose that the birth of God can be understood by a carnal intellect and believe that the mystery of His Majesty can be resolved by human reasoning, we will, if God permit, offer a refutation later on. In the meantime, however, let us prove by divine testimonies both that Christ is God and that Mary is the Mother of God.

— Ca. A.D. 430: John Cassian, *The Incarnation of Christ*, bk. 2, chap. 2, in FEF 3:200, no. 2054.

This [Jesus] was certainly a wonderful Person, having the natures of God and of man, but truly conceived and born according to the flesh, inasmuch as the Virgin, in an indescribable manner, conceived and bore the God of heaven, and remained inviolate, Virgin and Mother,—she, of course, is truly designated by the angel "full of grace" and "blessed among women,"—because she neither had nor desired any commerce of man but, while retaining a virginity both of mind and of body, she received from Him whom she was about to conceive and bear the gift of uncorrupted fruitfulness and of fruitful integrity.

— Ca. A.D. 520: Fulgentius of Ruspe, *Letter of Fulgence and Fourteen Other African Bishops Exiled in Sardinia, to Various of Their Brethren* 17, no. 12, in FEF 3:288, no. 2242.

The course of this life having been completed by Blessed Mary, when now she would be called from the world, all the Apostles came together from their various regions to her house. And when they had heard that she was about to be taken from the world, they kept watch together with her. And behold, the Lord Jesus came with His angels, and taking her soul, He gave it over to the Angel Michael and withdrew. At daybreak, however, the Apostles took up her body on a bier and placed it in a tomb; and they guarded it, expecting the Lord to come. And behold, again the Lord stood by them; and the holy body having been received, He commanded that it be taken in a cloud into paradise: where now, rejoined to the soul, [Mary] rejoices with the Lord's chosen ones, and is in the enjoyment of the good of an eternity that will never end.

—A.D. 590: Gregory of Tours, *Eight Books of Miracles* 1, 4, in FEF 3:306, no. 2288a.

Saints and Purgatory

TODAY'S CATHOLIC TEACHING

Until the Lord shall come in His majesty, and all the angels with Him and death being destroyed, all things are subject to Him, some of His disciples are exiles on earth, some having died are purified, and others are in glory beholding "clearly God Himself triune and one, as He is"; but all in various ways and degrees are in communion in the same charity of God and neighbor and all sing the same hymn of glory to our God. For all who are in Christ, having His Spirit, form one Church and cleave together in Him. Therefore the union of the wayfarers with the brethren who have gone to sleep in the peace of Christ is not in the least weakened or interrupted, but on the contrary, according to the perpetual faith of the Church, is strengthened by communication of spiritual goods. . . .

For after they have been received into their heavenly home and are present to the Lord, through Him and with Him and in Him they do not cease to intercede with the Father for us, showing forth the merits which they won on earth through the one Mediator between God and man, serving God in all things and filling up in their flesh those things which are lacking of the sufferings of Christ for His Body which is the Church. . . . Fully conscious of this communion of the whole Mystical Body of Jesus Christ, the pilgrim Church from the very first ages of the Christian religion has cultivated with great piety the memory of the dead, and "because it is a holy and wholesome thought to pray for the dead that they may be loosed from their sins", also offers suffrages for them.

—Vatican II, *Lumen Gentium*, no. 49, 50.

CATHOLIC TEACHING IN THE EARLY CHURCH

[Christ] we worship as the Son of God; but the martyrs we love as disciples and imitators of the Lord; and rightly so, because of their unsurpassable devotion to their own King and Teacher. . . . We took up [Polycarp's] bones, more precious than costly gems and finer than gold, and put them in a suitable place. The Lord will permit us, when we are able, to assemble there in joy and gladness; and to celebrate the birthday of his martyrdom.

—Ca. A.D. 155: *Martyrdom of Polycarp*, chap. 17, no. 3, chap. 18, nos. 2–3, in FEF 1:31, no. 81.

[Speaking of the parable of the Rich Man and Lazarus] In short, if we understand that prison of which the Gospel speaks to be Hades, and if we interpret the last farthing [Mt 5:26] to be the light offense which is to be expiated there before the resurrection, no one will doubt that the soul undergoes some punishments in Hades, without prejudice to the fullness of the resurrection, after which recompense will be made through the flesh also.

—Ca. A.D. 210: Tertullian of Carthage, *The Soul*, chap. 58, no. 8, in FEF 1:145, no. 352.

Lawrence and Ignatius, though they fought betimes in worldly camps, were true and spiritual soldiers of God; and while they laid the devil on his back with their confession of Christ, they merited the palms and crowns of the Lord by their illustrious passion. We always offer sacrifices for them, as you will recall, as often as we celebrate the passions of the martyrs by commemorating their anniversary day.

—A.D. 250: Cyprian of Carthage, *Letter to His Clergy and to All His People* 39 (34), no. 3, in FEF 1:229.

[At the Eucharistic celebration] we make mention also of those who have already fallen asleep: first, the patriarchs, prophets, Apostles, and martyrs, that through their prayers and supplications God would receive our petition; next, we make mention also of the holy fathers and bishops who have already fallen asleep, and, to put it simply, of all among us who have already fallen asleep; for we believe that it will be of very great benefit to the souls of those for whom the petition is carried up, while this holy and most solemn Sacrifice is laid out.

— Ca. A.D. 350: Cyril of Jerusalem, *Catechetical Lectures*, lec. 23 (*Mystagogic* 5), no. 9, in FEF 1:363, no. 852.

What is more timely or more excellent than that those who are still here should believe that the departed do live, and that they have not retreated into nothingness, but that they exist and are alive with the Master? . . . Useful too is the prayer fashioned on their behalf, even if it does not force back the whole of guilty charges laid to them. And it is useful also, because in this world we often stumble either voluntarily or involuntarily, and thus it is a reminder to do better. For we make commemoration of the just and of sinners: of sinners, begging God's mercy for them; of the just and the Fathers and Patriarchs and Prophets and Apostles and Evangelists and martyrs and confessors, and of bishops and solitaries, and of the whole list of them, so that we may set the Lord Jesus Christ apart from the ranks of men because of the honor due Him, and give reverence to Him, while keeping in mind that the Lord is not to be equated with any man, even if that man live in a justice that is boundless and limitless.

— Ca. A.D. 375: Epiphanius of Salamis, *Panacea against All Heresies* 75, 8, in FEF 2:75–76, no. 1109.

There is an ecclesiastical discipline, as the faithful know, when the names of the martyrs are read aloud in that place at the altar of God, where prayer is not offered for them. Prayer, however, is offered for other dead who are remembered. For it is wrong to pray for a martyr, to whose prayers we ought ourselves be commended.

— Ca. A.D. 400: Augustine of Hippo, *Sermon* 159, no. 1, in FEF 3:29, no. 1513.

A Christian people celebrates together in religious solemnity the memorials of the martyrs, both to encourage their being imitated and so that it can share in their merits and be aided by their prayers. But it is done in such a way that our altars are not set up to any one of the martyrs,—although in their memory,—but to God Himself, the God of those martyrs. Who, indeed, of the presiding priests assisting at the altar in the places of the saints ever said "We offer to you, Peter, or Paul, or Cyprian"? What is offered is offered to God, who crowned the martyrs. . . . That worship, which the Greeks call λατρεία [*latria*] and for which there is no Latin single term, and which is expressive of the subjection owed to Divinity alone, we neither accord nor teach that it should be accorded to any save to the one God.

— Ca. A.D. 400: Augustine of Hippo, *Against Faustus the Manichean*, bk. 20, no. 21, in FEF 3:59, no. 1603.

You say in your book that while we live we are able to pray for each other, but afterwards when we have died, the prayer of no person for another can be heard; and this is especially clear since the martyrs, though they cry vengeance for their own blood, have never been able to obtain their request. But if the Apostles and martyrs while still in the body can pray for others, at a time when they ought still be solicitous about themselves, how much more will they do so after their crowns, victories, and triumphs?

— A.D. 406: Jerome, *Against Vigilantius*, no. 6, in FEF 2:206, no. 1396.

Temporal punishments are suffered by some in this life only, by some after death, by some both here and hereafter; but all of them before that last and strictest judgment. But not all who suffer temporal punishments after death will come to eternal punishments, which are to follow after that judgment.

— A.D. 426: Augustine of Hippo, *The City of God*, bk. 21, chap. 13, in FEF 3:105, no. 1776.

There is no doubt that . . . [there are] lesser sins which, as I said before, can scarcely be counted, and from which not only all Christian people, but even all the saints could not and cannot always be free. We do not, of course, believe that the soul is killed by these sins; but still, they make it ugly by covering it as if with some kind of pustules and, as it were, with horrible scabs, which allow the soul to come only with difficulty to the embrace of the heavenly Spouse, of whom it is written: "He prepared for Himself a Church having neither spot nor blemish" [Eph 5:27]. . . . If we neither give thanks to God in tribulations nor redeem our own sins by good works [cf. Jas 5:19–20], we shall have to remain in that purgatorial fire as long as it takes for those above-mentioned lesser sins to be consumed like wood and straw and hay [1 Cor 3:12]. But someone is saying: "It is nothing to me how long I stay there, so long as I go on finally to eternal life." Let no one say that, beloved brethren, because that purgatorial fire itself will be more difficult than any punishments that can be seen or imagined or felt in this life.

— Ca. A.D. 542: Caesarius of Arles, *Sermon* 179 (104), nos. 3–5, in FEF 3:283, no. 2233.

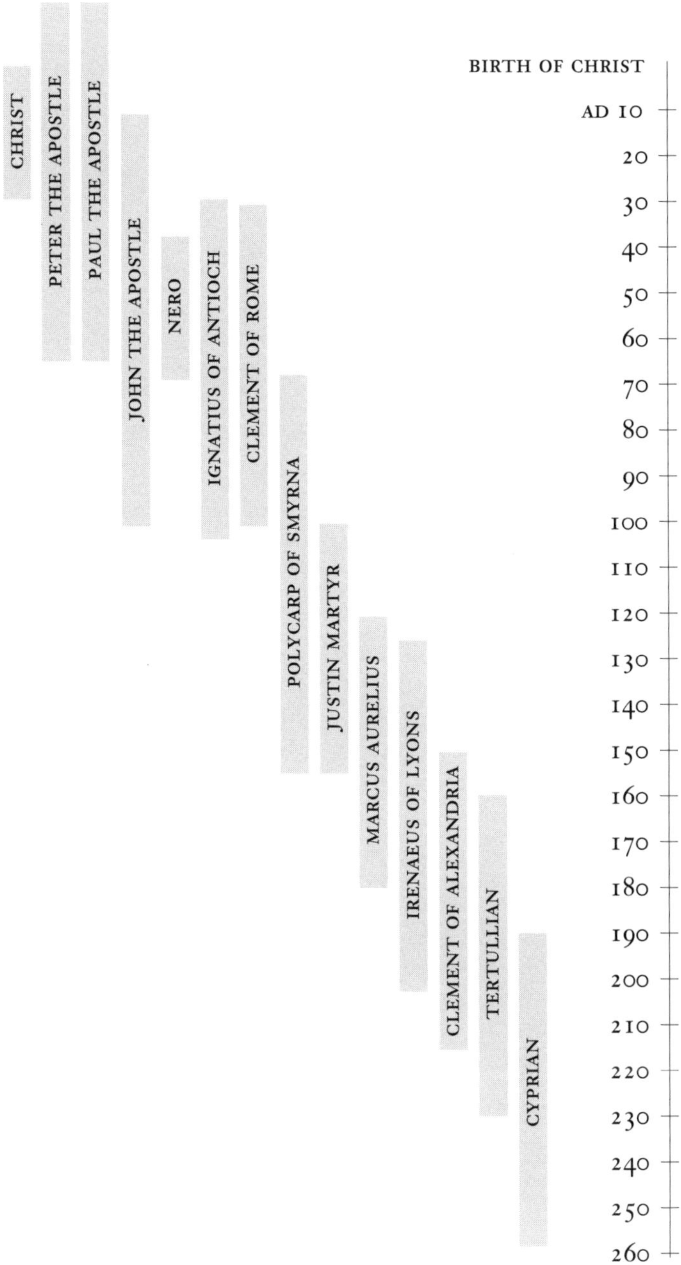
BIRTH OF CHRIST
AD 10
20
30
40
50
60
70
80
90
100
110
120
130
140
150
160
170
180
190
200
210
220
230
240
250
260
CHRIST
PETER THE APOSTLE
PAUL THE APOSTLE
JOHN THE APOSTLE
NERO
IGNATIUS OF ANTIOCH
CLEMENT OF ROME
POLYCARP OF SMYRNA
JUSTIN MARTYR
MARCUS AURELIUS
IRENAEUS OF LYONS
CLEMENT OF ALEXANDRIA
TERTULLIAN
CYPRIAN